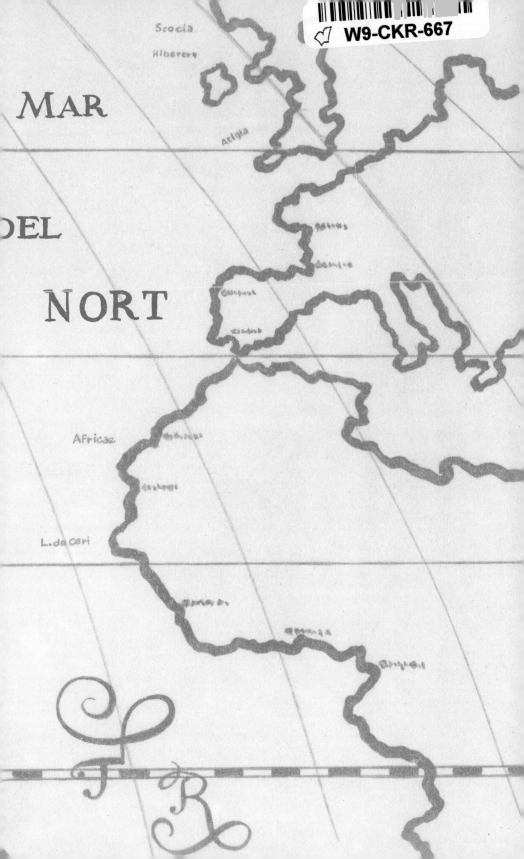

OGLETHORPE'S FOLLY: THE BIRTH OF GEORGIA

OGLETHORPE
Engraving by C. Burt, adapted from mezzotint of c. 1744

Oglethorpe's Folly

THE BIRTH OF GEORGIA

Webb Garrison

COPPLE HOUSE BOOKS
Lakemont, Georgia
30552

Orglethorpe's Folly: *The Birth of Georgia*. Copyright © 1982 by Webb
Garrison. All rights reserved. Printed and bound in the United
States of America. Published by Copple House Books, Road's End,
Lakemont, GA 30552. ISBN 0-932298-30-3

Library of Congress Cataloging in Publication Data

Garrison, Webb B.
  Oglethorpe's Folly.   95510

    Bibliography: pp.221-26.
    Includes index.
    1. Oglethorpe, James Edward, 1696-1785. 2. Georgia — Gov-
ernors — Biography. 3. Georgia — History — Colonial period, ca.
1600-1775. I. Title.
F289.G27   975.8'02'0924   [B]   82-5191
ISBN 0-932298-30-3   AACR2

PREFACE

Samuel Johnson, a long-time friend of Georgia's founder, wanted the world to know his story. "I know of no man whose life would be more interesting," he said. "If I were furnished with the materials, I should be very glad to write it."

He couldn't possibly have been speaking of the one-dimensional and less-than-human James Edward Oglethorpe who stalks grimly through the pages of some volumes that deal with him. An early biographer dubbed him "a paladin of philanthrophy." Unfortunately, the label and the stereotype that it evoked came into general use.

Today Samuel Johnson would have more than enough material with which to write the story of his friend's life. Tens of thousands of colonial records, British documents, letters, and other short materials have been published in addition to lengthy diaries and journals. Much unpublished material is available on microfilm.

Sifting through an almost overwhelming quantity of source material, a clear conclusion emerged from the mists of Georgian England and Trustee era Georgia. *So much attention has been paid to the deeds of Oglethorpe the "imperial idealist" that Oglethorpe, the man, has been somewhat overlooked.*

So the goal of this inquiry linked with the 250th anniversary of Georgia's founding is high. It seeks to discover and to reveal Georgia's founder as a three-dimensional person. He was a philanthropist but he was much more: a petty gentleman with blood coursing through his veins and ambitions churning in his head. In the finest and best sense, as well as in some self-centered aspects, he was a soldier of fortune.

5

Many persons risk something or much in pursuit of their goals, while deliberately holding something in reserve. Few have been willing or able to risk everything. Oglethorpe did. He lost many of his battles and was soundly defeated in some of his campaigns. Yet he emerged from the wars a victor on every front. That he fought for fame and fortune as well as for the dispossessed and for the glory of imperial Britain adds to his reality as a person, rather than diminishing it.

Gregorian or New Style dates are used throughout. However the 11-day correction required for absolute precision is made only for the all-important year 1732/33. Unless otherwise indicated sums of money are in pounds sterling and are rounded out to the nearest pound.

Gratitude is due to so many persons that a list of acknowledgements would be unduly long. A very special "thank you" is due, however, to the editors and staff members of The Atlanta *Journal-Constitution* and to readers of "Southeastern Scrapbook" therein. Their warm response and encouragement were significant factors leading to a decision to undertake this long but thrilling odyssey. A great debt of gratitude is owed to distinguished Georgians who read and evaluated pre-publication copies. Many of the illustrations were generously provided by: the University of Georgia Libraries, Oglethorpe University, and the Georgia chapter of the American Institute of Architects.

Hopefully, through these pages Americans in general and Georgians in particular will arrive at new appreciation of a complex and sometimes vulnerable man who has no close counterpart in our heritage.

Webb Garrison

Atlanta, 1982

CONTENTS

New and Accurate ACCOUNT

OF THE

PROVINCES

OF

SOUTH-CAROLINA

AND

GEORGIA:

With many curious and useful Observations on the Trade, Navigation and Plantations of *Great-Britain*, compared with her
most powerful maritime Neighbours in an-
tient and modern Times.

LONDON:

Printed for J. WORRALL at the *Bible* and
Dove in *Bell-Yard* near *Lincoln's-Inn* ; and Sold
by J. ROBERTS near the *Oxford-Arms* in
Warwick-Lane. 1732.

(Price One Shilling.)

Title page of booklet that lured many colonists to Georgia

James Oglethorpe is almost universally regarded as author of this highly imaginative
1732 booklet. More than any other single early printed piece, this served to gain the
support of the British public for the Georgia scheme — and to lure great numbers of
persons to the colony.

ILLUSTRATIONS

Chapter 1

A HERITAGE OF GLORY AND SHAME

December, 1696 — April, 1723

James Edward Oglethorpe, soon to become Jamie within the family circle, was baptized 24 hours after his birth on December 22, 1696. Ninth and last child of Sir Theophilus and Lady Eleanor Oglethorpe, their fifth son arrived just ten months after Fanny and about 90 days before their father turned 46.

Oglethorpes had been land holders, petty gentry, fighting men and office holders since the Norman Conquest. In recent decades they had tasted unprecedented glory that was repeatedly mingled with defeat, humiliation, loss, and shame.

Sutton Oglethorpe, grandfather of the infant, inherited the family estate in Bramham, Yorkshire, barely eight years before civil war broke out in 1642. Fiercely loyal to King Charles I and holding the rank of colonel in the royalist forces, Oglethorpe angered Oliver Cromwell's followers. In 1651 he was arrested and placed on trial. There was no doubt of the outcome; found to be an unswerving royalist, he was fined £20,000. His sequestered estates fell into the hands of William Fairfax, leaving the long-proud family virtually landless and penniless.

Matters took a different turn when the monarchy was restored under Charles II, in 1660. Theophilus Oglethorpe, born shortly before his father's arrest and imprisonment, fought as a private gentleman in one of the king's newly-created troops of lifeguards. His military advancement was rapid. Eventually he was knighted and made a brigadier-general. Then his ruler rewarded him with

11

grants of land forfeited by enemies of the crown. With profits from enterprises that ranged from coal mining to the lending of money to the king, in 1688 Sir Theophilus purchased Westbrook manor in Godalming, County Surrey. Once more the family belonged to the ranks of landed gentry.

Before the year's end King James II, brother of Charles I, abandoned the throne and England and fled to France. Stubbornly loyal to James, Sir Theophilus was stripped of his military command and was for a time a fugitive in hiding before taking refuge in France. From popular Latin for "James," Oglethorpe — and every other outspoken follower of James II after his abdication — was termed a Jacobite.[1] Significantly for him and for his youngest son, Sir Theophilus was branded an "undesirable Jacobite" in 1698 after returning home from France. Given to him by Secretary of State James Vernon, that label made him subject to arrest or exile as well as potential confiscation of what little property he had managed to salvage. Seven years earlier his name had been prominent among those listed as conspirators who were charged with high treason.

In spite of danger to his person and property he did not again flee. Instead he boldly stood for Parliament from the "pocket" borough of Haslemere. Most voters were tenants on the Oglethorpe and Molyneux estates,[2] so victory came fairly easily. He sat in the House of Commons a bit less than four years, until his death in 1702.

Fatherless at age five, Jamie grew up under the strong hand of Irish-born Lady Eleanor, who survived her husband by 30 years. One of her sons, Sutton, lived only seven weeks. Another, James, died at 12 months.[3]   Hence the matriarch had, in effect, two families. A gap of a dozen years separated Fanny and Jamie from Eleanor, youngest of the cluster of five children born at nearly annual intervals beginning just one year after Eleanor Wall left her native Tipperary.

Lady Oglethorpe's Irish temper flared most frequently when matters of state were involved. Even more strongly than her husband she espoused the cause of James II and his descendants. When his foes dubbed James "The Pretender" to the throne of England, Lady Oglethorpe schemed and plotted and worked even harder for his restoration. It is not accidental that in the Stuart papers her most common code name is "Old Fury."

Small wonder that Westbrook manor gained more than local notoriety as a hotbed of Jacobite activity. At first orally and then in pamphlet form a fantastic tale circulated among the credulous. According to it, at the death of the infant Prince of Wales in 1688, an Oglethorpe baby was substituted for him. Had it been true, the story would have meant that the man who for years vainly strove for England's throne as the Old Pretender (James III) was blood brother to Jamie Oglethorpe.

Lady Eleanor could have been no more ardent a Jacobite had it been her son, rather than the man she regarded as England's rightful soveriegn, who played the role of absentee ruler from a quasi-court in France. Three of her daughters entered the inner circle of that court. Anne, 16 years older than Jamie, served as a courier between France and England and was once arrested for entering her homeland without a pass. James III made her Countess of Oglethorpe in 1722. Eleanor, one year older than Anne, became the Marquise de Mézières. Molly, barely nine months her senior, married the Marquis de Bersompierre. Even Jamie's only playmate, Fanny, also went to France where she married Jean Francois de Bellegarde. From their voluntary exile Oglethorpe's sisters spent more than a quarter of a century in a day-dream world. Politically dangerous however fanciful, their goal was restoration of the line of James to England's throne.

Sons of Sir Theophilus and Lady Eleanor were as thoroughly indoctrinated as were their daughters. Lewis, born in 1681, succeeded to his father's seat in Parliament. His brief and colorless career as a lawmaker was punctuated by a duel. Sick of an England that was ruled by a "usurper of the crown," rather than by her exiled "rightful monarch," Lewis went to the Continent as a soldier of fortune. At age ten Jamie learned that his big brother had died of a leg wound sustained in battle.

Theophilus, junior, second of the Oglethorpe sons, took the place in Parliament that was vacated by Lewis. His tenure was also brief and undistinguished. Chucking the whole business he also fought for a time on the Continent before joining the Jacobite court of Saint Germain, France. There his sisters were already high in the favor of the man they regarded as England's true king. Theophilus greatly pleased James III, who made him Baron Oglethorpe of Oglethorpe. Since his newly-elevated follower had no son, the Old Pretender graciously decreed that the hereditary title should be inherited by his brother.

Jamie, who never claimed the Jacobite-conferred title, left few records of his boyhood days. He spent much of every year in London with his mother. As he grew older and was permitted to venture out alone, he became accustomed to cries of vendors hawking lottery tickets. He learned to distinguish the noises and smells of the crowded streets and to feel the vibrations of London Bridge under his feet.

At home in County Surrey 35 miles south of the great city the bold ridges and high valley of Haslemere were regions to be explored during early adolescence. Awesome Gibbet Hill, not far from Westbrook, afforded a breath-taking view of the steep and picturesque valleys that scored Hindhead and Blackdown ridges. Only a few miles to the east was 0° 0' 0'' latitude — so designated by scientists at the Royal Observatory in Greenwich. It was natural to regard Godalming as being very close to the heart of the world. From this region as a center, time was measured — along with distance east and west to the ends of the earth.

Chartered by Queen Elizabeth I in 1575, Godalming was already ancient when Jamie roamed about the village. Located just over the hill from Westbrook, the church of Saints Peter and Paul dominated the region. Its spire made a permanent impression upon him. Though never an ardent participant in worship, Oglethorpe had deep reverence for structures whose architecture proclaimed them to be dedicated to the Almighty. Without becoming a fervent supporter of the established church, he considered organized religion to be an integral and an essential aspect of community life.

Always-ambitious Lady Oglethorpe managed to secure for Jamie an appointment as ensign in the foot guards at age 13. This "paper commission" was torn up four years later when he was made (again on paper) captain of foot. He clearly did long for a military career but at about age 17 Eton College took precedence. He stayed there just long enough to qualify for admission to Oxford University, whose Corpus Christi College he entered in July, 1714. Spires that dominated the skyline of the venerable city strengthened childhood impressions from Godalming.

In Oxford the youngest son of ardent Jacobites found himself in a hotbed of political activity. Queen Anne's death, which came within weeks after he reached the city, triggered Mar's rebellion of 1715. James III landed at Peterhead in a last futile attempt at personal invasion and recapture of "his kingdom." George I, a German-speaking prince descended from James I, gained the crown that Oglethorpe and many others believed the rightful heritage of the Stuarts. Oxford, perpetually in turmoil, was marked by brawls and by a riot started by Jacobites who refused to celebrate the birthday of King George.

How long James stayed at Oxford is unknown. His name may have remained on the register for months after he followed the example of his sisters and brothers and shook the dust of England off his feet. He spent part of 1716 in France. There he managed to join the forces of Prince Eugene of Savoy who was preparing a campaign against the Turks. Much later, Napoleon listed Eugene in the top rank of battlefield geniuses. As aide-de-camp to the prince the youthful expatriate took part in the crucial battle of Belgrade, August, 1717. He emerged without a scratch but the servant who always stayed at his side was killed.

Decades later he regaled Samuel Johnson with anecdotes of his European military career. Johnson's Boswell faithfully recorded a tale according to which James first publicly displayed the steel temper for which he later became noted. As the chief actor in the drama recalled the incident, a high-ranking member of Eugene's entourage deliberately flipped wine into Oglethorpe's face. Smiling and congratulating the German at his skill in playing practical jokes, the youthful Englishman — so he said — exclaimed: "That's a good joke, but we do it much better in England!" Simultaneously he tossed a full glass of wine into the face of the startled general, who was too taken aback to issue a challenge.

When the campaign against the Turks ended shortly after the battle of Belgrade, James set out for Turin, Italy, in order to visit his brother Theophilus — soon to be made a baron by James III. During a period of weeks or months James and his brother paid court to the Old Pretender, now exiled in Italy. James found him "a pretty youth" and clearly counted him as a devoted follower. Leaving Italy, Oglethorpe visited his sisters in France.

It was as a never-say-die Jacobite and potential rebel against his sovereign that James returned to England early in 1719, at age 23. He lived quietly at Westbrook manor with his mother and his sister Molly. Suddenly, in 1722, he emerged from obscurity by announcing that he would stand for Parliament from Haslemere. He offered himself, not as a supporter of an exiled Stuart, but as a true and loyal subject of His Majesty King George I of the House of Hanover.

What forces and factors led a once-ardent Jacobite to reject a cause espoused by his family for decades — turning his back upon his heritage? There are no positive answers. Documents of the era do not even hint as to precisely when and why James Edward Oglethorpe switched his allegiance. Clearly the still-powerful Lady Eleanor concurred in the decision or even initiated it — for the domineering matriarch sensed that the Jacobite star was fast setting.

James III had personally participated in a 1715 attempt at recovery of the throne. Led on the battlefield by the Earl of Mar, it had been a dismal failure. Thousands of Scottish Highlanders who participated in the revolt were punished by being transported for life to the American colonies.

Still the Jacobites hoped and plotted. Cardinal Giulio Alberoni, also prime minister of Spain, was among the most astute diplomats in Europe. He had personally negotiated the marriage between Spain's Philip V and Elizabeth Farnese. With James Butler, second Duke of Ormond, Alberoni plotted for a new invasion of Scotland on behalf of the Catholic Stuarts. It matured to the point that they seriously discussed landing a Spanish expedition there. When this scheme collapsed Lady Oglethorpe realized that a change of allegiance would afford the family's only hope of recouping lost wealth and power.

As a Jacobite nobleman Baron Theophilus Oglethorpe would risk forfeiting the small family estate even if he chose to show up in order to try to gain title to it. His stipend from the family — £100 per year — was so small that the Earl of Mar wondered how he managed to live. Yet he had no intention of returning to England, ever.

James, 15 years his junior, had not burned his political bridges behind him. By changing his political stance he could live as lord of the manor during his mother's lifetime and claim it as his inheritance upon her death. Furthermore, the seat in Parliament briefly held by three earlier Oglethorpes offered an opportunity not to be dismissed lightly.

With the possible exception of Molly, about whom little is known, every child of Sir Theophilus and Lady Eleanor Oglethorpe was highly motivated toward prestige, power, and material success. Did they, individually and collectively, consciously or unconsciously, yearn to regain or even surpass the lost glory and wealth of the family?

Almost certainly that was the case. Altruistic motives were usually visible components of Oglethorpe's attitudes and loyalties. Yet he nearly always demonstrated by deeds his determination to win fame and fortune like that won — and lost — by his grandfather and his father.

An initial step toward his ultimate goal was the decision made in a feverish national climate of risk-taking to stand for Parliament. Haslemere borough had two seats. For practical purposes they were the property of the Oglethorpe and the Molyneaux families. After having held them for a century these landed gentry placed the seats

Godalming, Surrey, England, 1779

Dominated by the spire of the Church of Saints Peter and Paul, the village of Godalming was James Oglethorpe's boyhood home except for time he spent in London.

All his life, he showed deep reverence for religious leaders and himself had strong faith. But he never was especially interestsed in corporate worship, and had no strong attachment to any branch of Christianity.

on the market. Purchasing them through a broker the Earl of Lonsdale paid £24,000 for the borough — which was abolished as a result of the Reform Act of 1832.[4]

Four candidates entered their names in the election of March, 1722. Ballots were divided as follows: Oglethorpe, 46; Peter Burrell, 45;[5] More Molyneaux, 25; and Lord Blundell, 24. At least one newspaper incorrectly announced the election of Blundell and Molyneaux, and defeated candidates drew up a petition of contest which was presented to Parliament without avail.

In days immediately preceding the election villagers expressed sharply partisan views. As a result the famous Oglethorpe temper flared. On Sunday, March 25, according to Oglethorpe's letter that appeared four days later in the London *Daily Journal*, vocal followers of his opponents chanced to meet him after evening service. Words were exchanged. Then at least four men drew their swords. Oglethorpe wounded Mr. Sharpe in the belly, disabled Captain Onslow's left hand and wounded him in the thigh. Then the unscathed candidate for office "bound up Captain Onslow's Wounds and sent for a Surgeon to him."

Election of James Oglethorpe and Peter Burrell to the Parliament of Great Britain was duly reported. Still the tension created by the political contest remained high. April 24, said the London *Daily Journal*, saw another display of temper. At about six in the evening the newly-elected M.P., allegedly overcome with wine, wandered into a tavern. There was a violent argument with a linkman, employed to carry a torch to light the streets. In the ensuing altercation Oglethorpe "drew his Sword and gave the Fellow a mortal Wound in the Breast." For this the budding lawmaker was committed to jail.

Records dealing with this homicide disappeared. Someone had enough influence to get Oglethorpe out of confinement in time to take his seat in the House of Commons on October 9, 1722.

Had there been no election-year brawls publicized in newspapers, many of his colleagues nevertheless would have looked askance at Oglethorpe. Throughout Britain his family's fidelity to the Jacobite cause was proverbial. No matter how fervently the fledgling M.P. might profess loyalty to the reigning sovereign he was always marked as a man to be watched with great care.

If he did not brood over two bloody fights in recent days, he was conscious that the affairs were still the subject of gossip. While deliberately moving 180° away from the political stance of every member of his family, he knew that some colleagues were ready to

Young Oglethorpe

James Edward Oglethorpe sat for this portrait — his earliest — about the time he decided to stand for Parliament, or shortly after his first election to the House of Commons.

In spite of his early and lasting enthusiasm for nearly every form of battle, this portrait — which hangs in the National Portrait Gallery, London — gives no suggestion that he was already a veteran of major European campaigns.

condemn him as a Jacobite without giving him a hearing. So the member from Haslemere bit his tongue and kept his silence for almost six months after Parliament convened.

April, 1723, brought him to his feet. The Rev. Dr. Francis Atterbury, Bishop of Rochester, was a notorious supporter of the Stuarts. He had played a minor role in an abortive 1720 effort to claim England's throne for Charles Edward — the Young Pretender. As a result the bishop, age 60, was arrested. First order of business for England's sixth Parliament was a bill calling for one year's suspension of the Habeas Corpus Act. Subsidiary to it but linked with it was a demand that Atterbury be banished.

Oglethorpe was excitedly conscious that he had few supporters. Speaking in the shrill voice that later came to be familiar to every listener to Parliamentary debates, he challenged his fellows to have mercy. Suffer the cleric "to stay in England under the watchful eye of those in power," he urged. Strongly-worded anti-Jacobite sentiments were included in his speech. He simply had to make it clear that his own loyalties differed from those of the man for whom he sought clemency.[6]

He was quickly and overwhelmingly shouted down and Atterbury was banished.

Never mind.

His spur-of-the-moment defense of a man with few friends had opened a great door. By supporting an under-dog Oglethorpe had at least been heard. Slowly but surely he began moving toward the role of champion of the oppressed, the abused, and the neglected. Perhaps he was not conscious that in a sense he began to use persons and causes as well to crusade for them.

In this dual role he was destined to seize and to exercise kinds of power that neither old Sutton nor his son, Sir Theophilus, ever gained.

Chapter 2

A RISE TO PROMINENCE IN AN ERA OF GRANDIOSE DESIGNS

April, 1723 — May, 1730

If Oglethorpe entertained any false notions about the precariousness of his position, they were soon dispelled. November 16, 1722, brought a message from the king himself. Lord Viscount Townshend delivered it to the House of Peers. His Majesty had learned that "many scandalous Declarations in print" had come into the kingdom from the continent. Hence it seemed appropriate to place before the peers an intercepted inflammatory message. According to the signature, it came from The Pretender himself.

A committee responded to the king's communication by framing a resolution whose heart was: ". . . the Paper . . . intitled, 'Declaration of James the third, king of England, Scotland, and Ireland, to all his loving subjects of the three nations, and to all foreign princes and states, to serve as a foundation for a lasting peace in Europe,' and signed 'James Rex,' is a false, insolent, and traitorous libel, the highest indignity to his most sacred majesty King George, our lawful and undoubted sovereign."

Despite his public posture, in private Oglethorpe clung to some of the principles for which his father fought and lost. He was keenly conscious that he was the inheritor of a tainted tradition and was sensitive to the overwhelmingly anti-Jacobite sentiment of his colleagues. So his maiden speech of April, 1723, that was delivered in the aftermath of the peers' resolution represented a calculated risk. There never was the slightest chance that his plea on behalf of Atterbury, Bishop of Rochester, would sway the verdict of Parliament. But his statement of defense might persuade some members to accept him as a mild high Tory rather than to shun him as a foe of the establishment.

What degree of success he had in his secondary endeavor, no one knows. Clearly — perhaps to his own surprise — he attracted startled attention. But for six years thereafter he remained silent upon the floor of the house. Perhaps some veteran colleague who took a liking to him gave him wise counsel. Perhaps he carefully assessed the total impact of his maiden speech. At any rate Oglethorpe now set out to win his spurs by quiet but strenuous service as a member of committees.

His first assignment, in February, 1724, was to a body with a lengthy title: "Committee to Inquire into pretended Priviledged Places and the best means to abolish them." No one expected it to do anything significant. Yet if it accomplished nothing else this committee brought him into first-hand contact with problems linked with debtors. Many such persons had been taking refuge in the royal mint in order to escape baliffs who sought them.

A year later he was named to a committee that studied proposals for the relief of insolvent debtors. Another group addressed the problem of providing jobs for the poor in the city of Gloucester. Almost simultaneously, in company with other M.P.'s, he probed the scandalous practice of impressment. Boys under 16 were regularly forced into apprenticeship for service as boatmen on the Thames.

By 1726 he had gained enough seniority and respect to become the tenth member named to a 61-man committee chaired by Sir Richard Hopkings. Significantly, Lords Morpeth, Shelburn, How, and Malpas — plus eight baronets — were listed below Oglethorpe when makeup of the body was published. Public safety, relief of shipwrecked sailors, land reclamation, and many other issues were considered by one or more of the 42 committees on which he served during his first five years as a lawmaker.

Many committees were incredibly large. As a rule most persons named to them gave only passing attention to any issue not high on their scales of interest. Actual work of a committee was normally performed by no more than one-fourth of those whose names were linked with it. James Oglethorpe was an exception. Whether or not personally interested in a given committee assignment at the onset, he tried to attend every meeting. Inevitably he made acquaintances and then formed friendships with a growing number of colleagues. Some of the ties so shaped had a lasting impact upon his career.

Perhaps as an effect of things he learned while serving on committees, he became interested in and then concerned about the plight of ordinary seamen in His Majesty's Navy. Late in 1727 or early in 1728 he set out to do something about the abuses with which he had become familiar. For the first time he tested the power of the printed word.

H. Whitredge printed and J. Roberts began selling to the public in 1728 an unsigned book of 52 pages. Its dual purpose was arousal of public opinion against activities of press gangs and persuasion of lawmakers to rise to the defense of seamen. How many persons knew at the time that Oglethorpe had penned *The Sailor's Advocate* remains an open question.

It created immediate interest, however, and was condensed in one of London's leading journals. A keynote of the booklet was the thundering assertion that "It is not the Timber nor the Iron of the *Ships* of War . . . but the Sailors who mann them, who are the strength of the NATION. . . ." No quick and drastic reform measures resulted, but public interest remained so keen that *The Sailor's Advocate* was still being reprinted half a century later.[1]

Concurrently with the sense of accomplishment that resulted from public interest in his booklet, Oglethorpe had another exposure to the pervasive problems of debtors. He went in person to The Fleet, London's famous and forbidding prison so-called because it faced Fleet Street. There he visited an imprisoned friend, Sir Thomas Rich, and was shocked beyond measure at what he saw. Soon afterward the matter of debtors and their welfare became not only personal, but also highly charged with emotion.

Aspiring architect Robert Castell wrote a treatise on *The Villas of the Ancients Illustrated*.[2] He dedicated the superb folio to the Earl of Burlington. Then he arranged to have it printed at his expense and sold by subscription to friends and patrons — a common practice of the era. Only a few copies were sold. His close friend Oglethorpe was among the handful who subscribed to two copies.

Plunged into debt by his unsuccessful venture as author-publisher, Castell evaded his creditors briefly. Then, exercising rights that were standard in 18th-century England, they demanded that the architect go to prison. Long-standing laws specified that "the person [body] of the debtor was the property of the creditor until the debt was discharged." This meant that regardless of the amount owed, any debtor could be thrown into a filthy prison that was operated on a fee basis.

On June 18, 1728, Mr. Justice Price committed Castell to The Fleet. There the office of warden had been purchased by Thomas Bambridge for £5,000. fee. Upon admission every prisoner was expected to pay the warden a £5 fee. If he had any cash left he was lodged in a "sponging house" named for the fashion in which it soaked up money very rapidly. Profits from charges for board and lodging went to the warden. In turn he was responsible for the pay of turnkeys and other subordinates.

Prisoners who could afford to do so paid stiff fees for the privilege of lodging outside the walls of the gaol but within specified limits called "The Rules of The Fleet." Affluent debtors had the privilege of walking at liberty within the yard. Some even exercised their trades while technically confined. Persons living within rules of The Fleet in the year Oglethorpe entered Parliament actually made good money producing and selling pornographic ballads.

When a prisoner's cash was depleted he was clapped in irons as a warning. Sometimes that was enough to persuade him to find more money. If he could not or would not produce the fees demanded by the warden, his treatment grew progressively worse. Eventually he landed in a dungeon so packed with desperate men that there was barely room to move. In such holes gaol fever was endemic; other more virulent diseases were often present.

Upon entering The Fleet, Robert Castell bribed the warden to get comfortable lodgings. When he could not continue his payment Bambridge ordered him into quarters where smallpox was raging. Castell protested; he had never been exposed to the disease, and feared for his life. No matter; into the contaminated area he went.

Soon after being forced into a pest-hole the architect contracted smallpox and died. He left "all his affairs in the greatest confusion, and a numerous family of small children in the utmost distress." In July, 1729, a few copies of *The Villas of the Ancients* were sold for the benefit of his widow and children.

Five months before the sale took place Oglethorpe went into action. His initial goal was prosecution of Bambridge, with the hope that the warden would be convicted of murder.

Long-established precedent dictated that certain issues should be initially considered by the House of Lords. So he persuaded the Earl of Stafford to call attention to conditions in The Fleet and to the plight of insolvent debtors in general. A resolution from the peers went to the House of Commons as a prelude to possible legislation.

Oglethorpe then persuaded his colleagues to establish a committee "to inquire into the State of the Gaols of this Kingdom and report the same with their Opinion thereupon."

At the head of the 96-man list issued on February 25, 1729, was Mr. Oglethorpe. Among the distinguished committee members were the chancellor of the exchequer and the master of the rolls; Lords Morpeth, Powlett, Inchequin, Percival, and Malpas, plus General George Wade and 23 baronets.

Few lawmakers envied the chairman his post. Opposition to reform of the penal system was deep, widespread, and firmly entrenched in places of power. There had been sporadic earlier and unsuccessful attempts to effect change. In the year of Oglethorpe's birth the shocking conditions of debtors confined to The Fleet had been described to the House of Commons by a member named Pocklington. Aldermen of London issued in 1702 a *Report of the Justices on the Abuses to Poor Debtors in Newgate Gaol*. An estimate framed in 1716 placed "total miserable debtors" in Britain's prison at 60,000.

One person who took early interest in debtors was the Rev. Dr. Thomas Bray, born in 1656. An inveterate organizer, he founded the two oldest English missionary bodies: The Society for the Propagation of the Gospel in Foreign Parts, and The Society for the Promotion of Christian Knowledge. At the turn of the century, when Oglethorpe was a toddler, Bray took active interest in the plight of debtors and other prisoners.

His fellow-workers came to be called Associates of Dr. Bray. They managed to distribute some tracts to prisoners but failed to get the interested attention of the public or of Parliament. Eventually they developed an interlocking relationship with pioneer leaders of the Colony of Georgia.

Parliament's 1729 committee headed by Oglethorpe included two associates of Dr. Bray — Lord John Percival, later First Earl of Egmont; and James Vernon. Vernon was the son of the secretary of state who bore the same name and who proscribed Sir Theophilus Oglethorpe. Egmont and Vernon were among the minority of gaol committee members who took their task seriously. Actual work of the investigative body was done by less than two dozen persons. When William Hogarth painted "The Fleet Prison Committee," just 15 bewigged lawmakers posed for him.

An initial report read on March 20, 1729, detailed shocking conditions found at The Fleet. His Majesty was begged to ask the attorney-general to prosecute six prison officials. Simultaneously, a four-man group headed by Oglethorpe began work drawing up bills asking for essential reform measures.

Three separate reports of which Oglethorpe was the architect were issued during the period that ended on May 11, 1730. Bambridge was relieved of office as Warden of The Fleet, but no prison official received severe punishment and no long-term sweeping reforms were instituted. Still, the Insolvent Debtors Relief Act of 1729 did temporarily better the condition of some imprisoned debtors. It also resulted in release of "many miserable wretches," whose numbers were variously estimated at a few hundred to 10,000.[3] To most who were released, freedom meant no more than an opportunity to wander the streets and fight starvation.

Oglethorpe's final recommendations, adopted without a dissenting vote, failed to effect permanent change in the English penal system. But they made his name familiar to the public and propelled him into a place of leadership in Parliament. Because of the highly unpopular nature of the task assigned to his committee, no one could have predicted such an outcome.

Analyzing this denouement, Lecky concluded that "He (Oglethorpe) would probably have remained an undistinguished Member of Parliament if it had not happened that among his acquaintances was a gentleman named Castell." That verdict is suggestive within limits but is greatly over-simplified. It fails to take into account Oglethorpe's complex personality and his deep-rooted drive to become much more than Sutton's grandson and Sir Theophilus' son. Had there been no Fleet and no Castell tragedy some other catalytic event would have released and channeled Oglethorpe's enormous life-long drive toward befriending the friendless, aiding the helpless, and ameliorating the conditions of the oppressed.

Immediate impact upon his career was as dramatic as it was unpredictable. While pursuing the gaol investigation he had learned how to secure Parliamentary appropriations: £700 in May, 1729, and an additional £400 one year later to fund his committee's work. Few investigative committtees received any funding whatever. Egmont, the wealthy Whig nobleman who had become an intimate of the Tory from Haslemere, calculated that Oglethorpe could be counted among the dozen "leading members of the House."

Shortly after the gaol inquiry was concluded England was rocked by scandals involving misappropriation of funds belonging to the Charitable Corporation. Created to offer loans at low interest, it was exploited by powerful officers. Failure of the corporation led the House to elect leading members to a committee charged with investigating the vast issues raised. His fellows showed their esteem for Oglethorpe by giving him the eighth highest vote for Charitable Corporation committee membership.

Oxford University, where he made no measurable progress toward earning his degree, honored herself by specially creating Oglethorpe a Master of Arts. Far more significant for his future and for the New World were associations formed during the period of gaol reform, plus deepening interest and new focal points for his already-strong urge toward humanitarian goals.

In a sense he was out of step with his era. It was an age of feverish speculation that fostered many grandiose designs — nearly all of which were profit-oriented.

Many aspects of life were remarkably stable; for example, there was no inflation. Neither were there any of the rapid changes soon to be brought about by the Industrial Revolution. Upward mobility in the highly stratified society was severely limited, despite the fact that some London shopkeepers "even had their own coaches."

Ferment was concentrated largely in political and economic spheres, rather than pervading every aspect of life.

In the aftermath of the Glorious Revolution of 1688, with James II still claiming the throne from exile, lawmakers had pushed through the Act of Settlement. This measure was ostensibly designed to provide for orderly succession to the throne — with all Catholic hopes supposedly crushed. Actually it placed severe limitations upon the power of the monarch. Divine right of kings, accepted as an article of faith as late as the time of James I, went out the window. For the first time Parliament became a truly powerful body with growing control of the budget.

Religious differences were heightened rather than reduced by a central paragraph of the Act of Settlement:

"Resolved —

'That King James II, having endeavoured to subvert the constitution of his kingdom by breaking the original contract between king and people; and, by the advice of Jesuits and other wicked persons, having violated the fundamental laws; and having withdrawn himself out of the kingdom; has abdicated the Government; and that the throne is hereby vacant;'

Resolved —

'That it hath been found by experience to be inconsistent

with the safety and welfare of this Protestant kingdom to be
governed by a Popish Prince.' "

No matter how faithful a man might be to the reigning sovereign, he
was barred from leaving his estate to Catholic heirs.

England and Scotland achieved legislative union in 1707, when
Oglethorpe was 11 years old. When Wales joined the fold Great
Britain emerged as a nation. England's earlier involvement in
struggles for military and economic supremacy culminated in the
Peace of Utrecht, April 11, 1713.[4] By every estimate it was then that
Britain became a contender for first rank among western powers.
This upward surge took place in little more than a decade.

For the moment France was the chief rival of Britain, but her
explosive move into the New World made Spain a foe with whom to
reckon once more. Under terms of the Peace of Utrecht, which
settled the War of the Spanish Succession, a French Bourbon
assumed the Spanish throne. Wealth of South America had been
pouring across the Atlantic for decades. During his long reign
Philip V had nearly unlimited resources with which to expand both
military and commercial fleets. Though it would not explode for
thirty years, a grenade had been lighted. Anglo-Spanish conflict on
the seas was inevitable.

British society was sharply and clearly divided into the haves
and the have-nots. According to one calculation the kingdom
included no more than 400 great landlords, half of them peers of
the realm, whose income was £3,000 per year or more.

At the bottom of the socio-economic scale were uncounted
masses of the wretched poor, whose cash income was too low to be
calculated. A maid-of-all work could expect annual wages of no
more than 30 to 40 shillings. At that she was immeasurably better
off than growing numbers of one-time farm laborers who, forced
from the fields, flocked to the cities to join the ranks of the
unemployed.

Between the great landlords and the servants were a handful of
successful shopkeepers whose earnings ran to perhaps £400 per
year. Landed gentry were of high social class but were little if any
better off in purchasing power. An estimated 15,000 families,
including that of Oglethorpe, owned considerable real property
but had median cash income under £500 per year.[5] Enormous
capital — a minimum of £30,000 — was required to move from
ranks of the petty gentry into the "great landlord" category.

Britain included at least 100,000 families who held small tracts of land in fee-simple or for life. Termed freeholders, males of such families were eligible to vote in Parliamentary elections. Provided that rental value of his land exceeded 40 shillings per annum, a freeholder could even stand for election. Few such persons had yearly cash income of £100, hence most lived just above the level of tenant farmers and servants in such households as Oglethorpe's Westbrook manor.

Since the nation was still overwhelmingly rural, the agricultural revolution drove increasing numbers of the desperately poor to seek refuge in a few urban centers. London, whose population was fast approaching 500,000 and who was soon to become the largest metropolis in Europe, was the mecca of Britain's desperate. Other fast-growing cities included Edinburgh (35,000), Bristol and Norwich (20,000+). Increasing significance of North America was underscored by the fact that, very soon, fast-growing Philadelphia would become the second largest city in the British Empire.

Prevailing attitudes toward the impoverished, nearly all of whom were locked for life in the stratum into which they were born, varied from callous indifference to benevolent despotism. A playing card issued about the time Oglethorpe made his maiden speech in Parliament expressed a major aspect of the latter attitude:

> The Poor when manag'd, and employ'd in Trade,
> Are to the publick Welfare, usefull made;
> But if kept Idle from their Vices Spring
> Whores for the Stews [brothels],
> and Soldiers for the King.

As a corollary of the principle that the poor must be kept hard at work because work is good for them, there was the conviction that the poor must have religion. It, too, is good for them and hence for society. Such views were never formally expressed in surviving records of Georgia's Trustees or in correspondence of Georgia's founder. Yet the Trustees in general and Oglethorpe in particular demonstrated by deeds that such ideas about the poor were accepted as fundamental.

One route — and only one — seemed to offer some hope for economic progress by a few poor. Covent Garden, alone, supported 22 gaming houses. In one of these a fortunate one might start with a few pence and enjoy a run of luck sufficient to enable him briefly to break out of rigid desperation.

James III, "The Old Pretender"

James III, son of the exiled Stuart monarch who fled as a result of the Glorious Revolution of 1688, set up a court in France.

Numerous members of the Oglethorpe family — including young James Edward — had personal contact with him.

For decades, Britain was in almost constant turmoil because Highlanders and others loyal to James III were forever devising a new plot to "restore Britain's rightful ruler to the throne."

Some sons of great landlords tried to improve their personal situations by borrowing against their expected inheritances. Baron Lyttleton charged that "all sons thought their fathers in their dotage at fifty, and proceeded to divide up the estates by means of post obits." There is no record of such borrowing on the part of Oglethorpe. His return to England and his change in political stance were, however, closely linked with anticipation that he would inherit Westbrook.

For many gentry of his class, living in a comfortable manor with a dozen or more servants but having little cash, lotteries seemed to offer a way up and out. Defoe raged, without effect, against the all-pervasive climate of risk-taking by persons of every economic group. "There has risen up in our age," he said, "a new-fangled fantastic credulity . . . whereby innocent, industrious and unwary people have been delivered into the ravening and polluted jaws of vultures and tygers."

Private lotteries proliferated to such an extent that they were envied and then seized upon by Parliament's budget-makers. As a result the government floated its own lotteries on a large scale. Net profit from a given state lottery seldom fell below £300,000. Managers of state lotteries issued packets of tickets, often in lots of 50, to members of Parliament on generous terms. Discounts were so great that re-sale of such tickets brought profits as great as £2 per ticket.

For those whose tastes did not run toward lotteries there were get-rich-quick schemes of every conceivable variety and of all dimensions. During the century of Oglethorpe's birth an enterprise involving great risk and promising large potential gain came to be termed a "bubble." This usage grew out of the fragile nature of the

venture, rather than the fashion in which notable ones were inflated
as rapidly as soap bubbles at the end of a pipe.

During the period in which Oglethorpe was making his decision
to seek a seat in Parliament a few months in a single summer saw
corporations of undisclosed size floated for such purposes as:

> Planting mulberry trees in Chelsea Park, plus
>   breeding of silkworms.
> Draining bogs in Ireland.
> Manufacturing oil from sunflower seeds.
> Importing Spanish jackasses in order to breed mules.

Other companies whose stock was hawked during this period
boasted of their size:

> Capital, two millions: for insuring of horses.
> Capital, three millions: for insuring to masters
>   and mistresses losses they may sustain
>   by servants.
> Capital: two millions: for erecting salt works.
> Capital: ten millions: for carrying on the royal
>   fishery of Great Britain.
> Capital, two millions: for importing walnut-trees
>   from Virginia.

For the investor who discarded these and many other possibilities
one promoter floated a company that offered "to carry on an undertaking of great advantage, but nobody to know what it is. Every
subscriber who deposits £2 per share to be entitled to £100 per
annum."[6]

Whether for a secret undertaking not revealed to purchasers of
shares in a bubble, for "a wheel for perpetual motion," or for
extraction of gold from sea water, most highly-speculative enterprises were relatively small in scale. Not so the South Sea Company.
Launched when Oglethorpe was 15, the chief promoter was Robert
Harley — soon to become Earl of Oxford.

Harley suggested that the company formed for the purpose of
gaining a monopoly in trade with South America should take over
£9,000,000 of Britain's national debt. Eventually the South Sea Co.
offered to fund the entire £51,000,000 debt at 5% for a century and
4% thereafter. Alarmed, directors of the rival Bank of England
offered the government £5,000,000 for the lucrative long-term

contract — but the South Sea Co. bid £7,567,000 and got it in April, 1720.

Launched as a legitimate trading enterprise, the South Sea Co. was designed to straddle the ocean separating the New World from the Old. Its change of course and acquisition of the national debt transformed it into a gigantic bubble — perhaps the biggest until the 20th century. At the beginning of 1720 shares of the company sold for £128.5 but had doubled in value by March. May saw the stock reach £550 and in June it approached £900. In July it passed £1,000 per share and briefly held at that level.

By that time insiders who had not already done so began to unload their holdings. During a period of less than 60 days shares fell from above £1,000 to £135. Dozens of smaller bubbles created in imitation of the South Sea Co. crashed along with it. In many cases stock of such enterprises could not be sold at any price.

Some speculators became wealthy. One of them, bookseller Thomas Guy whose stall was located at the intersection of Lombard Street and Cornhill — afterward famous as "the lucky corner" — sold out just in time. With part of his newly-acquired fortune he endowed famous Guy's Hospital.

Most who profited greatly from the debacle were company executives and insiders. Some of these who were implicated in the ensuing investigation were: Chancellor of the Exchequer John Aislabie, Joint Postmaster-general James Craggs, Secretary of State James Craggs, and Commissionary of the Treasury Charles Stanhope.

Aislabie, whose profits were estimated at £794,000, was expelled from Parliament and imprisoned. He and all other directors of the South Sea Co. had their estates confiscated.

So great was the fiscal crisis that the stability of the government was threatened. Desperate lawmakers turned for help to 44-year-old Sir Robert Walpole. Earlier serving as secretary of war and treasurer of the navy, he had been expelled from Parliament on charges of venality in office. When the South Sea bubble burst, he was paymaster of the forces. In the time of national desperation he was made first lord of the treasury and chancellor of the exchequer.

Walpole managed to salvage enough South Sea Co. assets to provide a fund of credit exceeding £40,000,000. This cushion softened the corporate fall sufficiently to enable it to remain in business until 1853.

For Walpole, an outspoken Whig, the South Sea debacle provided an opportunity to become "the right man, at the right spot, at the right time." His masterful handling of the crisis boosted him to undisputed top place in the government and made him Britain's first prime minister. Later decorated with the Order of the Garter and created First Earl of Orford, he was the nation's most influential man during a period of more than 20 years when George II sat on England's throne.

It was Walpole with whom Oglethorpe and his colleagues had to deal in most cases involving basic interests of the Colony of Georgia. "No man before or since," concludes John B. Owen, "has dominated British politics for so long."[7] During most of his period of dominance Walpole dispensed patronage — formerly the province of the sovereign — and controlled the cabinet, Parliament, and the Whig party.

Bursting of scores of small bubbles plus the biggest of them all did little, if anything, to reduce public interest in entirely different but equally speculative kinds of enterprises. For more than a generation before James Edward began to redeem the Oglethorpe family name, men had been fascinated with the possibility of winning quick wealth in the New World.

William Paterson, founder of the Bank of England, tried to establish a Scottish colony in the isthmus of Darien (now Panama) in 1698. His "Darien Scheme" wiped out his fortune. But a government grateful to him for his role as banker compensated him for his losses in the sum of £18,000.

Few who tried to float a New World colony lost so heavily as did Paterson. Most promoters did not go beyond issuing literature and stock. Sir Robert Montgomery, a Nova Scotian baronet, in 1717 projected for the unexplored region between the Savannah and Altamaha rivers a colony he called the Margravate of Azilia. He got a land grant from Carolina's proprietors, conditioned upon beginning settlement within three years. Then he published *A Discourse Concerning the Design'd Establishment of a New Colony to the South of Carolina, in the Most Delightful Country of the Universe.*[8] Beyond that he did little; the projected colony ended in dreams and talk without attracting even one settler.

Land of unknown extent and value lay to the south of Carolina, adjoining immense tracts claimed by France. Fast-growing Carolina could well use a buffer to protect it from Indians and French to the west and from increasing danger of attack by Spanish forces from Florida. So the region to which Montgomery vaguely looked became the focus of interest by others.

At least one unpublished map drawn up about the time Oglethorpe was winning his military spurs in Europe labelled the region

The Press Yard, Newgate Prison

A workman, hammer raised, is in the process of removing shackles from a felon. They are in the Press Yard of Newgate Prison. Removal of the shackles suggests that the prisoner has decided to come to terms with the warden and pay exorbitant fees for better treatment — though occasionally even persons of some substance served out their terms before having shackles removed.

Georgia — in tribute to then-ruling King George I. There is no evidence that this name was widely used, however. Ordinary persons plus most would-be colonizers who considered the region used Carolina as an all-inclusive label.

Lord John Percival, who "kissed the king's hand" on August 5, 1733, when the monarch made him Earl of Egmont, was among those who had more than casual interest in the still-unoccupied region. Records of Britain's privy council include a tantalizing reference dated November 19, 1728. According to it, at this early time Egmont and others had some vague notion about securing a Carolina land grant "for settling a Charitable Colony." Whatever their intentions may have been, they accomplished nothing at this time.

Prior to December, 1730, there is no hint concerning proposals that matured as the Georgia scheme. In a long letter of that month, writing to George Berkeley, Egmont spoke of a mutual friend. James Oglethorpe, he said, had earlier proposed to establish below Carolina a haven for England's oppressed.

Unlike Sir Robert Montgomery and other would-be colonizers, Oglethorpe did not act in a vacuum. During a conversation about work of the gaol committee he confided to Egmont, on February 13, 1730, the "unexpected find" of £5,000 soon to be available for charitable work.

A person identified only as a Milk Street haberdasher named King had inherited or accumulated a substantial estate. At his death he left £15,000 in the hands of three trustees. One of them, his heir, had delayed disposition of the fund in hope of securing all of it for himself. His fellow trustees had turned to the man propelled into the spotlight by his work on behalf of debtors. They were willing, they told Oglethorpe, to release one-third of the trust if it could be attached to an existing charity.

Oglethorpe and Egmont agreed that it was more than coincidental that a suitable channel for use of the King monies was already available. Years earlier, Dr. Thomas Bray had secured from Abel Tassin D'Allone a gift of £900. This sum was restricted to use in providing Christian instruction for negroes in the New World. Long before his death in 1730 Bray persuaded four of his associates to join him as trustees of the D'Allon fund. For this purpose he selected Egmont, who earlier gave him £200 for his many enterprises,[9] plus William Belitha, the Rev. Stephen Hales, and Robert Hales.

Associates of Dr. Bray should be enlarged in order to handle the anticipated £5,000, Oglethorpe said. At Egmont's request he joined the group and for a year served as its chairman. With the King money in the hands of such men something notable could be achieved.[10] It was to this end that Oglethorpe looked to far-away Carolina — about which he knew little more than the name and approximate location.

Chapter 3

CONCEPTION, GESTATION, AND BIRTH OF A GRAND UTOPIAN SCHEME

May, 1730 — June, 1732

A legend that refuses to die insists that Georgia was colonized by debtors newly released from English prisons. Origins of the myth are impossible to miss. Yet no careful analyst has found evidence that even one dozen such persons actually became pioneer Georgians.

Another fallacy that appears in most studies of Oglethorpe and his deeds has to do with the supposedly "intractible nature" of Georgia's founder. He certainly could be so stubborn that he sometimes nearly drove other persons wild. But when circumstances dictated a different approach he could be pliable — especially about details concerning a goal or plan. After developing the Georgia design he yielded to pressure or changed his own mind, not once but over and over. As it crystallized after months of effort and numerous modifications the scheme was only remotely like that first proposed.

Adaptation, compromise, and revision did not take place in isolation. Men who eventually shaped the Georgia colony were occupied with other things, too. During the first six months of 1730 the gaol committee issued its second and third reports. Parliament gave unanimous approval to proposed reforms on May 12. While moving toward that goal even the crusading chairman of the committee gave considerable attention to unrelated issues.

He enthusiastically supported a strong anti-Spanish resolution that was adopted by the Commons on March 13. Along with his fellows he gave perfunctory approval to the Royal African Company's annual £10,000 subsidy — continued until 1746. Later he was offered a seat on the board of directors of the once-profitable enterprise that specialized in providing Africans for the American colonies.

He had initially hoped and expected to see Thomas Bambridge, warden of The Fleet, convicted of murder — but came to realize that bigger issues were involved. So Oglethorpe spoke only once during the trial of prison officials and did not protest when all defendants were acquitted.

Georgia's founder had a long conversation with Egmont on Friday, February 13. Before they parted the member from Haslemere suggested that the anticipated King fund of £5,000 would serve nicely for their plan. Oglethorpe hoped "to procure a quantity of acres either from the Government or by gift or purchase in the West Indies, and to plant thereon a hundred miserable wretches who being let out of gaol by last year's Act, are now starving about the town for want of employment; that they should be settled all together by way of colony, and be subject to subordinate rulers, who should inspect their behaviour and labour under one chief head."

This first detailed proposal, though centered vaguely in the West Indies rather than on the North American mainland, was a product of gaol committee work. What more natural than to suggest, as well, that D'Allone Trustees be augmented from ranks of this committee in order to handle the new and larger fund?

Since the King estate was involved in litigation, it might be well to pick up from some other source the small amount of money believed sufficient to get the scheme under way.[1] On March 19 Oglethorpe called on Egmont to urge "that we might speak to Sir Robert Walpole for Lottery tickets for the advantage of" what — by now — was often termed "the Carolina Colony."[2]

A few days earlier the two lawmakers, supported by some of their colleagues, had made their first approach to Walpole concerning the possibility of an Act of Parliament. They wanted a Parliamentary charter "for the charitable colony we design to plant in [the] South [of] Carolina."[3] Walpole's initially favorable reaction was reversed overnight. He bristled with objections and told Egmont that the proposed colony should be a project of the king, not Parliament.[4]

With support still highly uncertain Egmont approached a relative and asked him to intercede with trustees of a £40,000 fund established by the late Thomas Tufton, Earl of Thanet. From it, suggested Oglethorpe's colleague, perhaps they could hope for £10,000. Once more the initiative brought a rebuff. Undaunted, Oglethorpe hammered away at "his project of sending a colony of poor and honest industrious debtors."

July 30 saw a meeting of the Associates of Dr. Bray, among whom Anglican clergymen were prominent. They agreed to seek land "on the south-west of Carolina" to establish their settlers. By now future colonists were usually described simply as "poor persons of London" who were not necessarily freed debtors.

Present at the July session was a high-ranking accountant of the South Sea Co. Also on hand was Captain Thomas Coram, a longtime member of Bray's parish and a veteran of New World travel. He gained approval of a proposal almost certainly discussed earlier with Oglethorpe and Egmont.

With time passing and no cash in hand, why not go to the public for help? Coram was authorized to explore this possibility in Tunbridge. As seed money to get the venture started Egmont handed over ten guineas. This gift was secured, through a friend, from the charity fund of the Prince of Wales. Robert Hucks, a wealthy brewer and M.P., approved of soliciting aid from the public but made no gift himself. James Oglethorpe came forward with £20.[5]

July saw England's privy council taking notice of a request from "a Group of Gentleman Petitioners" who hoped to be chartered as "The Corporation for Establishing Charitable Colonies in America." Their document "prayed His Majesty" for a grant of land "between the River Savana and Alortamalla" for the purpose of establishing a still vaguely-defined charitable colony. Petitioners also begged authority "to receive Charitable Benefactions of all those who are willing to promote the said Undertaking."

Referred to the board of trade with a memorandum pointing out that "the Citys of London and Westminster and places adjacent Do abound with great numbers of indigent Persons," the proposal got favorable reports. In spite of them no formal action was taken for a year. Meanwhile Oglethorpe was made a director of the Royal African Company — a potentially profitable post. He waited until January, 1732, to qualify by purchasing £1,000 of the company's stock.[6]

If public subscriptions would be needed in order to start the colony, as seemed increasingly likely, publicity was vital. February, 1731, saw publication in The *Gentleman's Magazine* of a pioneer story dealing with the proposed experiment. There is no record that Oglethorpe was responsible for this account. But when his colleagues agreed upon a publicity campaign it was the member from Haslemere who was named to head it.

March brought a new idea for financing the experiment. Seeking to establish a missionary college in Bermuda, Irish clergyman George Berkeley had secured substantial support. Yet his project still faced many obstacles. Perhaps he could be persuaded to shift to Carolina and divide the £20,000 promised him by the government. That was the heart of Egmont's suggestion, expounded to Berkeley in a letter of December 23.

This initial probe came to nothing. Significantly for the future, it envisioned Carolina as a region where colonists "may raise white mulberry trees and send us good raw silk."

In order to prepare the clergyman for Egmont's request, Oglethorpe contacted him earlier. He went into great detail about utopian plans for Carolina, stressing "charity to distressed pesons" rather than aid to debtors only. Christianity would surely benefit from the scheme, the politician told the churchman.

On the European continent Christianity was in fresh ferment. August had seen adoption of the Covenant of Salt by 100 representative Salzburghers. These folk were citizens of Salzburg on the Salza, famous as the birthplace of Mozart. Defying ecclesiastical authority their covenant led to an open rift with powerful Archbishop Firmian. Sixty days after being challenged Firmian issued orders requiring all Protestants who were not burghers to leave the archbishopric within eight days. Clearly, great numbers of these refugees — and not merely London's poor — would welcome a haven in Carolina or anywhere else.

Along with early reports about dispossessed European Protestants the fiercely anti-Catholic Parliament heard rumors of trouble in their nation's Charitable Corporation. Established in 1707 as an agency whose function was to lend small sums to merchants and artisans, it began with a capital of just £30,000. Fever of the times transformed it, too, into a bubble. By September, 1731, it had swollen into a fund of £514,370. Stock was held for speculative purposes by many notables and national leaders.

John Thompson, an official of the corporation, was said to have "run away with their books, and, it is thought, a great deal of their cash." Matters proved far worse than even pessimists had feared.

King George II

King George II, for whom Georgia was named, was keenly aware of his German heritage and was deeply interested in the plight of German Protestants. Unlike his father, George I, he spoke English — and as a boy served as interpreter for his father.

A seasoned horseman who liked to ride and hunt, George II fought in the battle of Dettingen, Bavaria, in 1743 — during the era in which Oglethorpe was fighting the Spanish. He was the last British sovereign to appear on a field of battle — and clearly admired the martial character of Georgia's founder. There is a remote possibility (wholly undocumented) that he may have secretly provided Oglethorpe with money — which would have had to be repaid in full.

With liabilities approaching £600,000 the Charitable Corporation was left with assets of no more than 2% of that sum.

Oglethorpe and 20 other lawmakers were elected by their fellows to form an investigating committee. Capital involved was small by comparison with that of the South Sea Co., but emotional reaction was at a high level.

Sir Robert Sutton, a distant relative of Oglethorpe, was deeply involved in the scandal. Though the member from Haslemere asked his colleagues to show mercy, Sutton was found guilty of fraud. He and Sir Archibald Grant were expelled from Parliament. Because many small investors were ruined, public interest was keen. Publications of the period gave detailed attention to every phase of the Charitable Corporation and its failure. Oglethorpe's role in the investigation was duly noted, but the press remained silent about his concurrent championship of ordinary enlisted men in the military forces.

Progress of the memorial seeking to charter a non-profit group to sponsor charitable colonies in America was very slow. Nothing like it had ever been presented to British leaders. Their experience with proprietary and crown colonies would have enabled them to deal promptly with a New World enterprise in which everyone involved hoped to make big profits.

Unique nonprofit emphases were not barometers indicating that Georgia's founder never sought personal gain. On the contrary, one of his paramount long-term goals was wealth.

Almost a decade before Oglethorpe became interested in the Carolinas, Swiss adventurer Jean Pierre Purry tried to establish a colony there.[7] He lacked financial backing and was frustrated by the powerful proprietors of Carolina, so his 1722 plan came to nothing. In 1731 he was back in London with a modified set of proposals. His ideas evoked such admiration from men associated with Dr. Bray that they subscribed £200 to aid Purry.

Oglethorpe listened with rapt attention as the Swiss promoter described the region close to the 33rd parallel. Just one degree of latitude north of present-day Savannah, the area was described as being blessed with an absolutely perfect climate. That meant many valuable commodities imported from the Orient could be produced there.

On December 4, 1731, a secret document was drawn up, signed, and witnessed. Written in French and lodged in Britain's Public Record Office but lost for generations, it was a contract between Purry and Oglethorpe. In return for a promise of one-fourth interest in the Carolina grant Oglethorpe agreed to put his influence and support behind Purry.[8]

Georgia's proposed charter was the topic of many secret discussions. As talk progressed the original idea of establishing a colony with the sole purpose of aiding London's poor was repeatedly modified and amplified. Petitioners led by Oglethorpe pressed for support of their views. But they had to deal with the attorney-general, the solicitor-general, the board of trade, the privy council and its committees, Sir Robert Walpole, the king, and Parliament.

Walpole, not George II, was the most powerful man in Britain. Still, the sovereign could delay action on some proposals indefinitely or kill them by indecision. He objected to various segments of the nearly-completed document submitted to him. Twice he gave tentative approval, then changed his mind or balked at signing anything. In this dilemma someone suggested that the new American colony be named for the sovereign.

It was not a novel approach. Carolina honored Charles II — from the Latin form of his name — when granted to eight of the king's favorites in 1663. Captain Thomas Coram had hoped in 1713 to establish a colony in the region of Maine's Sagadahoc river, now the Kennebec. He expected Fredrick Louis, Prince of Wales, to ascend the throne soon. So Coram offered to call the capital of his proposed province either New Hanover from the native land of the prince, or Augusta in honor of Frederick's wife.

After years of fruitless waiting Coram made a new approach. This time he suggested that the North American colony be called Georgia, in honor of then-reigning King George I. Formally presented to the board of trade in 1717, the proposal involved establishment of 30 or more Trustees with full governing powers. This plan was never implemented.

So the scheme by which the vanity of George II might cause him to approve a colony bearing his name brought the final shift from "Carolina" to "Georgia."[9] On April 21, 1732, the sovereign finally signed the long-awaited charter. It then had to go through the formality of "passing the Great Seal." With all signatures affixed on June 9, it was promulgated on June 20, 1732.

Lengthy and complex, the charter provided that "The Trustees for establishing the Colony of Georgia in America" would have full governing rights. Land between the Savannah and Altamaha rivers, extending westward to the South Seas, was to be under their control for 21 years. After that it would revert to the crown.

Stated purposes of the colonial experiment, expounded in minute detail, had grown from a single clear-cut goal to three separate but inter-related ones. Benefits were expected to accrue to "many of our poor subjects" — and to foreigners in like circumstances who were willing to become British subjects.

Increase in the "trade, navigation, and wealth of these our realms" was also envisioned in Georgia's charter. Long before it was issued men seeking it had become convinced that they had fixed upon a new Eden. Silk could be produced there at low cost and in vast quantities. Indigo, wine, cochineal, and a host of other things not produced in volume anywhere in Britain's realm would flow from Georgia. Thereby colonists would live in comfort and the empire would be enriched.

Last in sequence but perhaps first in significance to king and Parliament, it was noted that South Carolina had unprotected frontiers. Encouraged and probably aided by the French, Indians had frequently come in from the west to ravage the colony. Its southern border lay open, fostering a constant flow of runaway slaves to the haven promised them by the Spanish in Florida. Lot in life of "our above-mentioned poor subjects" would be improved when they settled in Georgia by royal permission. Soon they would simultaneously create a protective shield for rich and highly-developed South Carolina.

One provision of the charter was without precedent. No Trusteee could receive any "salary, fee, perquisite, benefit or profit whatsoever." Full religious freedom was promised to all except Catholics.[10]

Members of the Georgia Society were so sure of ultimate success that they tried to move into action before formal promulgation of the charter. One of them, George Heathcote, conveyed to Parliament their lastest scheme. It proposed that vagrants be bound as apprentices to invalid soldiers, then maintained in the colony for a number of years at government expense. For such a noble purpose it seemed appropriate to seek something not normally given to a British outpost — a Parliamentary appropriation.

Objections to the request for £10,000 were immediate and strong. Georgia never even came close to becoming an old soldiers' haven. Within less than a month after having been floated, this proposal was formally shelved on May 17. As a result Egmont ruefully recorded in his *Diary* the observation that "for want of money I find we shall be able to do nothing in pursuance of our charter this year."

Precisely how much money would be needed, even those who sought a grant didn't know. Estimates ranged below £5,000 as a minimum with which to start. Lord Carteret's proprietary claim upon Carolina still gave him one-seventh interest in land forming the new colony. It would be futile, he insisted, to begin with less than £20,000 cash and 1,000 settlers.

On June 29 an exuberant James Edward Oglethorpe brought the Georgia charter to newly-named Trustees. They had gathered in offices rented a few days earlier for £30 a year. Their utopia had been conceived as a haven for English debtors, to be funded by legacies. Months of compromise had shaped it into a refuge for worthy poor of whatever origin who would aid Britain's economic and military purposes. As modified in the interests of imperial Britain the Georgia scheme was woefully dependent upon public subscriptions and faced an uphill struggle for survival.

Chapter 4

A RASH DECISION, MADE IN HASTE

June — November, 1732

Initially-named Georgia Trustees, 21 males, already knew one another well. Ten had served together on the gaol committee. All had participated in the work of Dr. Bray's associates. Of the 11 who were not Members of Parliament, five were clergymen of the Anglican Church.

Clergymen threw their weight behind a proposal to mount a vigorous campaign designed to raise funds from the general public. This approach lent itself to vigorous interpretation from pulpits, to be followed by canvassing of parishes. Trustee Thomas Coram was a leader of the parish of St. Botolph Without Aldgate. Earlier he had envisioned using the parish approach to seek £60,000 with which to fund a colony he had hoped to establish in what is now Maine.[1]

Zeal — and a wide circle of acquaintances — would be required for success in leading such an undertaking. So it was to Oglethorpe that colleagues turned, assigning to him the task of preparing commissions that could be presented to solicitors. A group of non-trustee notables would help to get the movement off to a good start. Persons named for this purpose — without having been consulted about willingness to serve — were: Lords Tyrconnel and Baltimore, Sir Abraham Elton, Sir Roger Meredith, and Governor Robert Johnson of South Carolina.

An undated broadside which may have been struck from the printing press near the outset of the campaign, stipulates in part: —

> NOW KNOW YE that We the said Trustees . . . do authorize and appoint the said Minister, Church Wardens, and Gentlemen of the Vestry of the Parish [of St. Margaret, Westminster] . . . to take subscriptions and to gather and collect such Moneys as shall be by any Person or Persons contributed for the Purposes aforesaid and to transmit with all convenient Speed to us the said TRUSTEES [of Georgia] at our Office in Old Palace Yard Westminster the Moneys so collected together with the Names of the Persons and the Sums which each shall contribute . . .[2]

Directors of the Bank of England subscribed £300 and officials of the East India Company gave twice that sum. Another substantial boost came from the Trustees of charitable legacies left by the Earl of Thanet.[3] Small gifts — often £1 or less — were made by many church folk whose priests challenged them to support the new charitable colony. Detailed lists with names, dates, and amounts, are preserved in the *Colonial Records of Georgia*. Collectively, institutional and individual subscriptions amounted to less than £2,000 on September 14, 1732.

That was a far cry from the £12,000 now estimated as needed to make a start, with £10,000 having come to be accepted as the bare minimum. At the time they received their long-awaited charter "the Associate Petitioners" who sought incorporation had assets amounting to £159 13 shillings 5 pence. Yet once they became Trustees, Georgia leaders began interviewing persons who "wished to form an embarcation" as soon as a time of departure was set.

Refugee Salzburgers, now streaming into ports of western Europe, were suddenly seen as potential sources of revenue as well as manpower. Organized groups were hard at work collecting funds with which to aid these European Protestants. So on July 26, at the second meeting of the Trustees after they were chartered, a new working plan was approved.

Georgia leaders would approach "the collectors of charity for the Saltsburgers" and offer land in the colony-to-be plus one year's maintenance. To cover cost of their Atlantic passage plus 12 months of living expenses, sponsors would be asked to pay for refugees at these rates: £20 for man, wife, and their infants under age four; £10 for a single man; £5 for children age four to 12; and £7 ten shillings for each youngster between ages 12 and 18.[4]

Already it was apparent that some persons, among whom Oglethorpe was conspicuous, preferred to make designated gifts for special purposes rather than to contribute to the general support of the colony. To his colleagues the man who didn't yet know that he would lead the first contingent of colonists to Georgia suggested "employing an ingenious person . . . to search out medicinal plants and roots, and to make experiments of grain to be planted . . . and to instruct the colony in agriculture." There never was any doubt that this plan would get favorable action, for along with it Oglethorpe reported ear-marked subscriptions of £70 annually.

Interest in the "encouragement and improvement of botany and agriculture" proved even greater than expected. As a result, special commissions were issued to persons who wished to seek subscriptions supporting this aspect of the enterprise. Soon it became apparent that great number of friends of Georgia would stipulate that their gifts be used for religious purposes. No separate commissions were issued in order to encourage support of this phase of colonial life, however.

Numerous persons eager to aid the undertaking could advance gifts in kind more readily than in cash. So it was decided that such would be accepted and stored until they could be shipped across the Atlantic. Again, Oglethorpe led the way. His gifts in July, 1732, were: two dozen matted chairs, a map of the world, a map of England and Wales, two sheets of common seals of English and Welsh cities, two maps of North America, one map each of South America and Pennsylvania, and two globes "mounted on frames, with covers." A few weeks later he added a large table made of African mahogany.

Lord Tyrconnel gave a North Carolina carpet for use with the table.

A time would come when such gifts in kind would prove a nuisance and an embarrassment. For the present, anything and everything was received with gratitude.

In order to succeed, the enterprise must become well known to Englishmen in general and to Londoners in particular. As usual it was Oglethorpe who was asked to take full charge of this matter. He himself wrote and published *An Essay on Plantations* and almost certainly produced *A New and Accurate Account of the Provinces of South Carolina and Georgia*.

Production of booklets was only one aspect of his activity as a pioneer in the art of publicizing a cause through the medium of

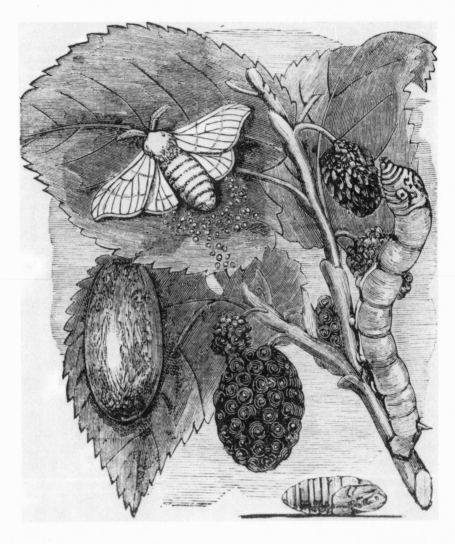

Stages of the silkworm's life cycle

Long before the Georgia scheme took final shape, leaders were giddy with dreams of wealth from silk. They were influenced by false ideas about the ease with which silkworms could be propagated.

This early engraving purports to depict the full life cycle of the silkworm — from egg to cocoon.

Seal of the Georgia Trust

Georgia has had numerous official seals. The first of these, issued to Trustees, was destroyed when the charter was surrendered before expiration. On one side, it depicted three stages in the life cycle of the silkworm.

print. Through his efforts newspapers and periodicals were "enlisted on behalf of Georgia to an extent which was never dreamed of" in any earlier colonial experiment.[5] His promotional campaign was far the most elaborate in early American history.

Work as public relations director for the experiment was only one of numerous posts filled by Oglethorpe in this formative period. Yet it had negative as well as positive facets. He was expected to take necessary measures "to prevent the Publishing in the News Papers anything relating to this Society that shall be disadvantagious to their Designs."

Prior to promulgation of the charter there were no public reports concerning the Georgia scheme. Oglethorpe began his blitz even before being formally assigned to the public relations post. Few literate Londoners remained long unaware of plans to shape an entirely new kind of colony. From June 20 through November 17, at least 30 accounts appeared in the press. They ranged from a three-page summary in *The Political State of Great Britain* to a dozen news stories in the *Daily Journal* and numerous long features in The *Gentleman's Magazine*.[6]

During their first year Trustees remained hard pressed for cash. Yet they spent £133, nearly 10% of all money received before the first embarcation for Georgia, upon "Stationary Ware, printing several Books and Accounts of the Designs of the Trustees, and publishing Articles and Advertisements in the Publick News Papers."

Many journalists borrowed verbatim from the exuberant language of Oglethorpe in his *New and Accurate Account*. According to it, climate and soil of the region were so wonderful that one American chieftain in Florida, 300 years old, had a father then living who was 50 years his senior.[7]

Benjamin Martyn, unpaid secretary to the Trustees, had been authorized to prepare and issue a detailed statement. He called it *Some Account of the Designs of the Trustees for Establishing the Colony of Georgia in America*. Martyn's ardor was beyond question; he was the originator of a scheme to erect in Westminster Abbey a monument to Shakespeare. Yet he proceeded much more slowly than did Oglethorpe. His book didn't appear until 1733; at once, a second printing was made in order to distribute a copy to every member of Parliament.

First-draft material that went into Martyn's report, plus everything in Trustee minutes, was wholly familiar to Oglethorpe. Through him, detailed optimistic reports of plans for Georgia were made available to the press.

Impoverished Londoners plus persecuted European Protestants selected to go "on the charity" would have their passage paid in full. Once in Georgia each head of a family would receive a grant of 50 acres of land. Tools and equipment furnished to such persons would include: a musket with bayonet, a hammer, a hatchet, and a handsaw; a spade and two hoes; a gimlet, an iron pot, a pair of pothooks, and a frying pan. A full year's maintenance would be provided by: 300 pounds of meat; 114 pounds each of rice, flour, and peas; 44 gallons of strong beer; 64 quarts of molasses; 18 pounds of sugar; 30 pounds of salt; 12 quarts each of soap and lamp oil. Each adult male would receive bedding plus two pairs of trousers, two pairs of "country shoes," and one well-crafted pair.[3]

To many who heard of these plans, they sounded like heaven on earth. Yet Britain stood to profit greatly from each colonist.

Careful calculations indicated that in London 100 poor families earned a total of about £1,000 per year. Simply to keep body and soul together they had to consume goods worth twice as much.

In the delightful country of the golden isles annual earnings of the same 100 families would run to at least £60,000. Of their own produce they would consume about £20,000. They would buy from Britain everything they did not themselves produce. So these 100 heretofore burdensome families would yield to the empire a net balance of trade amounting to £40,000. Net increase over London earnings would run to £50,000 annually. Multiply this 100-family unit by dozens or scores, and any dunce could see that "the rich and industrious" at home would benefit enormously from a flow of colonists to Georgia.

That was just a beginning.

Future years would see silk, wine, cotton, almonds, olives, rice, and other products flow to the home country in an ever-growing stream. National gain from Georgia silk, alone, would be a minimum of £100,000 per year. Therefore, "England will grow Rich by sending her Poor Abroad."

Small wonder that promoters of the Georgia scheme were ecstatic. So were would-be colonists. Contemplating his future Phillip Thicknesse, an early applicant for passage at Trustee expense, was "filled with infinite delight." Joseph Fitzwalter exulted that upon reaching Georgia he and his fellow colonists would literally be in "the promised land."

Hordes of hopeful ones found their way to offices of the Georgia Trust. Though some were rejected out of hand, 90 days after the charter had been issued "upwards of 500 Persons" were registered as potential colonists.

Clergymen fanned this forest-fire of public excitement. They
extolled the virtues of a colony so worthy that "all good Christians
should assist in so good and laudable a Design, in providing for so
many honest poor Families." Many sermons were printed, some of
them at the expense of Trustees.[9] In parish after parish "Gentlemen
were so fully convinc'd of the Charity and Excellence of this
Undertaking, that they resolv'd, with great Unanimity, to collect
from House to House for the Promotion of it."

Authority of planners was limited in some respects. They could
not name a governor; that right was reserved by the crown. Yet they
realized that a set of regulations was essential. For this purpose they
established still another committee that was headed, once more, by
James Oglethorpe.

Some index to reasons for Trustee willingness to delegate
leadership to one man may be found in records of their meeting of
August 3, 1732. On this occasion each Georgia leader was given an
opportunity to bring forth names of influential persons he considered
to be "desirous to encourage the design." Oglethorpe's list ran to 23
names. All other Trustees, combined, provided just four more.

Highly influential Egmont, whose wealth is indicated by countless
diary entries, had the ear of both Walpole and the king. He knew in
late April that the charter would be issued. Reflecting upon the
future he concluded of the enterprise to which he was wholly committed except for his purse and his person that "The chief of our
business for a twelvemonth will be only to get in subscriptions and
settle schemes for our proceeding, which may be left to committees.
I grant it will be a great while before we can proceed to anything of
good purpose."[10]

As first president of the Georgia Corporation he was, therefore, taken by surprise at news that reached him at Bath on September 18, while he was on vacation. Captain Coram rushed there to inform him that in his absence Trustees had "concluded to send a small number of persons over, and that Mr. Oglethorpe resolved to go with them."

Egmont's joy that Oglethorpe would sail with the first contingent of colonists was mixed with doubts. He felt it a mistake "that they should send any away so soon."

Reaction of Egmont to the greatly-accelerated schedule adopted without consulting him provides some insight into the abruptness with which James Edward Oglethorpe reached a decision personally to accompany Georgia's first European settlers. Upon departure from England he took along a large supply of personal belongings and provisions that he judged likely to be needed in the New World. Clearly he had not reached the decision to go when he made August gifts of a table plus maps and other gear designed for use at an undetermined time in the future.

Importance of one factor affecting his decision cannot be assessed. One day before the Georgia charter was promulgated, Lady Eleanor Wall Oglethorpe died at her house in Westminster. James had long served as squire of Westbrook manor; now he became sole proprietor of the family estate.[11]

For a decade he had worked tirelessly in his role as inheritor of a strangely mixed set of family traditions. Now, at age 36 and unmarried, for all practical purposes in England he was The Oglethorpe Family.

He decided to go to Georgia with full knowledge that though he represented the Trustees, he would not have the title or authority of a colonial governor. It was already clear that Trustees who remained in England would reserve to themselves the power to make policy decisions. They had demonstrated their desire to deal with administrative details, however petty, despite the four or more months that would be required for an exchange of information between London and the colony.

Money was still desperately short. Needs of the first year would have to be met from yet-to-be-collected gifts. Numerous persons had indicated eagerness to become colonists and some had been interviewed, but none had been selected to go. There was a general understanding that English common law would prevail; yet no statutes designed for specific conditions and needs of Georgia had been adopted. Worst of all from the viewpoint of veteran travellers, neither Oglethorpe nor any of the persons likely to accompany him had any first-hand knowledge about the colony.

How woefully ignorant and gullible Oglethorpe was is indicated by near-ecstatic comments in his *New Account*. "The Air is healthy, being always serene, pleasant and temperate, never subject to excessive Heat or Cold, nor to sudden Changes. . . ." Georgia's soil, he wrote, is "impregnated with such a fertile Mixture that they use no Manure. . . ."

No part of the world has a greater variety or number of fishes. Georgia's oranges, lemons, apples, pears, peaches, and apricots "are so dilicious that whoever tastes them will despise the insipid watery Taste of those we have in *England*" and are grown in such numbers that "they are given to the Hogs in great quantities." A person who doesn't wish to raise his own cattle and fowls or to shoot them in the woods may purchase meat from Indians at ridiculous prices — a 40-pound wild turkey for two pence, or a whole deer's flesh for six pence.

Oglethorpe's decision to go to Georgia was made so hastily that it came as a surprise to his most intimate co-worker. Even those colleagues who rejoiced that he wished to sail as soon as possible regarded his personal embracement of the embarcation as being rash, even downright foolhardy.

Chapter 5

SEVENTY-NINE DAYS: ENGLAND TO GEORGIA

November 17, 1732 — February 12, 1733

Waiting for the last formality — receipt of orders to sail — Oglethorpe chafed at what he considered unreasonable delay. Virtually single-handed he had alternately cajoled and threatened those Trustees who wished to proceed cautiously. For him it was now, or never. When he made that clear, opponents of haste either yielded or gave up active roles in the Georgia enterprise.

Detailed articles of agreement were speedily framed. Then they were explained to each prospective colonist before finalists in the contest for places on the first ship signed or made their marks. With their families these persons were now aboard the frigate *Ann*.

Arrival of documents enabled Georgia's founder to leave London on Wednesday, November 15, 1732. His destination was Savannah, already officially named and allotted five thousand acres at a site yet to be selected.

Owned by merchant Samuel Wragg and commanded by Captain John Thomas, the 200-ton *Ann*[1] lay in the Thames at Deptford, about four miles below London. Her papers called for transportation of passengers, provisions, equipment, and miscellaneous gear to Beaufort in Carolina. That was the nearest deepwater port to the new colony that as yet existed only on paper.

To the *Ann's* owner and master, passengers were freight for which the trans-Atlantic voyage would yield £4 per head. An adult was counted as one head. For juveniles there was a sliding scale of charges, so that the total number of heads was substantially less than the entire passenger list.[2]

58

Provisions that the *Ann's* owner had agreed to put aboard, measured most often in 100-pound units, included: beef, pork, bread, fish, peas, butter, suet, plums, and — of course — water. Enough was provided for a six-week passage, but there was no surplus for use if the ship suffered delays.

Some of the food needed for the voyage went aboard alive: sheep, hogs, and a great many ducks and geese.[3] According to The *Gentleman's Magazine* the cargo included "10 Ton of Alderman Parsons' best Beer,"[4] allowing about two quarts per week for each adult. Stay-at-home adventurer Egmont concluded after an initial check that nothing was wanting in the way of provisions, medicines, tents, and weapons.

Books there were aplenty. Men who had labored in association with Dr. Bray before becoming Georgia Trustees were convinced that no New World enterprise could prosper without the printed word. At least initially, the Rev. Stephen Hales, D.D., was the most ardent leader in solicitation of books for Georgia. For the first transport he assembled:

40 Bibles printed in minion (very small type)
60 Testaments printed in long primer (somewhat
   larger than minion but still hard to read)
100 copies, *Book of Common Prayer* (minion)
50 copies each, *Duty of Man, Christian Monitor
   and Companion, Christian Monitor and Answer
   to Excuses*, and Bishop Gibson's *Family Devotion*
72 copies of the Psalter and an equal number of
   spelling books
100 each, horn book, primer, and *A.B.C. with Church
   Catechism*
700 Lewis's *Catechism*

Had he been challenged, even Hales would have conceded that the first Georgians would hardly have need for seven copies each of Lewis's *Catechism*. Precisely how many copies of what books went with the *Ann* it is impossible to determine. When the vessel was loaded to capacity Trustees arranged with a Mr. Plumstead "to provide Freightage by the first Ship bound for Carolina, for the remaining part of the Peoples Baggage."[5]

Oglethorpe's personal provisions and equipment, loaded and stored separately, included abundant food and drink plus at least one dog — a black bitch.

English ships of Trustee era Georgia

This engraving depicts the harbor of Falmouth, England, as it was believed to have appeared during the 1730's and 1740's. Vessels shown are larger than the *Ann*, however.

Because all of the ships used to transport colonists to early Georgia were small and privately-owned, there are no known contemporary sketches of these vessels.

In a rare burst of generosity tight-fisted Egmont provided £20 "for the use and Relief of the Necessitous Women and Children on board the Ship in their Passage to Georgia." According to the *Daily Post*, that sum was inadequate to meet emergency needs of those who were "in want of Shifts, Shirts, Stockings, Shoes, and other Necessaries." An anonymous female donor responded to the crisis with a gift of five guineas.

Yet as measured by the standards of London's poorest, families selected to launch Georgia were by no means destitute. Trustees took action on October 3 by which the embarcation was limited to 35 families. Oglethorpe and a few colleagues interviewed about 600 men. In a period of less than three weeks they selected as finalists 100 heads of families — not the most needy, but those judged most likely to be successful colonists. Then they sifted the candidates once more in order to make final choice of 35 families.

Trustees later gave a detailed account of this sequence of events. According to it the 114 selected to go on the *Ann* were for the most part "in decayed Circumstances, and thereby disabled from following any Business in England; and who, if in Debt, had leave from their Creditors to go, and such as were recommended by the Minister, Church-wardens, and Overseers of their respective Parishes."

Emigrants were assigned to their shipboard quarters by lot. Each family space was furnished with a wooden cradle for sleeping.

While women and children worked at the task of arranging their living quarters, sergeants of the guard drilled adult males. No one knew what Georgia would be like, but it was essential to be competent in the use of "Musquets, Bayonets, and Swords." Danger from the French and their Indian allies was very real — perhaps even more pressing than that from Spanish to the south.

That is why the original concept of a utopian society of farmers and artisans had already given way to that of a self-sustaining military fiefdom. In Georgia every landholder must be prepared to

take up arms at an instant's notice. Drills, practice with arms, and other military exercises were continued on a regular basis throughout the voyage of the *Ann*.

Thursday, November 18, brought a contingent of seven Trustees to Deptford. They inspected the vessel and noted with approval that canvas curtains had been provided in order to give some privacy to each family's quarters. Cargo was found to be packed tight and strong.

Events had moved so rapidly, once Oglethorpe decided to go and to go at once, that his colleagues feared some colonists might have lingering doubts or serious unanswered questions. One by one, families came before Trustees in the great cabin and stood while they were quizzed. Learning that one woman had just borne a child, Trustees provided two guineas "to make ye Company merry ye day of the Christng."

Her anchor was weighed at 8:00 A.M. on November 17 and the *Ann* prepared to sail. Already, she was more than a week behind schedule. But wind proved so slight that no significant progress was made on the first day. Two males took advantage of the delay to change their minds and leave the ship.

Tardy sailing of the *Ann* raised questions about adequacy of food supplies, laid in for a voyage of six weeks. As a precaution the vessel took on more sheep and hogs plus several dozen more fowls. This required a cash outlay of more than £52. By providing it Oglethorpe began on a small scale a practice that would later loom large beyond belief. When all other resources were exhausted he habitually purchased essential items from his own funds, expecting to be repaid in full after rendering an accounting.

Manuscript records that include lists of persons aboard the tiny vessel are not in total agreement. Charity colonists plus employees of the Trust numbered about 114. There is no record to indicate that even one passenger on the *Ann* was a debtor who had formerly been imprisoned.[6] Significantly from the perspective of those who first formulated the Georgia scheme about three years earlier, males old enough to have gained experience at their trades but young enough to bear arms headed all of the families who became the first Georgians. Most heads of families were in the age range of 35 to 50 years.

Vocations represented on the passenger list included that of carpenter, wig maker, apothecary, wheelwright, tailor, merchant, cloth worker, baker, gardener, basket maker, vine dresser, flax and hemp dresser, and stocking maker.[7] Though perhaps not regarded as important at the time, at least nine passengers were listed simply as "servant."

Servants were nearly equally divided between males and females. On the average they were more than a decade younger than their masters. Mary Cormock, who went with carpenter Noble Jones, was but 11. Inclusion of so many servants clearly indicated that the first embarcation would not form a one-class society. Instead the colony would begin its life with at least three distinct socioeconomic levels: masters, servants, and yeoman farmers plus artisans. A fourth class made up of self-financed adventurers would develop almost at once.

This early evolution of a colonial caste system was not planned. It stemmed in part from the enthusiasm with which Oglethorpe recruited persons with specials skills, some of whom wouldn't have considered going without servants.

From the beginning it had been taken for granted that colonists must have the guidance of a resident clergyman, accustomed to being provided with a "living" from the government. Just 11 days before the *Ann* sailed the Rev. Henry Herbert, D.D., attended a meeting of Trustees and to their surprised delight "charitably offer'd to go without any allowance." He was one week behind surgeon William Cox, 41, who agreed to care for the sick and wounded during the first year for no reward "except that his House should be built, and Land tilled" by joint labor of charity colonists. Each such person owed the community one day's work each week. Another volunteer, an engineer, went along to supervise the building of a fort.

An Italian who was skilled in the silk industry, hence vital to long-range plans, was included in the first contingent. He was recruited by Trustees, but an artisan who planned immediately to launch production of potash had applied for the opportunity. Paul Amatis, selected because he represented himself as understanding the nature and production of raw silk, was first on one list of passengers. Timothy Bowling, potash maker, was second.

For the safety of the ship's company eight men, selected by Oglethorpe, were divided into two watches for all-night patrols of the *Ann*. They visited the craddles to see that things were quiet and orderly. They kept an eye on the dogs and fowls, and took special care to safeguard the vessel from fire. After eight only the sick were permitted to burn candles "& that in Lanthorns," while smoking was limited to those whose pipes were fitted with caps and who would promise to fire them up only on deck.

The Duke of Newcastle

The Duke of Newcastle, who served as secretary of state for many years, was wealthy and influential. He gave his blessing to the Georgia enterprise very early; during years of turmoil, it was to Newcastle that Oglethorpe addressed many of his questions, reports, and pleas for aid.

Oglethorpe was in constant contact with individual colonists. Still the long voyage that followed a standard route to Carolina gave the expedition's leader time to reflect upon things already accomplished — plus uncertainities ahead.

Long-time control of land had been assured, he was confident, by establishment of "inheritance by tail-male." This now-clumsy legal term was clear to settlers, who knew that a man's widow or daughter could never gain more than a fractional interest in improved land. If a land owner died or quit the colony without leaving behind a male heir, his land reverted to the Trust so that it could be re-assigned to another male. This system was designed to guarantee that every holder of land would be available for military service.

From the beginning of enlistment of colonists, tail-male restrictions were a major source of uncertainty and complaint. Four who had been selected for the first embarcation pondered the matter and because of it decided to step aside and yield their places to others. Later it became a central issue in widening rifts between Georgians on the ground and Georgia leaders who saw the colony only from the perspective of London's streets.[8]

Stability of the colony in the making was greatly enhanced, according to Oglethorpe, by a regulation that banned slaves from Georgia. No other New World enterprise had a comparable statute. A set of very practical considerations — not strong anti-slavery sentiment — influenced the thinking and the decision of Georgia's founder. In turn, he persuaded colleagues to support the unusual policy.

"The first Cost of a Negro is about Thirty Pounds," wrote Georgia leaders by way of explanation for the anti-slavery stance they took. According to their calculations such a sum "would pay the Passage over, provide Tools and other Necessaries, and defray the Charge of Subsistence of a white Man for a Year."

A second consideration was equally important. Slaves, said Oglethorpe and his colleagues, were notoriously prone to take up arms against their masters at the slightest opportunity. In the case of Georgia the risk was compounded by proximity to Spanish Florida, where runaway slaves were offered a haven.

Exclusion of slaves and later of free blacks as well was a conspicuous deviation from policies that prevailed in other British colonies. Fine! Georgia was never intended to be a carbon copy of other colonial enterprises! Cost what it might, exclusion of slaves from Georgia would make it a better place to live.

Oglethorpe was keenly conscious that he did not go as governor. He sometimes brooded over the limitations set upon his authority, but usually ended by deciding that he would act as though he had whatever powers he felt it necessary to exercise. No charity colonist would dare to challenge him . . . and his fellow Trustees would be 3,000 miles away. Already it was apparent that Oglethorpe's colleagues were reluctant to delegate authority, even to their own representative. Acting as a corporate body they had already taken care of such key Georgia appointments as those to offices of bailiff, tythingman, conservator of the peace, and recorder.

Because of his keen personal interest Georgia's founder took special pleasure in seeing to it that a botanist was hired. William Houstoun, who received a salary advance of £75 upon signing a contract, did not sail on the *Ann*. Instead he followed Trustee orders and set out on a journey to Madeira, Jamaica, and some of the Spanish colonies in order to gather vines and seeds plus roots or cuttings of plants judged likely to prove profitable in Georgia.

Clearly it was to the great advantage of the colony that the powerful Duke of Newcastle, secretary of state, had agreed to send formal communications to governors of both the Carolinas, Virginia, Maryland, Pennsylvania, New Hampshire, and Barbados. Since it was not penned until November 8, Oglethorpe probably was unaware that this official request for aid made no mention of debtors or paupers or worthy poor or oppressed European protestants. Rather, Newcastle's circular letter stressed potential advantages to Britain's trade and navigation. Additonally, said the secretary of state, successful colonization of Georgia would add significantly to "the strength and security of H[is] M[ajesty's] Colonies in America."

Oglethorpe doubtless saw and approved an earlier letter. It went from Trustee secretary Benjamin Martyn to Governor Robert Johnson of South Carolina. When written on October 18 it appeared that "an imbarcation of eighty or thereabouts of his Majesty's natural born subjects" would sail on November 7.

Settlement of these persons in Georgia would "greatly redound to the security and advantage" of South Carolina. Hence all possible aid was requested. Specifically, Trustees ventured to hope that the well-established colony would provide 20 negro laborers and four pairs of sawyers to help clear the site of Savannah.

No matter where he should decide to build it, the town launching the new colony would not be precisely what Oglethorpe had originally conceived. Other major changes aside, it was already certain that non-English settlers would come soon. How German-speaking Salzburgers would fit into the pattern of the British enterprise, no one knew. With them or perhaps even before them would come a number of adventurers.

Such persons would not be dependent upon the Trust for passage or support. They would be sufficiently prosperous to bring servants with them. From the first they would form a social class quite distinct from that made up of charity colonists eligible to receive 50 acres of land each. Most adventurers sought and gained assurances that they would be granted up to 500 acres, each.

Long before the *Ann* reached her destination the rate at which adventurers applied for and received large grants of Georgia land began to accelerate. They brought numbers to the colony and revenue to the Trust. But these colonists were quick to balk at vexatious regulations and were vocal in their complaints about decisions of their leader. Oglethorpe was, after all, very much like them — an adventurer who happened also to be a Trustee in residence.

Aboard the *Ann* these developments were in the future. For now the expedition's leader was deeply involved in personal concerns of members of his company.

Flax- and hemp-dresser John Warren, 34, and his wife Elizabeth, 27, were accepted as charity colonists about the time their fourth son was born. Preparations for the voyage occupied so much of their time and energy that they neglected to have the baby baptized. It was for this as yet un-named son that a merry-making fund had been contributed.

Six days after the anchor was weighed, finally out of sight of land, members of the ship's company assembled for a ceremony. Having consented to be godfather to the infant, James Edward Oglethorpe stood with the family. The Rev. Henry Herbert reached the proper point in the ritual and asked the parents to name their child. Though the boy had been born on land and had not yet set foot in Georgia, the father spoke with enthusiasm: "Georgius Marinus!"

No doubt about it. Georgia's founder had been busy with his daily administrative chores, his planning, and his remembering. But he was not too busy to select a name for a hemp-dresser's son. No isolated incident, his action was typical of this Member of Parliament throughout his career as functional head of a colony. Indeed, later analysts' chief criticisms of Oglethorpe the administrator have centered in his personal handling of details that most persons would have relegated to subordinates.

For him it was natural and spontaneous to go into the hold on November 21 in order to visit every cradle. He found many passengers seasick, so with surgeon Cox at his side saw to it that these received wine or chicken broth or sage tea. He found four beds so foul that he ordered them taken on deck to be aired.

Before this bedding was taken back below the *Ann* passed the Tropic of Cancer. Seamen followed an age-old ritual by demanding "a pound and a bottle." This gratuity had for decades been exacted from passengers on their first voyage into such waters. Colonists were bewildered; they had little or no money with which to comply. Captain Thomas loudly insisted that if they failed to pay they should get the standard penalty — a severe ducking.

According to terse notes made on the spot by colonist Thomas Christie, Oglethorpe halted the folk ceremony of the sea. He ordered seamen to cease bothering colonists and "promised the Ships Crew to give it 'em in money when he came ashoar."

Oglethorpe intervened again when sawyer James Wilson, seized by fellow passengers and informally convicted of having given a sheep's head to a dog, was brought to the gangplank for punishment. Though there was little doubt of Wilson's guilt, Georgia's founder ordered him to be released.

Aware that the hold included pregnant women with keen appetites, Oglethorpe did not so much as taste the fine dolphin he caught. Instead he gave it to the mothers-to-be.

This gesture that was indicative of his life-long concern for women was followed in just four days by a display of temper. Numerous future Georgians had gathered on deck for burial at sea of Robert Clark's infant son, the second human casualty of the voyage. Earlier, an infant had died and numerous fowls plus a few animals had perished. With the body of the Clark infant committed to the sea by chaplain Herbert, mourners remained clustered closely together. An unidentified person — almost certainly a member of the ship's crew — threatened to throw water on them. Hearing the threat "Mr. Oglethorpe came behind him & gave him a good kick on ye arse."

He made many visits to the hold to see the sick. When surgeon Cox expressed doubt that the ship's provisions included food that some sufferers craved, he ordered his personal steward to provide whatever was needed from his own stores. Presumably he also provided the mutton and broth plus a pint of punch per person with which the ship's company celebrated his birthday.

There is no record of the frequency with which Oglethorpe participated in a central activity of the voyage. At frequent intervals — sometimes twice within 24 hours — chaplain Herbert called colonists together for prayers and a sermon. Unlike Egmont and clergymen who served as Trustees, Oglethorpe never was a regular church-goer. He wholeheartedly concurred in carefully-framed principles by which religion would be an integral aspect of life in Georgia. But for the colony's founder this emphasis was not rooted in conventional piety plus loyalty to the Church of England. Rather it stemmed from a deep but seldom-articulated conviction that "religion is good for the people — it helps to make fine citizens of them."

If there were special prayers of thanksgiving on January 23,[9] excitement of finding ground at 21 fathoms so absorbed Thomas Christie that he made no mention of a religious service. Next day, after a run of 60 miles, the *Ann* dropped anchor in Charles Town harbor. Four guns were fired. At this well-established signal of the sea, a pilot came aboard.

Oglethorpe ordered land-hungry colonists to remain on their ship. During the ten hours that the *Ann* lay at anchor he went ashore and learned what colleagues at home had known for weeks by means of a letter from Governor Johnson. Carolina not only welcomed the planned settlement to her south; the well-established and prosperous colony would give every possible assistance to newcomers. Already, the South Carolina Assembly had voted to provide boats with which to proceed from Port Royal to Georgia. In addition lawmakers made their new neighbors a gift of 105 head of cattle, 24 hogs, and 20 barrels of rice. Equally important, colonial rangers of the Independent Company were lent to Oglethorpe so that he would have a temporary military force from the first.

Preceding the *Ann* by a few hours, Oglethorpe reached Beaufort, hard by Port Royal. He quickly arranged for use of a military

Part of Charles Town Harbor

This view of Charles Town Harbor, prior to 1739, reveals that the old and wealthy port
city was already a busy center of commerce when voyagers aboard the *Ann* caught sight
of it. Some of the buildings depicted are still standing.

At this stage of the enterprise, Savannah had been named but no site had been selected.
Even after a start had been made in building the town, no one knew whether or not water
in the Savannah river was deep enough for ocean-going vessels.

barracks as temporary quarters by his followers. Since Captain
Thomas was not familiar with coastal waters, a seasoned pilot had
been brought aboard the ship for the week-long trip to Port Royal.
Once there Georgia storekeeper Thomas Causton was ecstatic at
being on solid ground again. But he wrote his wife that he was
surprised to find Beaufort's "gallant and generous" people lived in
houses "all of Timber and very few have Glass Windows or Brick
Chimneys."

While some colonists recovered from seasickness and their
comrades sorted out their belongings, their leader went by boat to
the mouth of the Savannah river. Colonel William Bull of Charles
Town accompanied him, along with a party of Carolina rangers. As
the site for Savannah they chose a spot about ten miles from the sea,
high above the river on Yamacraw bluff.

A small band of Indians headed by aging chief Tomochichi
made the region their tribal home. After negotiations between the
Englishman and the native American led to an exchange of title,
Oglethorpe laid formal claim to a small section of coastal land.
Whatever his shortcomings as colonial administrator may have
been, readiness to deal with Indians and skill in arriving at
understanding with them marked Oglethorpe's American career
from beginning to end. He dealt with Tomochichi through Mary
Musgrove, the mixed-blooded wife of a trader who operated a post
on the river.

Yamacraws whom Tomochichi led did not themselves constitute
a significant military force. Yet their chief was influential because
other Indians leaders held him in high regard. Partly through
Tomochichi's influence, partly as a result of Oglethorpe's enlightened
policies in dealing with native Americans, during his era of
leadership the Georgia colony experienced unequaled cooperation
and even aid from tribesmen.

Back in Beaufort in time for a service of thanksgiving on February 8, Oglethorpe joined his followers in feasting upon New World bounty: turkeys, hogs, punch, beer, and wine and abundance. Most of their heavy cargo was packed into a 70-ton sloop. Colonists then crowded into five pettiaguas — small boats especially constructed for use on inland waterways — for the final leg of their journey. They went ashore to sleep on February 10 and again the following night. Then they spent the morning of the twelfth working their way toward the site chosen by their leader.

During the afternoon of February 12 Georgia's first English settlers disembarked and took a look at their new home. During their journey up the Savannah river they had already discovered that huge trees abounded; the task of making a clearing would be much harder than anticipated. Soil was sandy and far less rich than they had hoped; marsh land couldn't possibly be cultivated.

Carolina rangers led by Captain Francis Scott, who had gone with Oglethorpe when he selected the site of Savannah and had remained camped there, fired shots as a welcome. While waiting for colonists the Carolinians had cut steps into the face of the steep bluff, some 40 feet above water level, against which the town's edge would rest.

Before settlers succeeded in getting any significant amount of cargo up the bluff, Tomochichi and some of his Yamacraws made an appearance. They greeted their white-skinned allies with an awesomely-strange dance that included many "antick postures." Then with Mary Musgrove as interpreter they talked with some of the newcomers for half an hour.

At their first meeting Oglethorpe had presented gifts to the aging chieftain. Now, as a seal of their pact of friendship, Tomochichi responded by presenting to the white man a buffalo skin. On its inner surface was painted the head of an eagle. Indians showed no sign of hostility and returned quietly to their own camp once the ceremonies were over. Still, colonists who hadn't seen a native American before chattered nervously about them as they resumed their interrupted activities.

With night not many hours away it was imperative to raise all four of the big tents that would, for now, provide their only shelter. Tomorrow would be soon enough to survey the territory and begin the tedious work of clearing a spot on which to build.

For the leader of the expedition the night was a never-to-be-duplicated watershed. Seventy-nine days out of London[10] . . . and totally surrounded by strangeness. So many leagues from the familiar sounds of London's streets, and so remote from a fatherless boyhood. Nearly half a world away from the invisible line close to Westbrook manor that ran through Greenwich to mark the point from which all distances and all time were measured.

He would stay a few months — long enough to see that affairs were progressing as planned. Then he would return to occupy again the highly-prized seat in Parliament that he had already held longer than any other Oglethorpe.

Not within the memory of anyone alive had another Englishman launched a New World colony, and none in existence were remotely like his. Whatever friends or foes might think of a latter-day Sir Walter Raleigh, surely the stigma of a Jacobite heritage would be erased when Georgia proved herself to be a sparkling jewel serving to enrich the commerce and enhance the power of imperial Britain.

If anyone in England harbored thoughts of this sort he failed to record them. Leaders of the Georgia enterprise simply noted tersely that "James Oglethorpe, Esq., one of the Trustees, went with the colonists at his own Expence to settle them." Even Egmont confided to his voluminous diary no word of admiration or praise for his risk-taking colleague except an observation that Oglethorpe's sudden decision to go to Georgia revealed his "public spirit."

Chapter 6

THE WORLD TURNED UPSIDE DOWN: OGLETHORPE IN
GEORGIA

February, 1733 — March, 1734

Yamacraw Bluff in February offered a climate far from the ideal
one that had been anticipated. Oglethorpe's hasty and ill-prepared
departure had been made by choice. He fervently hoped that
colonists would reach Georgia in time to plant crops for harvesting
in the summer and fall of 1733.

On the scene, though, housing was as urgent as planting. For
now, only a fraction of the colonists could be put to work preparing
fields.

February 21 found Oglethorpe writing a brief report to far-away
Trustees. His decision to place Savannah about ten miles from the
sea, he said, rested partly upon the "healthy situation" he found
above the high river bank.

Under their leader's direction workmen laid out the settlement
with precision — almost as though it were an estate of a wealthy lord
in suburban London. As a result Savannah became America's first
pre-planned city. Thomas Causton, magistrate and store keeper,
proudly wrote home that the "beautifully laid out" community was
marked by "an agreeable uniformity."

Each group of ten single-house lots was called a tithing and was
placed in charge of a tithing man. Tithings were grouped into wards
that were headed by constables and were interspersed with squares
plus markets and sites for public buildings. Special locations were
selected for a church and a cemetery.

74

To first-time visitors one feature of Savannah stuck out like a sore thumb. At the edge of the bluff and near the center of the rapidly-emerging town stood a big tent that was sheltered by a clump of trees. This wet and windy canvas shelter was Oglethorpe's only residence in Georgia during the first four years of the colony's life.

Back home in County Surrey he lived like a bloody lord in servant-filled Westwood manor. Here he refused to occupy a clapboard house even when some stood empty. Had he been pressed to explain the paradox Georgia's founder would have said simply that he wished to put himself "last among many."

Deep inside, he wanted to be known and accepted as made of such tough stuff that no Georgian would dare to cross or challenge him. Simultaneously and paradoxically he revelled in being called Father by deferential charity colonists. Nothing pleased him more than the annual colony-wide celebration of his birthday. By insisting upon remaining in a cold and drafty tent when he could have had the best house in Savannah, he demonstrated his fatherly concern so vividly that it was not necessary for him to talk or to write about it.

Specialists who have analyzed the town plan, wholly incongruous for a wilderness setting, have concluded that Savannah formed a special kind of monument to Oglethorpe's friend Robert Castell. According to this view the community plan mirrored the formal gardens that were depicted in *Villas of the Ancients*. It was this book that sent an architect to debtor's prison and death — triggering Oglethorpe's passionate inquiry into gaols and subsequent rise to leadership in parliament.

Lots in Savannah were of uniform size, 20 by 30 yards. Houses were designated to be 24 feet long and 16 feet wide. Log foundations raised them 30 inches above the ground. Lumber was sawed by hand on the spot. Had not William Bull brought experienced sawyers and their tools from Carolina, it would have been impossible to take pride in the fact that four houses were under construction by the middle of March.

Simultaneously, work proceeded on another vital aspect of the colony's life. Long before the *Ann* sailed, Georgia leaders had agreed that a public garden must be established at once. A ten-acre tract lying between Savannah and the river was chosen for this purpose. Like the settlement, it was laid out in squares.

Very early, many squares were planted with white mulberry trees. Eventually 40,000 of them were being nurtured in what came,

Parliamentary election of the Oglethorpe era

British elections, especially when one or more candidates couldn't conduct a lengthy campaign, were often frenzied affairs. William Hogarth's engraving that depicts "Polling the Hustings" gives some idea of the way in which a contest caused village feelings to run high.

James Oglethorpe, Member from Haslemere of the House of Commons, clung to a precarious margin of support in spite of frequent and lengthy absences from Britain.

He received a great deal of help from Speaker of the House Arthur Onslow — but was dealt "a near mortal blow" by the son of the Earl of Egmont, who chose to offer as a candidate for one of the two Haslemere seats.

inevitably, to be dubbed the Trustees' Garden. Other cities, including Charles Town, had botanical gardens earlier — but Savannah's was America's first that had no goal except the public good and was totally cultivated by a communal labor force.

Soon orange trees lined many of the walks in the garden. Vines of many kinds were planted, along with patches of indigo, cochineal, flax, and hemp. According to Baron von Reck, peaches were being grown there as early as 1734 — supporting the contention that the Trustees' Garden gave rise to the peach industry in Georgia and then in the entire southeast.

Though emphasis was upon exotic and hard-to-cultivate plants, botanists responsible for this unique feature of colonial Georgia did not neglect more humble things. They experimented with various kinds of peas, cabbages, and other familiar European plants such as beets and wheat.

If cultivation of peaches and — perhaps — of upland cotton began here, failure was more common than success. Olive trees refused to grow. Figs flourished, but produced little usable fruit. Barilla seeds sprouted and yielded promising-looking plants but these never became the eagerly-anticipated rich source of potash that was expected. Bamboo plants and madder roots proved well adapted to the soil and climate, but little use was found for mature plants.

According to a very early account in the *South Carolina Gazette*, a prominent topographical feature of the botanical garden was a

huge "mount of earth." Later discovered to be an Indian burial mound, it was long regarded as supporting the claim that Sir Walter Raleigh had visited the spot, and had built the mound as a marker. Perhaps Oglethorpe sometimes sat on the mound to re-read marked passages in Raleigh's *Journal*, which he brought with him when he boarded the *Ann*.

During early months the man who dreamed of being a latter-day Raleigh had little time for reading. Protection from enemies was as vital to the colony as shelter from the elements. Oglethorpe personally supervised the arrangement of cannon into a small battery, completed about the time the first two clapboard houses were finished. Powder plus shot were soon stored in a hastily-erected magazine. Wooden palisades 17 feet high would, it was hoped, be satisfactory as temporary defensive barriers.

About the time the first houses were ready for occupancy, wealthy Charles Town merchant Samuel Everleigh came to see how the colony was progressing. As a special treat he brought Oglethorpe a bundle of asparagus. Immediately the overseer of the colonists, as he often termed himself, divided the asparagus among pregnant women "without reserving any for himself." Later the man whose childhood had been spent among females made special provision for widows. Many of them were assigned to houses where they could best function on their own. So a chimney, costly in labor and hence often the last feature added to a dwelling, came to signify "a widow is inside."

Males, regardless of marital status or age, got no special privileges. They were divided into three gangs, each with designated tasks. One group cut trees to clear the site of Savannah. Another built defensive fortifications, and the third tried to prepare ground for spring planting. No colonists were experienced farmers and only a few knew how to handle saws; progress was painfully slow.

Carolina rangers were hired to build a fort on the Ogeechee river at a site that straddled a path often taken by Indians en route to raid Carolina. Their work proceeded fairly rapidly until the river jammed and made transportation impossible. This dilemma caused them to abandon Fort Argyle, named for Oglethorpe's good friend the Duke of Argyle. When a second Fort Argyle was started five miles away the earlier site was dubbed "First Fort." A sturdy guardhouse in Savannah, "commanding the river both ways," rounded out initial physical arrangements for the colony's protection.

Military drills began on February 22, before the first house was framed. Within 90 days the colony's population had swelled to 160, of whom 70 were able to bear arms. Each potential defender was issued a musket plus a bayonet and a cartridge box with a belt. Indian or French attack was a far more pressing threat than it had seemed from offices of the Georgia Trust in Westminster, London.

From the perspective of London Georgia's founder had viewed the task of clearing ground as almost absurdly easy. "Half a Dozen strokes of an Ax" around the base of a tree would kill it, he then believed. After girdled trees stood for a time, acre after acre would be felled by the first brisk gust of wind. With 5,000 acres set aside for Savannah by Trustee action, the proud new town should be completed in one season's work.

On the site big clusters of pines, many 100 feet tall and few under 70 feet, presented unexpected problems. No significant amount of land was cleared for planting during the first year. At the time Savannah's home sites were assigned to pioneer settlers on Saturday, July 7, more than half the town was still covered with trees. Most cleared land was dotted with big stumps.

Streets were designed to run due north-south and east-west. They had been cut for only a few hundred yards when colonists were given their land. Each man received a town lot for a dwelling plus a five-acre garden plot. Then he was assigned enough farm land to bring his total to the 50-acre maximum. No deeds were executed until December 21.

As a tribute to South Carolina the chief public square was named for the colony's governor, Robert Johnson. Colonel William Bull was thanked for his services to Georgia by having the main street bear his name. Though much of Savannah existed only on paper, 16 tithings mostly named for Trustees were formed into four wards.

Pioneer historian William B. Stevens described the climax of morning activities on July 7 in idealized fashion: "Having apportioned out to the inhabitants their several lots, and settled, in an amicable way, all differences as to choice and locality, the people, at noon, sat down to a plentiful dinner, provided by Oglethorpe; and made the day festal, with the thanksgiving of the lips, and the gladness of the heart."

During the afternoon Oglethorpe really did make some hearts glad by taking his first step toward delegating some authority. He surrendered their commissions to bailiffs, tithingmen, constables, and conservators of the peace — who had been named to their posts before the *Ann* sailed. A town court was set up, complete with recorder and registrar, and was ordered to convene at six-week intervals.

Trustees had furnished Oglethorpe with extra copies of signed commissions, with names omitted, for use in the event an officer did not perform his duties or died. Eight of these blank commissions were filled out and delivered to successor officers during the first year Georgia's founder spent in the colony.

Death came early and stayed late. By a twist of fate the first to succumb was Dr. William Cox, the colony's physician. He came as a volunteer without pay, but was provided with a residence and servants to cultivate the land attached to it.

Determined if possible to get some public good out of individual bad, Oglethorpe ordered a military funeral for the civilian physician. For the first time the machinery of the ward/tithing system was tested by a call-up of males. With Savannah's only bell tolling mournfully, minute guns were fired. Then ceremonies ended with a volley of small arms.

Mrs. Cox, pregnant, was left with children Eunice and William to rear in one of the few houses already provided with a chimney. When the baby arrived in October she was christened Mary, but lived only ten days.

Another essential leader of the colony, also a volunteer, became ill in time to receive the ministrations of Cox. He was diagnosed as having a severe case of bloody flux, probably brought on by cold and damp while sleeping in a tent. Medications provided by Cox seemed to have little effect upon the Rev. Dr. Henry Herbert. Hence he left the colony in early May and took passage for England on the *Baltic Merchant*. Barely a month out of Charles Town the clergyman died at sea.

Life rather than death became central on March 28, when Mrs. Hanna Close gave birth to the colony's first child. Grateful to providence for their anticipated good life in this new land of plenty, parents named the girl Georgia. Soon she received from South Carolina planter James Hume a silver boat and spoon —earlier promised to the first child born in the buffer colony. Georgia's father, Henry, died when the girl was six months old. Two weeks later, just before the end of 1733, Georgia went to her grave, too.

Scurvy, ague, and dysentery — treated with salitrum seeds when they were available — stalked the land. James Goddard, a sturdy carpenter just 38 years old, died in early July. His wife followed him within two weeks. Since orphans could not be left to care for themselves, nine-year-old John Goddard was bound out as apprentice to public gardener Joseph Fitzwalter. His sister Elizabeth, age five, was placed by Oglethorpe in the care of wig maker James Carwell and his wife Margaret.

There was astonishingly little demand for perukes in the land of sand and pines. Hence Georgia's founder had earlier placed the Carwells "on subsistence." That is, they were fed and clothed from the colony's store that was operated by the Trust. In order to keep them going with another mouth to feed, a cash allowance of £3 per year was added to their subsistence when they took Elizabeth. This arrangement lasted just 60 days. Margaret Carwell, age 32, died in September, so her ward was re-assigned.

At least twice death paid two visits to a single family in one day. Flax and hemp worker William Littell, age 31, and his five-year-old daughter, Mary, died on July 12. Two months later Margaret Carwell — who had taken the Fitzwalter orphan into her home — died on the same day as her infant daughter.

Before fall brought blessed relief from the stifling heat Father Oglethorpe, as many charity colonists habitually dubbed him, had seen one out of every nine pioneer Georgians consigned to the strange, sandy earth. There was special consternation during periods when each successive day saw a funeral — as during the August hot spell when "five of them dyed within one week."

Singly or in clusters, at intervals of a few days or in rapid-fire succession, each instance of death heightened fears of survivors and weakened the colony. Always there were personal affairs to be settled.

Joshua Overend, whose only work experience in England was as a dealer in fabrics, left behind an unusually large quantity of clothing at his death. Carefully itemized, it included three coats and a jacket plus two pairs of breeches, two pairs of stockings, five ruffled shirts, a damask nightgown and three caps — each made of a different kind of cloth. His widow in England was entitled to lifetime use of the empty house and half of his tract of farm land — if she cared to come in order to claim it. She also would have inherited Overend's steer, cow, and calf had it not been necessary to sell them in order to pay his accumulated debts of slightly more than £1.

No matter what crisis or issue confronted him, Father Oglethorpe seldom lacked a sense of sure knowledge that give him firm convictions. No man to bite his tongue under any circumstances, he told everyone who would listen that rum was the chief culprit causing the little cemetery to fill so rapidly.

Did his own drunken bout that led to the death of a stranger and a term in prison enter into his views? If so, they were reenforced by observations of what he considered to be cause-and-effect sequences.

Gasping for breath as he lay dying on July 29, 42-year-old

Salzburgers in flight

According to a very early print, German Protestants driven from their homes used this prayer:
> O Lord, let our flight not occur in winter;
>   this used to be my plea and the aim of my wishes,
>
> but now I am content to go even in wintertime,
>   because God's warm love will cover us.

Some of them actually did journey to the Georgia colony at the height of winter. Theoretically British, they clung tenaciously to inherited dress and to their own language.

carpenter Thomas Milledge choked as he thought of the five children he was about to leave behind. As Oglethorpe reported the matter to Trustees in London "he confessed he contracted 'a burning Feaver' at the Indian Trading House; he there drank Rum Punch on the Wednesday, on Thursday was taken ill and on the seventh day, dyed."

It didn't matter whether or not such evidence would hold up in court. Having previously convicted rum, Oglethorpe had no difficulty finding fresh evidence with which to frame new charges. Armed with the death-bed indictment plus his own conclusions about many other fatal or debilitating ills, Georgia's founder set out to stave every rum barrel in the colony.

A source of particular frustration was the all-important Indian trading post barely 15 minutes' walk from the heart of Savannah. There John Musgrove and his wife Mary, both vital to the colony because of their skill as interpreters, ignored Oglethorpe's ideas and his prohibitions alike. Rum was profitable so they sold it to anyone who could pay for it. This situation changed not a whit when Trustees later elevated the prohibition of strong drink from an official policy to one of only three laws ever established for Oglethorpe's Georgia.

Whatever caused death to stalk the colony — rum, contaminated water, high temperatures to which former city dwellers were not accustomed, flies, gnats, lice, malaria, or factors unknown — impact of the terrible toll was softened by arrival of ship after ship bearing new bands of hopefuls. Some vessels had only a handful of passengers; others brought dozens. Only a few English charity colonists in addition to those aboard the *Ann* came during the first year. Most were artisans, foreigners seeking any haven however desperate, self-supporting adventurers, and servants — lots and lots of servants. Many of the latter were indentured to the masters they accompanied; others were servants of the Trust.

Just three months after the *Ann* started on her epoch-making voyage, the *Volant* followed with left-behind equipment, supplies, more of Hales' ever-present books, and four passengers —two artisans and two apprentices. After 11 weeks, in early March the vessel hove in sight of Savannah's lookouts.

She was followed by the tiny 110-ton *James*, one of whose passengers was former ship's captain Botham Squire. More important to the colony, she brought Italians self-described as highly skilled in both the propagation of silk worms and the processing of raw silk. In May, Captain Yoakley of the *James* claimed from Oglethorpe the "handsome prize" offered to the first vessel that unloaded in Savannah rather than Charles Town or Port Royal.

On July 7, the day land was first allocated, more than two dozen new settlers arrived on the *Pearl*.[1] Most of them were sent by Oglethorpe to establish an outpost at Thunderbolt. One of these persons, potash maker Roger Lacy, didn't bring quite the entourage he had hoped to have. Trustees listened eagerly to his ambitious plans for producing silk and his arguments about his need for workers. They agreed to let him take over 20 charity children who would serve him as indentured servants until age 24. For reasons unknown this entrepreneur failed to get his supply of cheap labor, but came on to Georgia, anyway.

To the total surprise of all Georgians, July 11 saw their ranks swelled by arrival of the *William and Sarah* with 39 Portuguese and three German Jews. No end of consternation had been stirred up earlier in London. Quite early, Trustees appointed three Jewish citizens as solicitors of funds for Georgia. They learned, too late, that funds raised in Britain by these agents would be diverted to refugees who were neither British nor Protestant.

Trustees would have stopped the voyage of the Jews had they been able to do so. Angry at having been tricked, they fired off instructions to Oglethorpe — aware that the contraband colonists would probably reach Savannah weeks ahead of their letters, but less than sensitive to problems their orders would create there.

Oglethorpe knew his colleagues at home too well to fail to anticipate their reactions. Yet he acted as though he had no notion that the Jews would be unwelcome. He received them with courtesy and openly rejoiced when he found among them a physician who stepped into the void left by the death of Dr. Cox. Under the treatment of Dr. Samuel Nunez, who favored cold baths and cooling drinks, none who followed his orders died. Some who were sickest experienced "wonderful recoveries."

When London's instructions finally arrived, Oglethorpe blandly ignored them. At one stroke he altered the makeup of the community by accepting one-fourth as many European Jews as the *Ann* had brought English Protestants. He allocated land to them and nodded assent when they produced their prized Torah, Hechal, and circumcision box as a prelude to asking permission to establish Mickva Israel synagogue. Soon a Jewish burying ground was established by this, America's oldest, Jewish congregation in the south.

Canny Oglethorpe said nothing about such matters in letters to Trustees. He was careful to stress, however, that one Jew was believed to have decided "to become a Christian of the Protestant variety."

Just one month after unexpected arrival of the Jews, the relatively large *Georgia Pink* delivered 84 more persons to Savannah. Her hold was crammed with tools and supplies plus an all-important chest full of what Trustees dubbed "trinkets." This merchandise, designed to be used as gifts to the Indians, was valued at £20. Inevitably, this vessel also brought Bibles, prayer books, and such all-important tomes as *The Duty of Man* and *The Great Importance of a Religious Life.*

In September the *Susannah* brought a few more colonists plus a silver chalice and paten for the yet-to-be built Savannah church. The Rev. Samuel Wesley, a long-time personal friend of Oglethorpe and father of Charles and John who later came to Georgia, was responsible for the ecclesiastical ware.

December 15 saw arrival of the *Savannah*, whose 132-name passenger list included Dr. William Watkins, surgeon, and a blue-blooded but impoverished Irish emigrant, William Wise. Wise was not enthusiastic about Georgia, but decided it was better to come to the new land than to starve at home. Fearing loneliness on the voyage and in Savannah, he reputedly smuggled a woman of easy virtue aboard his vessel. Trustees got wind of these doings in London, and sent urgent letters ordering that Wise be shipped back.

Oglethorpe acted as though he hadn't received these instructions.

In spite of the high death rate, a census made in January, 1734, revealed that 437 persons in Georgia were "receiving the support of the Trustees." It is not clear whether or not that total included a special group of new arrivals. Survivors of an entire shipload of Irish convicts, approximately 40 in number and near starvation, were forced into Savannah by a severe storm "at the turn of the year." Oglethorpe purchased their service as indentured servants at £5 per head. He put some of them to work upon the Trust, or communal, farms. One man was assigned to the service of each magistrate, and others were divided among the widows — for whom they worked as farm hands.

Reconciliation of head counts by Oglethorpe and by Trustees in London is impossible. Records of the latter were maintained according to the colony's operating year, which ended on June 9. According to their accounts, 237 British and 104 foreign Protestant settlers had been sent on the charity by June 9, 1734.[2]

Since Trustees had no responsibility for welfare of private adventurers and their servants, no tally of such persons was kept. According to careful calculations based upon records of land grants, 195 adventurers and 77 of their servants were in Georgia by June 9, 1734.

Most adventurers were artisans or petty gentry. They had no guarantee of food, clothing, or other necessities. In this respect they relieved Georgia's founder of a great many headaches. But Oglethorpe soon found such settlers to be bolder, less docile, and more argumentative than charity colonists. They often ignored his instructions which, they pointed out, didn't have the force of law. Trustees made land grants in London, with the location of each tract left up to Oglethorpe. Some of those who claimed 300 or 500 acres quickly found their land to be badly situated. Too stubborn to alter an allocation once it had been made, Oglethorpe fumed as he watched some angry adventurers abandon the colony after a few days or weeks in order to head for Carolina or points farther north. At other times he vainly wished that all self-supporting emigrants would pull up stakes and leave, instead of remaining to make trouble.

From the outset of his suddenly-undertaken journey of adventure, the Member from Haslemere had confidently expected to return home after a few months in the colony. His seat in Parliament would be up for re-election early in 1734. Nothing he had already attained or hoped to gain was more highly prized. Before landing at Savannah in February, there was every reason to expect that he would no longer be needed after June. When he found that he could not leave as he had planned a recurrent theme of his letters — almost petulant at times — expressed the hope that, finally, he could make ready to leave the colony.

Had he encountered no other problem that was not foreseen from offices in London, the pressing issue of food for the hungry would have forced him to revise his schedule. Deer, turkeys, ducks, geese, doves, and squirrels abounded in the forests — but charity colonists had no skill in hunting and little time to learn.

As part of the contract between Trustees and emigrants, all whose expenses were paid were guaranteed subsistence — but no cash — for the first 12 months. Eventually the standard yearly allowance for an adult male came to be: 312 pounds of beef or pork; 104 pounds each of rice, flour, and either peas or Indian corn; 16 pounds of cheese; 12 pounds of lamp oil; 1 pound of spun cotton. Females and children got fractional allowances; servants received less meat and more rice.

Plans called for the colony to be self-sufficient by the end of the first year, and prosperous enough to begin exporting its surplus plus special products at the end of the second year. Some fortunate settlers to whom Oglethorpe assigned fertile land that required little clearing did manage to grow a few potatoes, peas, and other vegetables in 1733. Others discovered their tracts to be part pine barren, part marsh, part pure sand that might be 20 feet deep.

Food was plentiful in markets of Charles Town, but prices rose with demand. A quantity of rice, part of Carolina's initial good-will gift to the new colony, had seemed immense when received. It was soon gone, however, and Oglethorpe had to start buying rice, too. Small wonder that a constant refrain, slightly varied in wording but identical in meaning, runs through his early letters to colleagues in Britain: "I have been obliged to make many new expences here."

Trustees, zealously watching every shilling, wanted their representative to send an exact statement of what it would cost to keep a family on subsistence for a year. Oglethorpe reported that he could not tell them. Some colonists needed or deserved more than others, and prices fluctuated sharply. Men trying to project the future growth and financial support of their scheme fumed and protested at such an off-hand response to a basic question.

Charles Town visitor Samuel Everleigh estimated in the spring of 1733 that about ten acres had been sowed with grain. He privately doubted that the colony could survive without corn, but was certain that persons accustomed to city life would be unable to grow and harvest it. For such an undertaking the Carolinian considered blacks essential — and a cardinal principal of the Georgia experiment was "no blacks, now or ever."

Especially among the self-supporting adventurers, Oglethorpe's followers complained bitterly about this policy. Presence of black sawyers brought by Col. Bull seemed to aggravate the situation, so Oglethorpe sent these experienced workmen away, too.

New Jerusalem church — where Salzburgers worshipped

Unlike most Georgia colonists, Salzburgers got the privilege of selecting the site of their own community. They called it Ebenezer, but soon had to move to New Ebenezer.

New Jerusalem church was erected in 1767 — nearly half a century after these European Protestant refugees sought and found a haven in Georgia.

A decade later Georgia had not achieved self-sufficiency. Staples were brought to Savannah from regions as distant as New York. Inevitably, prices were boosted by shipping charges that were added to base rates. Salt pork was used in large quantities because it cost less than fresh meat. But use of it brought nutritional problems, especially when it was eaten with little except hominy or grits.

Genuine success, without a precise parallel in any other British outpost on the continent, was achieved in the effort to gain and to keep good relations with native Americans. Like other aspects of the Georgia experiment, this received wide and favorable attention in the press of England.

Reporting in detail about a colonial dispatch dated May 20, 1733, the *Gentleman's Magazine* noted that about 50 "Chief Men of all the Lower Creek Nation" had gathered in Savannah for a parley with Oglethorpe. Some native leaders travelled as long as five days in order to be present. As a special gesture of hospitality — not unmixed with showmanship — Georgia's founder insisted upon receiving his guests in a recently-completed dwelling.

A treaty was drafted with the aid of interpreter Mary Musgrove. Under its terms the Indians "freely gave up their Right to all the Land they did not use themselves." In addition they "offer'd to go and attack the *Cheroquees* who they heard had slain some *English*, if Mr. *Oglethorpe* would Command them, declaring a love for him and his People."

Then it was Oglethorpe's turn to be generous. "A Laced Coat, Hat and Shirts were given to each of the Chiefs, some Cloth for their Attendants, a Present of Gun-Powder, Irish Linnen, Tobacco, Pipes, Tape of all Colours, Bullets, and 8 Cags of Rum to carry Home to their respective Towns."

Monday, May 21, saw formal agreement upon a pact of alliance,

friendship, and commerce — designed to last as long as the sun shines or the waters run in the rivers. Inscribed upon vellum and ornamented with water-color birds and festoons, the treaty was duly sent to England. Trustees formally ratified it in October. Land ceded to Oglethorpe then and later exceeded 1,100,000 acres — enough for 200,000 charity colonists.

Long before Trustees assented to the agreement, Oglethorpe proceeded as though it were in full force. He consistently kept his word, to the letter, in dealing with Indians. Sometimes he was accused of treating them more kindly than his down-and-out countrymen. From the beginning of his friendship with Tomochichi, Georgia's founder hoped — without fulfillment — that the aging chief would become a convert to Christianity.[3]

Equally important in the view of Oglethorpe, it appeared likely that Tomochichi could recruit Indians to strengthen Georgia's fighting forces. Here the aging chieftain succeeded admirably. Among the Yamacraw, alone, two companies of volunteers were raised and put under the command of Tuskenca and Skee. Later, Tomochichi's nephew, Toonahowi, played a significant role in struggles against the Spanish.

For the present Oglethorpe had his hands full without facing armed foes. Few of his followers were satisfied with the system of land tenure, an issue that erupted even before the *Ann* sailed. Some who had been selected to go on the first ship turned down the opportunity because they wanted full inheritance rights for females as well as males. Prohibition of rum to Europeans — relaxed in the case of native Americans — was a source of endless headaches in spite of the fact that beer and ale were relatively abundant. Especially when their hand-to-mouth existence was compared with that of flourishing Carolina planters, Georgia's first settlers felt woefully abused because they couldn't own or even borrow slaves.

Couple these three basic issues with frequent disappointment at land quality, climate, scarcity and cost of food and supplies, arbitrary ways of Father Oglethorpe, distance from home, sickness and death, competition between charity colonists and self-supporting adventurers with their servants . . . and it is easy to see why grumbling never ceased. Georgia's founder labeled this reaction "Petulance," and tried to ignore it.

Things were bad enough when he was present, which was only a fraction of the time. Business required frequent trips to Charles Town and outlying settlements had to be started. Much of Oglethorpe's energy went into trips through the forests, probing for evidence of enemies and seeking to gain full understanding of the region. Hector Beaufain, who went on one excursion early in 1734, found that it required "much ado to follow Mr. Oglethorpe, for he walks the woods like any Indian."

Whenever Oglethorpe was absent from Savannah for a few days, malcontents got their heads together. They plotted about leaving the colony in a body, and pondered the possibility of lodging a group protest with Trustees in London. Georgia's founder didn't mince words. He castigated all who complained as having "grown very mutinous and impatient of Labour and Discipline."

His return home was postponed again and again.

On the ground, Georgia had proved to be quite unlike the paradise he himself had depicted to prospective settlers. So the anniversary of his arrival found him determined to leave, regardless of consequences. He began making arrangements for others to take over some of the many roles he had been filling. Thomas Causton was authorized, not in writing but in a cautious oral statement, to serve in Oglethorpe's place as on-the-ground representative of the Trustees. Carolina friends were requested to notify him when ships arrived.

When word came that a vessel was in port he hurried to Charles Town and made ready to embark. Then he learned that a contingent of German-speaking Salzburgers was expected to arrive momentarily. Henry Newman was secretary of the Society for the Promotion of Christian Knowledge, and hence was influential in channeling funds of that group to Georgia's needs. He had expressed a strong desire that Oglethorpe be on hand to meet the persecuted European Lutherans when and if they came.

So the return home was postponed once more.

British interest in the Salzburgers had reached a high level before the *Ann* sailed in 1732. It took a year for Trustees to agree upon a plan of action. When they finally came to a decision in September, 1733, they — as usual — went overboard. Samuel Urlsperger was authorized to gather 300 of the Salzburger, or Bertoldsgoden, refugees to form a huge embarcation for Georgia. Trustees sent the *Purisburg* to Rotterdam for these Europeans in November. When the vessel sailed from Dover on January 8, her passenger list of 73 included 47 Salzburgers who went at the expense of the S.P.C.K. Leaders were Baron Georg Philipp Friedrich Von Reck plus pastors John Bolzius and Israel Gronau.

They reached Charles Town on March 7, 1734. With Oglethorpe at their head they arrived at Savannah on March 12.

From the earliest hint that foreign Protestants might be added to the British poor who went to Georgia, it had been stressed that such persons would be expected to become subjects of His Majesty the king. They would mix and mingle and intermarry with native-born Britishers. Hence in a generation or two they would add significantly to the number of His Majesty's loyal subjects in the New World.

Oglethorpe was fully aware of this line of reasoning. Yet, once more, he had to deal with reality that differed from theory. Salzburgers balked at the notion of settling in Savannah. They wanted their own community, where they could use their native language and follow their inherited customs.

Georgia's founder did not attempt to force integration of Germans into the established English setttlement. Instead he took the newcomers up the Savannah river and let Von Reck select a site for their settlement. According to the *Journal* of the German leader the spot he picked was "21 Miles from the Town of *Savannah*, and 30 miles from the Sea, where there are Rivers, little Hills, clear Brooks, cool Springs, a fertile Soil, and plenty of Grass." Germans dubbed the place Ebenezer — meaning "place of help," or "divine haven." Like other new Georgians they soon discovered that their haven was less idyllic than it seemed to be at first look.[4]

Six days after Ebenezer was selected and named, James Edward Oglethorpe set his face toward home.

A long-familiar military tune called "The World Turned Upside Down" ran through his head over and over. Everything really was topsy-turvy. It seemed long, long ago when an anticipated legacy had fostered dreams of a Utopian community to be peopled by England's debtors and other worthy poor.

For the present Father Oglethorpe had a stomach full of such folk. What's more, money wasn't coming at a level sufficient to maintain the colony. If the scheme was to survive, a big and steady source of support must be found. Not a chance of getting from Parliament that kind of money for a charitable colony, as such.

Georgia's founder vividly remembered the sermon preached by the Rev. Samuel Smith at the first annual meeting of future Trustees in February, 1731. Smith, a man of the cloth and of peace, had been wise enough to underscore sentiments already being voiced by some. Georgia's settlers, said he, would constitute "Frontier Garrisons against any Foreign Power that may invade [the Carolinas], and secure the dependance of the Provinces to the Crown . . ."

During a bit more than one year on the ground, that argument in support of the Georgia scheme loomed much larger than it did in London, even to the most ardent imperialist. But if the colony was to develop military strength it must have a seasoned leader. Who better to assume that role than a veteran of European campaigns, one who had fought and studied under the great Prince Eugene himself?

Already transformed in imagination from philanthropist to commander-in-chief, Georgia's founder was confident that he could find money and men. He had settled upon what he expected to be a splendid way to regain the interested attention of all England. Once national interest was brought to focus upon Georgia, the colony's strategic military location would serve as a lever with which to pry open the vaults of Britain's treasury.

Chapter 7

OGLETHORPE'S COMRADES BEGIN TO
FLEX THEIR MUSCLES

London: November, 1732 — June, 1734

Shortly after her passengers boarded the *Ann*, comrades whom Oglethorpe left behind convened for yet another conference. From the start of the Georgia enterprise they had made a basic assumption. All policy issues concerning the colony, it was agreed, must be considered and settled in the Palace Court, old palace yard, Westminster — or some other convenient meeting place. Collectively, the Trustees constituted the Trust. Full power of government resided in the Trust alone.

Had they dealt only with major policy matters, the unpaid work of the Trustees would have been far less time consuming. Men far from the scene of action and often ill informed about what was happening there insisted on dealing with minor and often petty adminstrative details.

Meetings were frequent and lengthy. Small wonder that a handful of enthusiasts conducted practically all business. Men named to the Trust because of their influence in the church or in Parliament or because of their wealth attended relatively few meetings. Some permitted their names to remain on the roll for a year or so, then resigned.[1]

James Vernon ranked first in faithfulness. During 20 years he attended and participated in 712 meetings. No man to bite his tongue, he took one side or another in practically every discussion.

94

Twelve years older than Oglethorpe, from adolescence he was accustomed to power. At age 14 he became groom of the bedchamber to the Duke of Gloucester. When Oglethorpe was five, Vernon was named envoy extraordinary to the court of Copenhagen. After one term in Parliament he became commissioner of excise in 1710 and retained the office for life. Also clerk of the council for 40 years, he was in constant intimate contact with Britain's top leaders.

Vernon never failed to remember that his father, James, had served as England's secretary of state. In that capacity the elder Vernon proscribed James Oglethorpe's father as a Jacobite and an enemy of the crown.

Long before he began to deal with Oglethorpe, Vernon worked as an associate of Dr. Thomas Bray. This relationship plus his great influence in the Society for the Propagation of the Gospel in Foreign Parts eventually brought him into the circle of men hoping to establish a colony in Georgia. Vernon continued to work actively for the New World enterprise long after Oglethorpe ceased to play an active role in the Georgia Trust.

John, Lord Viscount Percival and later Earl of Egmont, attended 614 meetings of Trustees and their committees. But he became disenchanted with the movement in 1742 and quit it for good. Often ridiculed as pompous, he took his seat in the Irish House of Lords when Oglethorpe was 19. He was elected to the House of Commons in 1727 and served on the gaol committee. Like Vernon, he was a long-time supporter of Thomas Bray. He also had close ties with George Berkeley — whose ambitious plans for education of New World blacks came to nothing.

Henry L'Apostre, Esq., and William Heathcote, Esq., were named to the Trust in 1733. Neither had a major role in the decision-making process, but L'Apostre faithfully trudged to 526 meetings and Heathcote attended 84.

The Rev. Samuel Smith was involved in 470 sets of deliberations, and the Rev. Stephen Hales managed to be present at 300 meetings in spite of his prodigious output of time and energy in the collection of books for Georgia. Captain Thomas Coram, only Trustee who had been in the New World prior to 1733 and a zealous adherent of Bray, had strong opinions that he was quick to voice. He later became noted as a result of launching the Foundlings Hospital. Oglethorpe served on its board of directors after he cut all ties with Georgia.

Numerous men of influence were for a short or a long time members of the Trust; few took great interest in it. When Parliament considered affairs of the colony, names of such Trustees may have helped to sway a few votes: James Stanley, Earl of Derby; John, Lord Tryconnel; James, Lord Limerick; James, Lord D'Arcy; William, Lord Talbot; and Lord Signey Beauclerk. Sir Jacob de Bouverie, unimportant in working of the Trust, channelled into its coffers the largest recorded gift from a private source: £1,000 "to be expended in providing foreign and other servants for the benefit of the colony."

Though not a member of the Trust, Benjamin Martyn served quietly and tirelessly as its secretary, without pay. Harmann Verelst, who was paid a pittance, kept meticulous financial records and attended to some of Oglethorpe's personal affairs.

Haste on Oglethorpe's part made it impossible to attend to all essential matters before he set out for Georgia. Meeting on November 23 the Trustees present were: Egmont, Vernon, Smith, Hales, Coram, and five others — a better-than-average attendance. They ordered that their "Common Seal be affix'd to a Power to James Oglethorpe, Esqr to appoint such Commander, or other Office or Officers, as he shall think fit, to train and Exercise the Militia in Georgia." Dispatched by messenger, this instrument caught up with the *Ann* where her commander waited for a fair wind in order to sail.

Then and always money was a critical issue. On November 23 plans were made to ask the Society for the Propagation of the Gospel in Foreign Parts to give immediate aid. It was a logical move; conversion of the Indians was an obvious and an emotion-charged goal central to the launching of the Georgia scheme. Even so small a sum as £70 per year, the society's usual allowance for a minister, would be of assistance. It would help greatly while Trustees waited for the development of the Savannah glebe by communal labor. This 300-acre tract, allocated to the church, was expected to meet many needs of the religious establishment as soon as it was "sufficiently improved for a Minister."

Unexpected problems erupted before the end of the month in which Oglethorpe and his followers sailed. Trustees learned of a new threat to the unborn colony. "One Thomas Bacon, a Square Well Set Man, about forty Years of Age, thick Lips, pale face, and dark brown hair," had reached London from Saint Augustine in September. He offered himself as a pioneer Georgian, but sailed for Carolina without waiting for a decision from his application.

An urgent letter to Oglethorpe warned that Bacon was believed to have hurried to Carolina "to discover the State of the Colony [of

Georgia], and give Information thereof to the Spaniards." Trustees expressed a hope that the admiralty could be persuaded to station a sloop of eight guns off the Georgia coast, as a protective measure. They did little or nothing to implement that hope, however.

Other applicants for passage to Georgia who couldn't possibly be Spanish spies brought headaches that had not been anticipated. Some were rogues who tried to pose as members of the honest poor. To avoid trouble from creditors, it was decided to publicize names of all Georgia applicants in the newspapers at least a fortnight before their scheduled departure. Prospective colonists were required to prove that "they do not run away from their wives and families to leave them a burthen on the parish."

About 60 days after Oglethorpe sailed, his colleagues interviewed a group of eight carpenters. To the chagrin of Trustees it was learned that one man wouldn't be able to work at his trade even if sent to the colony at the expense of the Trust; he had sold all of his tools in order to satisfy some of his creditors. Another carpenter didn't even own a bed on which to sleep. Individually and collectively this group of artisans evoked the Trustee reaction: "miserable objects, most of them."

Concurrently, Count Zinzendorf's petition for aid to exiled Schwenkfelders was rejected. This time there was no negative reaction to qualification of applications — but money on hand was inadequate to meet needs of colonists already on their way to Georgia.

Prospects for sending some Salzburgers were better, because the S.P.C.K. had special interest in these folk and already had the financial support of numerous persons of wealth.

It was absolutely urgent that lawmakers be persuaded to back the Georgia scheme. So Trustees voted in March to order 600 additional copies of Martyn's *Reasons for Establishing the Colony of Georgia*. Thereby, every member of Parliament could be provided with the booklet.

Contributions from parishes and from the general public were frequent and generous by comparison with those made to any comparable enterprise. Oglethorpe's public relations blitz continued to have a significant impact long after he had left Britain. But when compared with needs of the colony, receipts from this source were small and woefully slow in coming. By the time Georgia's founder returned from his first voyage to the colony, the total received from church folk and Britishers at large was only £4,200.

Worse yet, some of this money — entirely too much of it in the opinion of a few Trustees — was designated to foster the spiritual welfare of the colony. In lists of gifts kept by Verelst, "The Religious Uses of the Colony" appeared over and over. Many small sums sent by the pious were for such specific purposes as: the maintenance of a catechist in Georgia; support of Swiss and Palatine refugees; purchase of a surplice; and construction costs of the planned Savannah church.

To decline any gift, whether of earmarked cash or of goods and equipment, might offend the giver. Besides, some commodities saved outlay of always-scarce cash. William Grimes made a small dent in the military budget by presenting 50 cartridge boxes with girdles, 50 belts, and 50 brass hilted hangers — short, slightly curved swords that were favored for use by many seamen. Samuel Wesley's gift of a pewter chalice and pattine would prove useful when religious services could be started. Henry Archer gave 22 dozen pairs of stockings; and the Duke of Montague sent 4 casks of nails, 1 cask of tools, 1 cask each of powder flashes, bayonets, and large spikes.

Along with commodities that were nearly as good as cash came many gifts of doubtful value and some that had no earthly use. Since any and all gifts were accepted, things not immediately usable were put in storage. Christopher Tower sent two gallons of lucerne seed. Richard Martyn gave a box of tellicherry bark. Robert More presented three olive trees in baskets. Philip Miller gave a tub of white mulberry plants and grape vines plus two packets of seeds from an Egyptian plant believed to be a good source of potash.

Samuel Skinner sent three large tubs of bamboo plants. Thomas Hyam presented some Neapolitan chestnuts for sowing in Georgia. His Grace, the Duke of Montague, sent a long chest of buttons and mohair.

Books poured in by the dozen and by the hundred. Many were bound, but others were in the form of unbound sheets. Most but by no means all were religious: countless Bibles and Testament of all sizes and styles; 178 copies, *Duty of Man*; 1400 copies, *The Great Importance of a Religious life*; 48 sets of sheets, *Faith and Practice of a Church of England Man*; 2 sets of sheets, *Select Discourses by Dr. Worthington*; 48 copies, *Companion for the Sick*. Stephen Hales, indefatigable collector of practically anything printed, hauled more books to the Georgia office than did all other Trustees, combined.[2]

One benefactor, James Leake, is remembered only for his gift. On January 31, 1733, he joyfully pledged to present 1,000 spelling books — which he brought in installments. Stored upon receipt and added to the inventory of the Trust, some of these books were finally used. Eighteen years after the first of them were stored 200 copies were shipped to Georgia. In 1752, when Trustees were busy making arrangements to surrender their charter, colonists at Fort Augusta on the Savannah river recorded the receipt of "12 more of the spelling books given by Mr. Leake."

Stephen Hales was well represented in the shipment that reached the frontier trading post in March, 1752. As a result of his earnest solicitations in earlier years, Augusta settlers received: 50 copies, Dr. Thomas Gouch's *Showing How to Walk with God*; 20 *Help and Guide to Christian Families*, and 12 *The Young Christian Instructed*.

Consideration money, or initial fees paid by adventurers and self-supporting gentry who got land grants in Georgia, proved to be an unexpectedly good source of revenue. Five persons started a trend by paying £1 each on December 14, 1732. During the life of the Trust such consideration money, plus related fees, brought in more than £104,000. This usually-overlooked source eventually yielded five or six times as much as all cash contributed by individuals and parishes. Much of it was received comparatively late, however.[3]

Except for a few days after receiving a huge check from the treasury, Trustees were perpetually desperate for money from any available source. Their hope of receiving big profits from sale of lottery tickets had faded. So had the prospect of government support for old soldiers and for apprentices to be sent with them. Linked with the latter scheme was a proposal that the government pay the Trust £10 a head — more than twice the standard fare — for transportation of "vagrants and poor children." It was implicit in this proposal that such poor children would be indentured, also for a fee. Britain's leaders balked, and nothing came of these varied fund-raising ideas.

A number of schemes, originated by persons not associated with the Trust, were presented as offering quick profits. Most such proposals were floated early in the Georgia experiment, but get-rich-quick ideas never wholly subsided.

Adventurers as well as Trustees dreamed of easy fortunes to be gained from Georgia silk, wine, cochineal, potash, indigo, and other products. Trustees were barred by charter from making a personal profit, but opportunists outside the Trust had no such restrictions. Some paid consideration money, got land grants, and personally went to the colony. Others expected to employ agents, or made elaborate plans and proposals that never got beyond the paper stage.

Thomas Lowndes approached Egmont and Vernon with a daring scheme that seemed to have great potential. Lowndes was not greedy; he wanted only 8% of the money to be raised — but at first refused to divulge the nature of the venture in which he wished to involve Georgia leaders. Initially he said only that "It was not to be at the expense of the public, but an advantage to it." This secret enterprise would be a future source of annual income, in addition to yielding "a great sum of money" immediately.

Trustees wasted time and energy with Lowndes and in planning how best to use the anticipated revenue. Then they discovered that he wanted them to sponsor "erection of a Lottery in Edinburgh or Some Other Town in North Britain." When they backed away from his plan, Lowndes waited a few months before coming to them with another. Also secret, it promised huge sums — with his own share reduced to 6%. Nothing came of it, of course.

Colliers who specialized in unloading ships of coal felt themselves abused by "a set of ale house keepers" who had formed a protective society in an effort to hold wages down. Representatives of the workmen, aware that Georgia leaders had influence in the government, offered a working partnership. Trustees were asked to persuade Parliament to pass legislation regulating the society of ale house keepers. In turn, colliers promised that they would collect as royalty "a certain sum on every chauldron [of coal], which will amount to £26,000 per annum, which they desire may be applied to the uses of Georgia."

One scheme that sounded ridiculous was quite sound. Andrew Duché informed Trustees that he was "the first Man in Europe, Africa, or America, that ever found the true material and manner of making porcelain or China ware." In return for financing of his capital needs, he would establish his factory in Georgia. By means of it he promised to give immediate employment to "100 poor people in the Town, & many more," as well as fostering the export trade of the colony. Duché went to Savannah without the requested aid, established a factory, and prospered so greatly that he tried to build a public wharf at his own expense. He almost certainly discovered Georgia kaolin and put it to profitable use.

Colonel Samuel Horsey, who later established a settlement in Carolina and became deputy-governor of the colony, pointed Egmont to another special-interest possibility. Investors and speculators had spent "near £7,000" in an effort to gain control of British properties once held by Catholics and forfeited to the crown. Yield from these estates was estimated at £20,000 per year. Though owners had been outlawed, "gentlemen who prosecuted that affair" faced technical legal obstructions in the effort for further recovery of them. If the gentlemen making up the Georgia Trust would gain title to these popish properties and then turn them over to investors, they, in turn, would channel one-third of their profits to the charitable colony. After several high-level discussions this potential source of revenue was reluctantly abandoned as being "more rational than feazable."

Someone in the Georgia Trust discovered that a fund had been created in 1709 for the relief of poor distressed Palatines. Many of these inhabitants of an old German Empire state along the Rhine, later a part of Bavaria, were then refugees. An unspent balance of £22,000 was held by trustees of the Palatine fund. Why not use all of it for the Georgia enterprise?

This scheme, too, came to naught. But it pointed Trustees toward a promising target — money designated specifically for some of the 30,000 Salzburgers recently exiled.

Income from all sources never met the needs and wants of the colony. As a result one Trustee very early began taking risks. Soldier-of-fortune James Oglethorpe used whatever means necessary, including his own funds, to pursue his goals. Before the sailing of the *Ann* an entry that would recur many times appeared in *The Journal of the Trustees for Establishing the Colony of Georgia in America*: "sums to be deducted out of the money due to Mr. Oglethorpe."

From the time the charter was issued in June until October 25, 1732, Oglethorpe received funds with one hand and disbursed them with the other. He gave a formal accounting in preparation for departure. Almost as soon as his accounts had been certified, he began advancing or lending his personal funds when no cash belonging to the Trust was available. During the struggle with Spain this practice, initially involving relatively small sums, mushroomed into a frenzied devil-may-care spate of borrowing from anyone who would lend to him.

Even more than affairs of the colony as conducted in London, Georgia in her infancy presented on-the-ground needs that could not wait. They must be met promptly, or not at all.

Writing from Charles Town in May, 1733, Oglethorpe informed his colleagues that he had drawn bills in the amount of £198 upon English shippers Peter and J.C. Symond. About one-fourth of this sum presented no questions; it was for his own account. Georgia's founder realized that the balance might involve more cash than Trustees would have on hand when bills were presented for payment. Hence he reported in matter-of-fact fashion that he had "desired Mr. Symonds to accept of any bills that you shall not think fit to pay, and to pay them upon my [personal] account. I have ordered him money for that purpose."[4]

At this early stage of the experiment, it was apparent to Georgia's founder and to his associates that neither his funds, nor contributions from the general public, nor speculative ventures, nor legacies would keep the colony long afloat. There was one and only one potential source of large sums of money over a period of years. In order to guarantee Georgia's survival it would be necessary to secure annual appropriations from Parliament. That could not be done unless both the king and the prime minster were agreeable to such a plan, if not actually enthusiastic about it.

Among the Trustees, Egmont probably had the greatest entree to the crown. Yet it was Vernon who initiated a radical new approach to the Parliament that earlier rejected a Georgia plea. Diplomatic experience plus intimate ties with the S.P.C.K. may have caused the son of a secretary of state to develop a really-novel idea.

George II was more German than English. S.P.C.K. leaders were motivated by anti-Catholic as well as by humanitarian considerations. Why not at one stroke bring satisfaction to both the sovereign and the Protestant missionary society? It could be done, Vernon calculated, by seeking funds to aid German Lutherans rather than England's poor. After all, King George's countrymen had been forced into exile with no possessions other than clothes on their backs and small bundles of household gear.

Once Vernon developed the concept, Egmont made some preliminary soundings. He found Sir Robert Walpole "not averse" to a grant from some earmarked fund that the prime minister couldn't touch for ordinary purposes, anyway. Public subscriptions had already provided, through the S.P.C.K., about £4,000 for aid of the Salzburgers. This money went for transportation and support of the embarcation met by Oglethorpe as he waited in Charles Town for a London-bound vessel. Popular feelings had been aroused. Lawmakers, sensitive to wishes of their constituents and in many cases facing tough election contests, could perhaps be persuaded to take a fresh look at funds earlier derived from sale of assets on Saint Christopher's.

Extensive land grants on the island, late Saint Kitts, had been designed for missionary-philanthropic purposes that never were achieved. Abandonment of the enterprise and sale of land had resulted in accumulation of funds amounting to a bit more than £20,000. Horace Walpole, brother of the prime minister, agreed to speak in the House of Commons in order to second a proposal to give half of this money to the Georgia Trust. His support was conditioned upon an agreement that money from this source would be used only for the relief of Salzburgers willing to go to the colony and to become Englishmen.

By pre-arrangement, Sir Joseph Jekyll introduced the matter to Parliament and Walpole spoke in support of the plan. There was dissent and objection. But in the end an overwhelming vote put into the hands of Trustees in one lump sum the incredible amount of £10,000.

It was enough to prevent disaster for the moment. It provided a breathing-spell, however brief, from the never-ending task of seeking money with which to meet Oglethorpe's drafts. Far more important even than the huge grant was the precedent it set. Now the new colony represented an investment on the part of imperial Britain. In the future it would be argued that the empire could ill afford to lose what it had previously expended upon Georgia, so should provide additional funds.

Since the entire £10,000 bonanza would eventually have to be spent upon the Salzburgers, and upon them alone, the grant did not give long-term respite to Trustees. Except for an occasional token gift of no consequence, Trustees other than Oglethorpe invested nothing in the colony except time. Their pride was involved, of course. Financial failure would be humiliating — especially in the light of the tremendous favorable publicity given to their scheme.

So they relaxed not at all in their scrutiny of every invoice and draft, small as well as large. It was a source of both bewilderment and a growing sense of outrage that their self-appointed representative, Oglethorpe, spent money for which they were responsible without securing their prior approval.

What could possess the man, that he should be passing out hard-gained currency in order to buy information from persons spying on the Spanish? In the name of everything high and holy, what led the man to shovel out £200 for a shipload of sick Irishmen[5] — when total income of the Trust during its first 12 months was just £3,723? Why couldn't he make a reasonably accurate estimate of the numbers of persons who would be on subsistence, totally dependent upon the Trust, and what it could cost to keep them? Why did he pay rewards for "taking Outlaws and Spies"?

Sir Robert Walpole

England's first prime minister, Sir Robert Walpole, often was in a position to make or to break the Georgia enterprise.

He wavered, sometimes supporting and sometimes challenging Trustee requests for financial aid. During the crucial years in which Anglo-Spanish tensions were high, Walpole sometimes seemed willing to sacrifice Georgia for the sake of peace.

James Oglethorpe more than once spoke to him in wholly undiplomatic fashion.

Everyone realized that it was necessary to placate the Indians with presents. But was it absolutely essential to continue showering upon them such costly goods as blankets and muskets? How could a person, based in London, be sure that some money spent upon the Indians couldn't be better used for other purposes?

No one ever admitted it — at least, not for the record — but an obvious source of frustration was the difficulty of communication. Under the best of circumstances a query or a directive sent from London would be received, acted upon, and reported back to the Trust in a bit more than three months. That speed was rarely attained. At the other extreme, letters not lost at sea might bring a reply in eight or ten months. Especially in the case of official messages involving an agency of the government, writers often made two or three copies and sent each by a different vessel.

Quite early, the governor of South Carolina heard rumors that a colony might be established to the south. He immediately wrote to Trustees and urged them to place their settlement on the Altamaha river rather than on the Savannah. Dispatched long before the first embarcation, his message didn't reach London until Oglethorpe and the *Ann* were on the high seas.

Accountant Harmann Verelst wrote to Samuel Quincy in December, 1734. His letter reached Georgia late in May, 1735. Quincy's reply was received in London just before the end of the year. Though that schedule was extreme, underlying difficulties of long-distance command caused a weary and exasperated Oglethorpe, late in his Georgia stay, to tell his colleagues: "It is impossible to advise what should be done at the distance between this and Europe. Before I can send over a proposal, have it debated and receive an answer, the executing of it becomes out of season."

For their part Trustees became vexed with their representative almost as soon as he landed at Savannah. He started off on the wrong foot by offering to them what seemed lame excuses for irregular, tardy, and abbreviated reports. Writing from Yamacraw bluff in February, 1733, Georgia's founder stressed a theme that was destined to recur over and over in his letters: "I have a great deal of pains [many details demanding attention], [so] hardly have time to write to you. I don't expect [matters] to be otherwise 'till I see you again."

Just four months after the *Ann* sailed, his colleagues began to flex their muscles.

Vernon went on record as favoring a change in the system of land tenure — a matter about which he knew Oglethorpe felt very strongly. A stream of letters sent by Benjamin Martyn upon orders from the Trustees rebuked Oglethorpe for brief and infrequent reports, for,"drawing bills to the value of £250 without sending advice,"for doing little or nothing to discourage Jews from remaining in Georgia, and for not keeping them informed about his precise plans.

By June, 1733, Martyn was inquiring rather sharply in order to ascertain, if possible, just how long Oglethorpe planned to remain in the colony. Trustees in London didn't know it, but when they began in July to talk about the possibility of recalling their representative, he was chafing to leave but felt duty-bound to stay. Six months later Egmont privately speculated that his friend might hold secret instructions from the king — a factor that could account for his long silences and his high-handed use of money.

A carefully-worded Trustee resolution of February 6, 1734, was framed as though it were meant to be general. Actually, it was aimed entirely at Oglethorpe: "Resolved — Nemine Contradicente: That no Bills drawn by any Person Whatsoever on the Trustees be accepted or Paid without proper Advice given to the Board by the Person Who drew the Bill."

Oglethorpe never received specific notice that he would be called to task and minutely interrogated, but he knew. As he waited for the vessel that would take him away from a world turned upside down, he anticipated that his reunion with colleagues after an absence of a year and one-half would be tense and strained.

He was right.

Patience of the Trustees was exhausted. They had made up their minds no longer to tolerate the kind of representation he had been giving.

Chapter 8

A LONG LEVER AND A FULCRUM
ON WHICH TO REST IT

Oglethorpe in England: June, 1734 — October, 1735

Self-taught propagandist and public relations expert James Oglethorpe had counted heavily upon Georgia's natural wealth. A steady flow of products — the more exotic the better — from her fields and forests, would go far toward persuading his countrymen to fund the colony generously.

His first shipment, consigned to Trustees through merchant Samuel Baker as agent, reached London on July 18, 1733. As itemized in records of the Trust this consignment consisted of two barrels and three bottles. They contained: "Twenty-three Deer Skins, weighing 30 Pounds, Bears Oyl, and several Parcels of Sea Rod, Snake Root, Rattle Snake Root, Sassafras, China Root, Shumack, and Contrayerva [or 'counter-herb']."[1]

Also shipped from Charles Town in 1733, the second consignment of Georgia products consisted of a barrel containing 48 skins, along with two barrels of rice and "a parcel of Fins and other Curiosities" not enumerated. Captain Yoakley delivered this merchandise to London on August 29.

Two of the 71 deerskins from Georgia were used as gifts for messengers who ran errands for Trustees. When the remaining skins were sold they brought about £12. Rice was held until June, 1734, when the 700-pound shipment yielded £7.

Long before he started on his frequently-postponed return voyage to England, Georgia's founder knew that the colony could not become self-sufficient in the foreseeable future. Even he did not then realize that additional Georgia produce received by Trustees during the entire era of their charter would result only in listings such as:

March 7, 1734 — "the stem of a large Vine"

March 13, 1734 — a cask of potash made at Thunderbolt, near Savannah.[2]

June 26, 1734 — a case of snake root containing 94 pounds (of which 44 pounds were damaged) plus a 9-foot tulip-wood log.

July 3, 1734 — samples of Georgia timber: 14 pieces of red bay, three of ilex, two of mahogany, one each of ash and sycamore.

February 3, 1735 — "64 Hogsheads and 112 Barrels of Tar [actually, turpentine that arrived damaged], sold for less than the Freight & Charges, but the Bounty on Importation when received, is to make good the Loss by Sale."

April 3, 1735 — eight pounds of raw silk.[3]

July 23, 1735 — "a Cask, containing a Quarter of an hundred Weight of the Bark of a Tree, thought useful for the Dyers."

Deerskins brought the only significant revenue ever realized by the Trust from colonial products. A consignment of 75, of which only 16 were damaged, brought £5 in June, 1736. One year later seven cases, weighing 3,068 pounds, sold for slightly more than two shillings per pound to yield £415. Fifty sound skins, with total weight 84 pounds, brought £13 in December, 1740. In August, 1751, 1500 pounds of half-dressed deer skins were consigned to Trustees from Fort Augusta. They went aboard the *Charming Martha* at Beaufort. But Trustee records — by then carelessly maintained — include no mention of their arrival.

Far the biggest entry in Trustee accounts of sales came from 266 barrels of rice brought by the *Two Brothers* in 1736. This shipment brought £858 — which represented only a small profit whose total was not specified. Oglethorpe had bought Carolina rice for the store in Savannah. Having overestimated consumption there, the surplus was sent to London for re-sale..

Before turning aside from his long-planned return home in order to establish the Salzburgers at Ebenezer, Oglethorpe had conceived another scheme. If the products of Georgia were not precisely mind-boggling in their promise for the future, the colony did have unique assets. Her native inhabitants, he knew beyond doubt, were different from other American Indians.

It was unbelievable from his appearance and manner that the Yamacraw chief, Tomochichi, was about 90 years old. His age had to be accepted on faith, for he looked 60 at most. Here was living proof that Georgia's climate, water, and soil could provide an astonishingly long and healthy life!

Given these circumstancces, Oglethorpe reasoned that it would be absurd to probe into the life story of his friend. Far better to take him at his word and extend to him all the courtesies that his great age suggested.

Toonahowi, the aged mico's 15-year-old grand-nephew and adopted son, had shown himself "of a very apt Genius" at learning religious gems dear to the hearts of many Englishmen. These the youth joyfully recited at every opportunity, speaking with strange accents but in fully comprehensible English.

Ninety-year-old Tomochichi, potential convert Toonahowi, and a few other carefully-selected members of their tribes would be Georgia exhibits without equal. London had seen many American Indians, but none like these.

That line of reasoning led Oglethorpe to the calculated conclusion that he should and would take a band of native Georgians to England with him. Hence nine of them waited with him at Savannah for a ship that would take them to Charles Town as a point of departure. They boarded the man-o-war *Aldborough* on March 23. After a delay in the harbor their Atlantic voyage began on May 7, 1734.

Tomochichi spoke for only a handful of warriors. No matter; while in England he could "confirm the peace" with dignitaries of the empire. Toonahowi's keen mind and apt memory were not focused upon religious matters alone. His wide-ranging interests made him ready and eager to learn anything and everything English. That did not for an instant detract from the wonder and glory that this child of the Georgia forests was a prime candidate for conversion from the idolatry of his people. One day, God willing, he would stand straight and tall as a red-skinned Protestant subject of His Majesty, King George II.

A Trustee memorandum had been drafted in late March. Extremely vexed at his "laxity in keeping them informed," Oglethorpe's colleagues desired him to appoint a secretary. Happily, Georgia's founder did not receive this directive before he left Savannah with nine prized living products of Georgia, plus interpreter John

Musgrove. He had problems enough from realization that he faced growing hostility from members of the Georgia Trust and that Parliament had never been disposed to make a significant grant to any North American colony.

Their voyage, one month from Charles Town to the Isle of Wight, was made in near-record time. Yet it was long enough for Oglethorpe to perfect detailed plans for the campaigns he faced in Westminster Court and in Parliament. He took secret delight at his own foresight in having insisted on remaining in his tent even though Savannah was dotted with completed and partly-completed houses. Determined to show that he was tougher and hardier than the colonists whom he led, he had thereby also demonstrated his nearly-total lack of concern for his own welfare and interests. Men who did not like his ideas would be forced to give him their respect, however grudging it might be.

Before making a frontal assault upon seats of power in London, Oglethorpe paid a brief visit to his home in Godalming — about a day's journey from the capital by stagecoach. His sister, Anne, had returned from France in order to serve as lady of the manor after the death of their mother.

Money was more than ordinarily scarce at Westbrook. In an ordinary election year, the cost of a contest was roughly equal to annual returns from rental properties attached to the estate. This year, 1734, had not been ordinary.

Opposition to a candidate who was far away in Georgia had been so great that Speaker of the House Arthur Onslow reluctantly decided to put his influence behind Oglethorpe's bid for re-election. An early advocate of the Georgia scheme who never became a Trustee, Onslow's weight brought narrow victory in the contest for the seat from Haslemere. To Egmont, the speaker confided that this had cost him dearly — in concessions he was forced to make in the course of the contest. So much of Oglethorpe's own cash had been used that he took a no-win stance in a minor local power struggle. Knowing that he couldn't legally withhold it forever, the lord of Westbrook stubbornly refused to pay the £10 per year quit-rent that he owed to the Molyneux family, nearby political rivals.[4]

There was little time for Georgia's founder to deal with his own affairs, whether petty or significant. Friday, June 21, found him facing hostile colleagues in their Palace Court meeting room. Counting Oglethorpe, 15 Trustees — a near-record number — had turned out for the meeting.

Their terse *Journal* gives no hint concerning the gravity of the session, what was said, or how long it lasted. It reports only two items of business. A resolution was passed stipulating that "thanks be return'd to James Oglethorpe Esqr for the many and great Services he has done the Colony of Georgia." A cash-book entry noted that two barrels of rice from the colony had brought seven pounds one shilling and six pence.

Earlier the same day, the common council of the Trust, with ten members present, devoted its full attention to fiscal matters.[5] June 9, end of the operating year, had found them with cash on hand amounting to just £330. "A Case of Snakeroot being the Produce of Georgia" and delivered by Captian Yoakley, constituted an asset of undetermined value.

Egmont was particularly vexed that an earlier and more optimistic accounting had proved erroneous. On June 1 it had appeared that there might be a substantial balance of cash plus gifts receivable to carry forward into the new fiscal year. But his colleagues had failed to take Oglethorpe into account. Within days it was discovered that known drafts from him, unpaid and not included in computations, amounted to more than £3,700. How much more money the man had spent without receiving authorization or even bothering to give notice of actions taken, no one had the faintest idea.

By June 21 the total so owed was known to exceed £5,000.

Oglethorpe's free spending aside, the period would have ended with a deficit had it not been for the generosity of South Carolina. A year earlier the Carolina Assembly had voted a special tax on rum of three pence a gallon. By means of it lawmakers began to raise an anticipated £8,000 (Carolina currency) "for the speedier and more Effectual Relief of his Majesty's Subjects of Georgia."

Gifts from Governor Robert Johnson, Colonel William Bull, other Carolina leaders and the parish of Saint Andrew came to £1,239 — not counting cattle, rice, and other commodities contributed. Converted into sterling, the cash flow from Carolina amounted to £464 by the time Oglethorpe returned from Georgia.[6] At that time the unpaid portion of the Carolina grant to Georgia was slightly more than £3,000. This approximately equalled the only substantial money from British sources during 1733-34 — grants of £3,161 from King George II. These gifts, the only ones ever made directly to the colony by the monarch, were not without conditions. One grant of £574 could be used only to lend money to "100 foreign Protestants, Swiss, Grizons and Germans, for their Passage [from

Sir Arthur Onslow, Speaker of the House of Commons

Arthur Onslow, Speaker of the House of Commons, went to great length in order to secure Oglethorpe's re-election to Parliament.

Here he is shown in his seat in St. Margaret's Church, Westminster, London (parochial church of the House of Commons).

Europe] and Assistance in their Voyages to Savannah & Purrysburgh [Carolina Colony], plus costs of their settlement in the two southernmost North American colonies.

Trustees had no idea where to seek the money that would be required for their guests from Georgia. Yet they acted promptly when they learned from Oglethorpe that he would bring Indians with him. It was everywhere understood that they came partly in order to confirm the treaty of the previous year, partly because they were very desirous of instruction in the English language and in the Christian religion.

According to Georgia's founder all were members of American Indian royalty. Tomochichi and his queen, Senauchi, were unlettered but authentic counterparts of King George and Queen Caroline. Toonahowi would one day be mico of the Yamacraw. Hillispylli was war chief, or "principal man next the Sovereign" of the Lower Creeks, whose other representatives were: Apakowtski, Stimaleechi, Sintouchi, and Stingwykkie. Umpychi, chief of the Uchees, completed the roster.

Such persons must be treated with the courtesy and dignity due to their stations in life.

Splendid quarters were rented for them in Westminster, near the Georgia office. Blankets were bought, and accountant Verelst was instructed to ask customs house officials to forego duty on wine designed for their consumption. On their first evening in London, Trustees gave the Indians a "grand entertainment" that ended with a bonfire, ringing of bells, "and other Demonstrations of Joy and Gratitude."

By then the city was agog. Oglethorpe had taken time to write in some detail about the Indians and their attitudes. They positively would not tolerate adultery; a native American male found guilty of that offense had his throat cut. But when an Englishman made a present of a blanket to an Indian woman, seducing her to lie with

him, the noble Yamacraw did not seek to extend their laws to outsiders. They punished their countrywoman by cutting off her ears and hair, reported Georgia's founder, but said "they would be contented if we whipped the man" not belonging to their tribe.

With Egmont in the chair, Indians paid their first formal visit to the Georgia Trust on July 3. They were brisk and well-trimmed people, but they insisted upon bizarre dress. Noted Egmont: "[they] will not put on breeches, and [they] wear the shirts we gave them over their covering, which is only a skin that leaves their breasts and thighs and arms open, but they wear shoes of their own making of hides that seem neat and easy."

Tomochichi, who had been carefully coached by Oglethorpe during their journey, did not fail his tutor. Stopping frequently so that John Musgrove could interpret, the sovereign who looked little more than half his years explained that he did not speak well. When he was young he neglected the advice of wise old men, so remained ignorant. Now that he himself was old he wanted one thing before he died — to see his nation settled in peace.

Englishmen were good, he said, and he wished his people to live with them as good neighbors. Still, he would not have made the long trek to England had it not been for Mr. Oglethorpe — a man who had been kind to the Indians and had shown that he could be trusted.

According to Egmont's running account, Tomochichi ended his brief address by saying that he thanked God "(at which he pointed and looked up)" for a safe passage and hoped God would carry him safely back.

Egmont responded, paragraph by paragraph, and ended by commenting that "we all have the same God and fear him. That we lived under a good and gracious King, who does justice to all his subjects and will do so by his friends and allies."

When the formalities were over the Georgia leaders, to a man, were glowing with pride and delight. Mounting animosity toward Oglethorpe was forgotten in the triumph of the occasion. They called for wine and tobacco with which to entertain their royal guests.

Neither Egmont nor other key Trustees had been deceived. They knew that their guests commanded no more than 50 fighting men. But from Oglethorpe they had also learned that "they are a branch of the Crick Indians, who make above 600," and that "they are in alliance with eight other nations something like the Swiss Cantons, each governing themselves after their own manner." Minor royalty perhaps they were — but none the less royal.

Soon a formal message was dispatched to Sir Robert Walpole, asking when the Indians could be presented to the king. It would be appropriate, the letter added, to transport these members of visiting royalty in the coaches of the king — with sentries posted to guard them from any possible danger of insults from the crowds that were certain to flock to catch a glimpse of them.

Concurrently the financially-pressed Trustees took under consideration Thomas Lowndes' secret proposal — not yet even suspected to be sponsorship of a lottery — by which for 8% commission he promised to raise as much as £30,000 for Georgia without applying to Parliament.

A state visit was arranged for August 1. Sir Clement Cotterell served as messenger from the king and as master of protocol. Tomochichi and his party, who had been told to expect him, expressed regret that one of their number was indisposed and could not pay homage to the great king. Except for this warrior, who was in the early stages of a fatal case of smallpox, all were ready for the historic journey.

Tomochichi and his queen had consented to don scarlet outfits that were trimmed with white rabbit's fur plus gold lace. Their attendant warriors had begged to be permitted to wear their native garb. Oglethorpe assented, but prevailed upon them to add blue frocks. Faces of the New World envoys "were variously painted, some half black, others triangular, and others with bearded Arrows instead of Whiskers." Festooned with long, colorful feathers, they were escorted to places in three of the king's own six-horse coaches.

At the door of Kensington Palace they were saluted by the king's body-guard. Then the Duke of Grafton, lord chamberlain to the king, presented them to George II seated on the throne of Britain. According to a lengthy account in the *Gentleman's Magazine*, the visitors from Georgia insisted upon presenting several feathers to the sovereign.

Feathers of the eagle, swiftest of birds, constitute a sign of peace among the Yamacraw, explained Tomochichi. These feathers were brought across the great sea as a gesture of peace, renewing the pact made with Mr. Oglethorpe. Whatever words of wisdom England's king might care to share with him, the native American ruler promised, would be told faithfully to all the kings of the Creek nations.

King George II responded with an expression of gratitude and good will. Then the New World friend of Oglethorpe briefly greeted Queen Caroline "and her Majesty returned a most gracious

Tomochichi, native American who befriended Georgia

On his visit to London, Tomochichi had his portrait painted; now lost, the original was copied by several artists.

As head of the small and weak Yamacraw sub-tribe, Tomochichi was a petty chieftain. Yet his personal influence helped to extend Georgia's boundaries and to persuade Indian leaders to send fighting men who joined Oglethorpe's forces.

answer." Signalled to approach the queen, Toonahowi responded in English to her greeting. Then at a question from her he joyfully recited the Lord's Prayer, the Creed, and the Ten Commandments.

William, Duke of Cumberland and second in line to succeed his father as ruler of Britain, presented Toonahowi with a gold watch. Along with it he gave the American youth an exhortation to call upon Jesus Christ every morning when he looked at the timepiece.

A smashing success by every standard, the reception at Kensington was followed by one triumph after another. Dr. William Walker, Archbishop of Canterbury, received the native Georgians at Lambeth in spite of the fact that he was almost too ill to stand. To his disappointment, the prelate's questions about Christianity brought few specific answers.[7] Still it was a surprise to all and a spine-chilling thrill to every military leader present to hear what even Oglethorpe had not learned — Tomochichi's father was burned at the stake by the Spanish because he refused to accept baptism as a Christian.

Egmont entertained the New World dignitaries at one of his numerous manors, Charlton. There he provided music and dancing plus an opportunity to walk through an English forest. At the invitation of the Duke of Chandos they visited him at Cannons. Later they spent a few hours at Oglethorpe's Westbrook manor. Then they were shown the sights of Windsor and of Hampton Court. At Eton, Tomochichi got "a general huzza" when he suggested that the students be given a holiday.

All the great sights of London, including Greenwich Hospital and the Tower, were visited. On days when they did not travel, Tomochichi and Toonahowi often remained motionless for hours while Willem Verelst painted their portraits.[8]

Queen Caroline

Caroline of Ansbach, wife of King George II and mother of the Duke of Cumberland, had high regard for James Oglethorpe.

Queen Caroline graciously consented to leave off her royal finery in order to celebrate the king's birthday by wearing a dress made from Georgia silk.

Capitalizing upon unprecedented national fascination with the visitors from Georgia, Oglethorpe and his colleagues asked for money from the crown and got it. They received £20 per week for subsistence of the Indians. A supplementary appropriation of £723 covered all other expenses except gifts — which were valued at £422 and were also purchased with money from the treasury.

Before boarding the *Prince of Wales* in late October in order to return home, Tomochichi insisted upon making a royal gift of his own. He left at the Georgia office "25 Buck Skins, One Tyger Skin, & Six Buffalo Skins." After reaching home he sent back a letter of thanks in the form of a dressed buffalo skin richly decorated with red and black symbolic figures.

Whatever his age, the mico died at Yamacraw Village on October 5, 1739. He was given a military funeral. His pallbearers, one of whom was Oglethorpe, bore his body to an English grave in Savannah's Court House Square.

Tomochichi's triumphant visit to England was marred only by the death of a warrior from smallpox and by intermittent periods of drunkenness on the part of interpreter John Musgrove. Its smashing triumph as a public relations event of the first magnitude silenced, for the moment, the rising chorus of complaints about Oglethorpe's handling of Georgia affairs. Equally important, it crystallized national interest in the faraway colony and fostered a climate in which Britain's policy makers were prepared, for the first time, to listen attentively to Georgia voices.

No commander willingly goes into a major campaign with a single battle plan. If his first fails, the second can become a substitute. Should the first bring smashing victory, follow-up by the second can wipe out any remaining rear-guard resistance.

Tomochichi and his tribesmen had brought victory. It was time to crush the opposition with silk.

Two months before Oglethorpe left Georgia, his colleagues received by Captain Yoakley "A Trunk containing Eight large Pounds of Raw Silk, of three Sorts, viz Ordinary, Fine, & Superfine, which was sent to Sr. Thomas Lombe to be organzined [made into raw-silk thread and then woven into cloth]."

It was inventor-manufacturer Lombe to whose aid Oglethorpe had rushed almost a decade earlier, in a futile attempt to secure for him an extension upon a patent. Lombe had come to be recognized as England's foremost expert upon silk. Before Georgia was chartered he was among those who fervently hoped the "charitable colony" as originally conceived would become a major producer of the exotic material.

King James I, best remembered for the translation of Scripture that bears his name, had first set heads of Englishmen spinning with dreams of wealth from silk. Beginning in 1608, the monarch personally supervised a 14-year series of tests aimed at rearing silk-worms in England. It inspired at least one notable bubble but had no other economic impact. By the time James conceded that the island kingdom's climate was not fit for silk-worms, the New World offered a chance to try them under what was believed to be more favorable circumstances.

Mulberry trees were planted in the Virginia Colony very early. Some silk, though not of first quality, was actually produced there. By the time it was ready to be sold, about 1650, no Virginian was any longer making a serious effort to collect a special bounty of 10,000 pounds of tobacco. Parliament had offered that quantity of the New World weed to the person who first exported £200 worth of cocoons or raw silk in a single year. The prize was no longer worth seeking; tobacco had proved to be infinitely better suited to the soil and climate of Virginia than had trees required for rearing of silk-worms.

Driven from Virginia by tobacco, sericulture was launched in Carolina. Again there was a measure of success, especially in the Charles Town area. But the infinite pains and small rewards for production of silk made that program a competitor with production of indigo and of rice. Both of these commodities proved far more profitable than silk.

Britain waited nervously and hopefully whenever sericulture was tried. Annual importation of £500,000 worth of silk played havoc with the empire's balance of trade. Silk involved such high stakes that it justified a considerable degree of risk, to say nothing of heroic effort.

Before the Georgia experiment got under way, all leaders — including Oglethorpe — had hopelessly-distorted ideas about the climate of the region. Britain remained seriously troubled by purchases abroad. Exponents of the Georgia scheme had been greatly encouraged by their early contacts with Sir Thomas Lombe. Hence men seeking to establish a colony south of Carolina caught a severe case of silk fever. They were so eager and so hopeful that the common seal of the Trust bore silk-worms on the reverse.

In 1730-31, many were sure that Georgia could and would produce all the silk England could use — perhaps more. Careful sets of calculations yielded precise anticipated results. Besides helping to balance Britain's trade, silk from Georgia would give jobs to 20,000 colonists and an equal number of persons at home.

Land ceded to charity colonists in 50-acre tracts not only had restrictions concerning title; each grant carried a stipulation that 100 *morus alba*, or white mulberry, trees must be planted and tended. Mulberry seedlings and seed plus eggs of the silk-worm were sent by Trustees on the *Ann*. Paul Amatis, whose official position was listed as "gardener and silk care," was second only to Oglethorpe among persons included in the first embarcation.

Early and strong interest in Georgia's role as a producer of exotic goods had led to numerous special gifts that were designated for the support of botany and of agriculture. Part of the money used to create the Trustees' Garden in Savannah came from such special gifts. Though it had many other functions, the communal botanical garden was a nursery for white mulberry trees. Joseph Habersham secured and planted so many of them that he named his plantation "Silk Hope."

Expecting the colony to move quickly into processing of thread, Trustees sent skilled help in the form of Samuel Grey. An experienced throwster who knew the art of twisting delicate fibers into raw silk and then into thread, Grey took along two apprentices.

A standing committee of the House of Commons kept a hopeful eye upon the Georgia silk trade. England's board of trade had the all-important first shipment of eight pounds examined by experts. They pronounced the colonial product "excellent in every respect," and urged vigorous cultivation of it. Success in this endeavor, they underscored in a report, would be "the surest means of reconciling the colony to the affection of the public and procuring future aid from Parliament."

It was in this climate that master-strategist James Oglethorpe zealously pursued the second of his battle plans conceived in Georgia and refined while on the voyage home. His good friend Lombe took the raw silk from Georgia to his factory — England's finest — and there produced a quantity of organzine. Instead of putting it up for sale or placing it on display, Georgia's founder used it as a gift.

Caroline of Ansbach, Queen of Great Britain and Ireland, was already well acquainted with Oglethorpe. She graciously consented to an informal ceremony in which the silk was inspected by a veteran weaver before being examined by the queen. Nodding approval that was followed by genuine delight, she accepted the product of the colony about which she knew very little.

Sir Thomas Lombe used the presentation as an opportunity to inform the public in general and journalists in particular that he found the Georgia product superior to the Piedmontese, from France. He was especially emphatic in stressing the fact that fibers sent from Georgia had less waste than did French raw silk.

London and all Britain soon learned that Georgia silk would be used to make a gown for the queen. Nothing remotely like this had ever happened before. At last, Britain had a tangible basis for hoping to produce and to process her own silk!

Tomochichi, Toonahowi, their comrades, and eight pounds of silk had opened many doors. It was high time to enter these doors and try to move the immoveable. Georgia's strategic location was a long and sturdy lever. Present security and future expansion of imperial Britain formed a powerful fulcrum. With these Oglethorpe confidently expected to effect movement; if not the world, certainly Parliament.

While getting machinery ready for making his bold try, the founder of Georgia took the initiative with his colleagues. They must immediately take all necessary measures, he insisted, to make possible tighter control of the colony's internal affairs. Instead of the loose cluster of regulations laid down by Trustees, a body of laws should be enacted.

Always jealous of their authority, members of the Trust had time and again encountered difficulty with the crown and with the privy council. Members of this key body were not inclined to approve any colonial law until it had been debated and revised.[9] Since the crown had shown no inclination to veto Trustee regulations that lacked full legal force, Georgia leaders had been willing to settle for these private enactments. Without bringing formal motions before the body to which he belonged, Oglethorpe began a campaign whose goal was adoption of a legal code for Georgia.

Another interruption came in early March, 1735. Thomas Causton, acting as Oglethorpe's proxy on the basis of oral instructions, followed the practice of drawing bills of exchange upon the Trustees in order to meet pressing needs of the colony. Normally payable 30 days after sight, two such bills — for £70 and £300 respectively, both drawn in Savannah in December, 1734 — arrived in London a few days apart.

At the Trustee meeting of March 5, accountant Verelst presented these documents and ruefully reported that unrestricted funds in the bank were inadequate for payment. George Heathcote magnanimously offered to advance the money to pay these bills — as a loan, not a gift. He said he'd wait for reimbursement "till there shall be Cash sufficient."

If anyone questioned the urgency of creating a comprehensive legal system, doubts were dissipated by news that William Wise had been murdered. He was sent to Georgia in 1733 aboard the *Savannah*, after having been recommended by several bishops of the Anglican Church. Egmont had resisted giving approval to this man's application because of his shady reputation.

When word of disturbances caused by Wise among passengers on the *Savannah* filtered back to London, alarmed Trustees directed Oglethorpe to ship the man home at once. Ignoring this directive the founder of Georgia permitted Wise to settle on Hutchinson's Island — called by Oglethorpe one of the most delightful spots ever seen. Wise obtained the services of two Irish transport servants and seems to have prospered. His prosperity was cut short in March, 1734, by strangulation. All reports from the colony suggested that the Irish servants were perpetrators of the crime.

From the start, British common law had been accepted as the standard for Georgia. Yet the colony had no statutes of its own dealing with murder — or anything else. Oglethorpe's refusal to obey instructions concerning Wise was temporarily ignored. Clearly, he had been right in asking for a codified system of laws.

While Trustees debated, Thomas Causton and his aides put Richard White and Alice Riley on trial for the murder of Wise. Convicted in May, 1734, Riley was sentenced to hang by the neck until dead. After sentence was passed the prisoner was found to be pregnant, so the execution was deferred until after the birth of her child. Four weeks after a boy was born to Alice Riley she became the first Georgia woman to go to the gallows — on January 19, 1735.

Wise had been murdered and Riley had been hanged. Trustees voted a reward of £50 to Edward Jenkins and others for their services in apprehending the killer. But was the execution legal? Unprepared or unwilling to tackle so large an issue, the Trustees were sufficiently troubled to name a committee to fashion a system of laws for Georgia. Oglethorpe was designated as chairman of the law-framing body.

They worked swiftly, but concentrated upon matters the chair considered urgent. Murder was not high on Oglethorpe's priority list. As shaped by the committee and transmitted to the privy council and to the crown, where they won quick approval, three statutes were enacted. They were the only formal laws ever enacted for Trustee era Georgia and consisted of: "The Law to prevent the Importation and the Use of Rum and Brandies in the Province of Georgia; the Law for maintaining the Peace with the Indians in the said Province; and the Law for rendering the Colony of Georgia more defensible by prohibiting the Importation and Use of Black Slaves or Negroes into Georgia."

Some of his admirers have used the last of the three laws as a lens through which to view Oglethorpe as a colonial administrator. So considered he is likely to be hailed as having been "an eighteenth-century Abraham Lincoln" — an emancipator who was generations ahead of most of his contemporaries in his views.

Nothing in the record supports such a judgment. Georgia's founder sought and got legal prohibition of slaves in the colony because he strongly believed their absence would render Georgia more defensible. His utopian dream of a classless colony of free-holders, each of whom would be part of the military establishment, had faded but had not disappeared completely. Barred from becoming land owners and from serving in the militia, slaves were considered assets by gentleman adventurers. But when the large and general goals of a buffer colony were considered, blacks clearly constituted liabilities.

This early position, from which Oglethorpe never retreated, was supported by evidence found in the field. Spanish authorities offered — or pretended to offer — an idyllic haven for runaway blacks. Lured to Saint Augustine by promises, slaves took with them first-hand knowledge about streams, harbors, trails, and fortifications. Such information gave aid and comfort to the Spanish. Furthermore, slaves were notoriously inclined to armed rebellion. Their presence constituted a festering sore in every colony where they were found.

No slaves for Georgia — now or ever — said the short-term director of the Royal African Society.[10] When North America was viewed through the eyes of a soldier-of-fortune, it was instantly obvious that the southernmost British colony needed the strongest possible military machine.

Though Oglethorpe considered the prohibition of slaves in Georgia to be essential, this measure would not in itself guarantee an effective fighting force. Even if a small army of freedmen were available for deployment in the colony, Georgia would be impotent without a proper chain of fortifications. Hence Oglethorpe carefully detailed the basic needs: 18 forts, each manned by 40 men, plus two new fortified towns, would — for the moment — serve his purpose.

He held long private conversations with fellow members of Parliament judged most likely to support his plan. In order to implement it, he estimated that he needed a bare minimum of £25,800. When colleagues in the Trust learned of that estimate they warned him not to make it public. Premature disclosure of so ambitious a goal would certainly lead to defeat.

Not necessarily, responded Georgia's founder. He had secret information that the French governor of Mobile had sent a written threat to Governor Johnson of South Carolina. Ostensibly presenting a demand that deserters who had taken refuge in Carolina be returned to him, the French leader obviously — said Oglethorpe — would use the issue as a pretext for an all-out war.

It was in the light of this situation, known in London only to the government and to Georgia leaders, that their common council took action. A resolution of February 26, 1735, requested Oglethorpe, Talbot, Tower, and any other member who cared to do so "to attend the Lords Commrs of Trade and Plantations on a Conference desired by their Lordships in relation to the Defence and security of South Carolina."

At this point it would have been difficult or impossible to drum up substantial enthusiasm for saving Georgia. Carolina was a different matter. This colony was rich and thriving, vital to British interests on the continent of North America. For the defense of Carolina it might be prudent to act upon Oglethorpe's recommendations concerning his young and otherwise unimportant colony.

This, then, was the line of argument developed by Oglethorpe — who became the chief advocate and spokesman for it. He also masterminded the strategy by which a memorial from the provincial government of South Carolina followed the right path into the proper hands. Though addressed to the privy council, it was steered by Oglethorpe to the board of trade. Col. Martin Bladen, commissioner of that all-important body, himself introduced the Carolina document into the House of Commons.

Clearly, the threat to Carolina had major implications for policy toward Georgia. Hence the Georgia Trustees were ordered to spread before Parliament a complete record of expenditures in recent months.[11] When this precautionary move produced no surprises and no evidence of maladministration, the way was paved for a formal resolution asking that Oglethorpe's plan be funded.

Both Oglethorpe and Egmont were confident of a favorable reaction. Yet they assumed that the appropriation voted would be substantially less than that requested. To their surprise and that of Sir Robert Walpole, Parliament voted the round sum of £26,000 — £200 more than Oglethorpe had requested.

Subsequently a Mr. Heup saved Trustees the usual fees linked with any governmental grant. Better off by £656 because of his concern, Trustees magnanimously sent this petty official a gratuity of 20 guineas.

In the climate of jubilant victory that followed Parliament's action and prevailed for many months, it was almost — but not quite — incidental that Britain's queen wore a dress made of Georgia silk on October 30, the day of the king's birthday party.

Clearly, Georgia had entered a new era.

No longer primarily philanthropic, but still the focus of hopes for a thriving agricultural and mercantile outpost, the colony was about to become a military bastion of imperial Britain. Spanish posed real threats, but for the present the most imminent danger was felt to be from the French.

Then and always, Oglethorpe believed with all his heart and explained in detail to all who would listen that Georgia was the keystone of defense for all of British America. Should the southernmost colony be conquered, South Carolina would be next. Then North Carolina and Virginia would fall — with the ripple effect extending to the northernmost British possessions in the New World.

Regardless of how much or how little validity there was to this complex theory, "the crown in Parliament" — that is, Britain as a nation — now had a strong vested interest in Georgia.[12] Leaders of the colony were confident that with this sturdy base on which to build, it would be comparatively easy to get additional funding in the future.

They were right. During the life of the Trust, Parliament

pumped the incredible total of £401,886 into the struggling little colony below Carolina. This sum far exceeded the total of all governmental appropriations for all other North American colonies, combined.[13]

Would the radically-transformed colony prove to be worth so vast an expenditure? It was largely up to one man — Oglethorpe — to provide the answer to that question.

While he chafed at being required to complete his business in England before going back to Georgia to put that £26,000 to use, his colleagues were not idle. In June some of them became vexed that the S.P.C.K. had made direct contact with Oglethorpe rather than with the Trust as a corporation. Trustees decided, however, to defer any action on the issue "till he [Oglethorpe] should meet with us." Mindful of their earlier directive, they notified him that he must select a secretary to accompany him on his second journey to Georgia.

They had yielded to his insistence concerning prohibition of enslaved and free blacks in Georgia — fully aware that they were holding £1,190 designated for the conversion of blacks. Never forgetful that Oglethorpe was in some quarters still suspected of harboring Jacobite sympathies, his colleagues enthusiastically supported a plan for an embarcation of 250 Highlanders. More than any other persons in Britain, these folk were notorious for their unwavering Jacobite loyalty — and were doubly suspect because of the central role of Highlanders in a recently-attempted coup.

Closing months of the year brought together the greatest single contingent of future Georgians ever to leave England. The *Prince of Wales*, the *Symond*, and the *London Merchant* sailed under escort of the sloop-of-war *Hawk*. In accordance with Trustee directives, one of those aboard was the Rev. Charles Wesley, secretary-designate to Oglethorpe. Wesley's brother, John, went along as missionary to the colony.

With ample money in the bank and men like the Wesleys with him as aides, surely — this time — Georgia would bring her founder neither disappointment nor failure.

Chapter 9

UNEXPECTED STORMS — THE SECOND
VOYAGE TO GEORGIA

October, 1735 — January, 1737

Only seven men appeared for the October 10, 1735, meeting of Trustees. It would be Oglethorpe's last for many months. Since July he had made it known that he would return to Georgia with the planned great embarcation. James Vernon, his most persistent and vocal critic among close colleagues, presided over the skeleton session of the Trust.

Three days earlier Georgia leaders had received a bundle of messages from Savannah. Carolina, one correspondent informed them, "is grown extremely jealous of us" because of the lucrative Indian trade. As a result, payment of the unpaid balance of £8,000 (Carolina currency) pledged to the support of Georgia had been suspended.

A Scottish colonist informed London that he had received from Britain "a letter full of invectives against the Trustees." Part of the letter, enclosed, charged that government of the colony was "military, arbitrary, and tyrannical." Since the writer's name had been scratched out Trustees could only guess at his identity. Most thought it had gone to the New World from London. Some cryptic allusions prompted the suggestion that it was penned by Trustee Thomas Coram. He had abandoned the Georgia scheme in disgust because females were not given full rights of inheritance.

128

Never mind a troublesome letter from an old gossip. Scores of new settlers were already aboard ships bound for Georgia, or were waiting for embarcation. Their arrival in the colony plus the heartening effect of Oglethorpe's return would soon bring matters to right. Even the vexatious problems caused by a stream of accusations against the colony's storekeeper, Thomas Causton, would disappear once the reins of government were again in Oglethorpe's strong hands. His imminent departure on the *Symond*, with 123 fellow passengers, would launch a third and altogether better phase of the Georgia experiment.

In July a meticulous count had envisioned a great embarcation: 100 Highlanders, male; 100 male servants with 50 wives and children; 40 English males with 60 wives and children; 100 Austrians; not more than 100 Palatines; 43 Swiss Grisons who would go as servants; and 55 Moravians. The final group would go as self-supporting missionaries and would expect no aid from the Trust. Though numbers were revised somewhat during the following three months, the total who set out for Georgia with high hopes in the autumn of 1735 was very close to the estimate of the summer.

Yet the dates of most departures had to be postponed — not once, but over and over. October 27 found Oglethorpe and two ships in the Downs, still far from the open sea. While waiting at Cowes on the Isle of Wight, Georgia's founder reported that all passengers remained in good health "and behaved very orderly." If anyone was bored, it was his own fault. Charles and John Wesley and other clergymen in the company "were very zealous in discoursing on religious subjects."

In London, Trustees began to worry by October 12. It would be difficult now, they realized, for Oglethorpe to lay out two new settlements in time for planting of crops. Charity colonists would therefore require subsistence for two years rather than one. Most of the money from Parliament, though unspent, was budgeted for items included in the mandate of the lawmakers. While ships lay idle, even demurrage of £100 per month was a major item.

Aboard his vessel, Oglethorpe was not greatly concerned that unrestricted cash was again running low. But he chafed and fumed that Capt. James Gascoigne of the Royal Navy — assigned to an escort vessel — was tardy in reporting for duty. Oglethorpe didn't know that his comrades in London were vexed at just-received news. Wealthy Carolina planter Samuel Everleigh was leaving Georgia for good. He had found on one island "live oaks sufficient to build a thousand ships," but said he would no longer tolerate the system of land tenure or the ban upon blacks.

Embarking for Georgia at Gravesend

Artist's interpretation of the embarcation of John Wesley at Gravesend, in 1735.

The ship in which he crossed the Atlantic was part of a flotilla, whose commanders tried to keep in sight of one another during the long voyage.

Furious at endless delay that cost yet another week's fair wind, Oglethorpe lodged a formal protest with the Admiralty that led to Gascoigne's reprimand. That did not move the *Symond*, however. Writing again from Cowes on December 3, Oglethorpe reported to Egmont that most of those aboard were now sickly and that he himself was ill of a fever. After a final five-day delay, they sailed fully 60 days behind schedule.

Had he been superstitious, Georgia's founder would have known that human shortcomings plus repeated failure of the winds were omens that boded only ill. He didn't then imagine that his return to England would be made in the season of violent tempests — underscoring, as it were, stormy events of the twelvemonth.

Moravians were far the noisiest Georgians-to-be so far encountered by Oglethorpe. He shook his head in bewilderment at their frequent vocal expressions of piety, and found their enthusiastic singing a source of annoyance. Twenty of them, led by Bishop Nitschmann, were aboard Oglethorpe's vessel. They quickly became fast friends with Anglican priests also headed for the colony. During a furious storm in late January the Germans remained calm when most English travellers began to panic. Acording to John Wesley, Oglethorpe himself permitted the Moravians and the Anglicans to spend two or three hours in prayer with him — "after which the fury of the storm did not appear so terrible as before."

Count Nikolaus von Zinzendorf of Saxony, sponsor of the Moravians, had aroused considerable antagonism in 1734. He by-passed the Trust and made a direct approach to the S.P.C.K. Several Georgia leaders roundly condemned this practice. Egmont charac-terized the entire movement earlier called Bohemian Brethren as made up of "a lot of enthusiasts, miserably persecuted by the Papists, [who] desired only land and that we would defray the charges of their passage, intending to convert the Indians and relying on Providence." Himself a staunch and loyal adherent of

Moravians read Scripture and prayed during storms

German-speaking Moravians were highly enthusiastic in their worship. During stormy hours at sea, they gathered to read Scripture aloud and to pray.

Anglican clergyman John Wesley, already a deep-troubled and a searching person, was strongly attracted to these persons. They were highly influential in his later life.

the staid Church of England, the Georgia leader was automatically suspicious of enthusiasts. He feared that such persons were prone to "take it in their head that everything that comes uppermost is the immediate impulse of the Spirit of God."

Charles and John Wesley seemed to Oglethorpe to represent his kind of religious leaders — a bit stiff and pious, but wedded to the established church. He had long-established ties with their family and was pleased when the Rev. John Burton, a Trustee and an Oxford acquaintance, brought the brothers to the Georgia office.

Oglethorpe knew that both men had won degrees from Oxford. If he was aware that they had been instrumental in forming a campus group derided by fellow students as "the holy club," he considered that unimportant. When the Wesleys learned from Oglethorpe's own mouth that many of the people of Savannah were ignorant and licentious, they expressed interest in going to the colony as spiritual leaders. An opportunity to spend some of their time as missionaries among the Indians clinched their decisions; they were so eager to win converts among native Americans that they could hardly wait to reach Georgia.

Moravians, who had great influence upon Charles and John Wesley, remained in close contact with them after reaching the colony. A band of ten settled on a 500-acre tract on the Ogeechee river and within 18 months had started a school for Indian chilren. Since there were only a few blacks in Georgia, and they were there illegally, the Moravians began making plans for evangelistic work among the slaves of South Carolina.[1]

Charles Wesley, age 28, had been a natural choice to fill the office of secretary that had been created by Trustee mandate. Perhaps to blunt the impact of that action, on September 24, 1735, Oglethorpe was named Georgia's first commissioner of Indian affairs. On the same day the clergyman was made secretary of that

office. Hence it could honestly be said that Wesley went to Georgia largely in order to relieve Oglethorpe of tedious clerical duties — with his religious interests relegated to second place by Trustees.

John Wesley, brother of Charles and 15th child of Oglethorpe's friend Samuel Wesley, would receive through the Society for the Propagation of the Gospel the £50 annual stipend designated for the support of a priest in Savannah. As usual, James Vernon made the necessary arrangements with the S.P.G. From the first discussion of the possibility that he might be sent to Georgia, Wesley made it clear that his primary goal was not pastoral care of English settlers but conversion of the friendly Indians. Still, the S.P.G. stipend would require him to devote some time to the needs of Europeans. He went with half-formed plans to teach children as well as to guide their elders. Because instruction of children was scheduled on Sunday, Wesley is sometimes credited with having formed the world's first Sunday School while serving in Savannah.

If the Oxford M.A. did win Indian converts, they would make splendid exhibits for the British public in general and especially for those Anglican parishes that had contributed to the support of Georgia. Still, it was the religious welfare of charity colonists with which Trustees were primarily concerned.

From the outset of their scheme, Trustees faithfully assembled to listen to a sermon at their annual meeting. Their appeal for charitable gifts from the public was based partly on a promise that religious needs of the colony would have high priority. Much of the £15,435 collected from the public during the first four years of the Trust came from mass solicitation in parishes, or from persons with strong religious interest.

Nearly half of this money was earmarked for specific purposes. Some of it could not be used for years. A proposal that idle funds held in this fashion be transferred to the general account created a stormy protest that was led by Vernon and Egmont. Tempers flared in such fashion that both of these key Trustees considered resigning in the aftermath of the great embarcation. When they cooled off they decided not to take so drastic a step "till Mr. Oglethorpe be returned to England."

Late February, 1736, saw Vernon and Egmont gloating. Their colleagues "who so long opposed the appropriating 300 [additional] acres to religious uses only," for a proposed church at Frederica, were out-voted. In this moment of triumph for religious interests, no one involved had any notion that Oglethorpe — then on the high seas — would soon have new reasons to look askance at over-ardent clergymen.

Both as secretary of Indian affairs and as Oglethorpe's personal scribe, Charles Wesley immediately became deeply involved in the growing Georgia-Carolina conflict. Oglethorpe's shrewd work in London had resulted in a stipulation by which a Georgia license was required for trading in the colony. Charles Town merchants, at least 41 in number, had long reaped handsome profits from trade with Indians whose chief hunting grounds were below the Savannah river. They balked, protested, and filed formal complaints at the restrictions placed upon them through Oglethorpe's influence.

For a few weeks Charles Wesley kept London informed of this and other matters by means of reports more frequent and more detailed than any Oglethorpe ever sent. Soon, however, he became emotionally involved in his chief's personal affairs. Mrs. Thomas Hawkins, wife of the physician at Frederica, boasted to Wesley of her misconduct with Oglethorpe. A rival for the affection of Georgia's founder, Mrs. Welch, lodged similar complaints with the clergyman-scribe. For his part, Charles Wesley was incredibly naive and was already exhausted from having to spend so much of his time and energy with secular duties.

A religious service conducted by Wesley was interrupted by the arrest of Dr. Hawkins for sabbath-breaking — shooting game on Sunday. Oglethorpe credited the priest with having engineered the arrest, and branded him a mischief-maker. Wesley in turn labelled his leader an adulterer.

At a subsequent service of worship led by the priest only three persons appeared: two Presbyterians and a Baptist. Small wonder that within less than a month after reaching Georgia, Wesley's *Journal* for early April reflected his despair. "I was forced by a friendly fever to take my bed," he wrote. "My sickness, I knew, could not be of long continuance; but, as I was in want of every help and convenience,, it must either shortly leave me or release me from further suffering."

No one in Georgia and nothing in the colony pleased the clergy-man-secretary. He later conceded that Oglethorpe may not have been having affairs with two prominent women, simultaneously. But the damage could not be undone. On July 25 the priest tendered his resignation to Oglethorpe. Then he shook the sand of Georgia off his feet and set out for England bearing a bundle of dispatches plus his own lengthy summary of the state of the colony.[2]

Wesley's ship, the *London*, was caught in a violent storm. Word reached Britain that it had been lost with all aboard. Egmont fumed that this new vessel was so poorly built that she was said to have sunk

23" per day for three days before starting her voyage; "Yet the drunken captain would not unload his ship to stop the leaks." Though she really was badly battered, the *London* limped into port safely in December, 1736. Charles Wesley's first visit was to a friend who at that moment was reading a dispatch about his death at sea. "Happy for me, had the news been true!" he wrote in his *Journal*. "What a world of misery it would save me!"

His brother John, like him an Oxford M.A., was well pleased when 20 persons appeared for his first Georgia service of holy communion on March 13, 1736. He could not avoid noticing that 18-year-old Sophy Hopkey seemed more animated than other communicants. She, in turn, was sure that the priest looked at her in a special way.

One of the few eligible females in the colony, Sophy was not bothered by the clergyman's short stature or by his face that was already stern at age 33. To her he symbolized all that was exciting and romantic about faraway England, Oxford University, and the Anglican Church. Within weeks she put timidity aside and went to Oglethorpe. Responding to her query Georgia's founder told the young woman that he thought Mr. Wesley would like her best in white — the color symbolizing purity.

Radiant in pure white, Sophy Hopkey began attending early morning prayers at Wesley's house. Soon she was present at evening prayers as well. When she said she would like to learn French, linguist Wesley graciously offered to spend an hour a day teaching her. As chaplain to the colony it seemed fitting that he should inconvenience himself a bit for a girl who was often "the most affected of his listeners." Besides, her aunt was married to public storekeeper Thomas Causton who was also the colony's chief magistrate.

Soon the clergyman's diary, written in a code of his own devising, began to include more and longer references to Miss Sophy. He found himself frightened. Not all of his thoughts were directed to the salvation of his own soul and to the spiritual welfare of others. He had fervently hoped to devote much time to the conversion of Indians. These folk proved only casually interested; still, he felt guilty at giving so many hours to instruction of deeply-interested Sophy.

As the relationship of the priest and his parishioner grew more intimate, notations in Wesley's diary became more tortured. He and Sophy spent five or six days and nights together, travelling by boat the 100 miles from Frederica to Savannah. In bad weather they slept crowded together with the crew of four and the one other passenger. All were covered with sails to keep the water off them. During daylight hours Wesley entertained Sophy by reading to her from Patrick's *Prayers* and Fleury's *History of the Church*.

Had he been consulted, Oglethorpe would have had strong advice for the priest. He should follow his heart rather than his head. He ought to settle down in Savannah and rear a family of good Georgia citizens.

Wesley asked advice of no one except his new Moravian friends. They urged him to give up all notion of marriage. Less than fully convinced he cast lots in order to seek the will of God. With three alternatives provided, he drew the slip that said: "Think of it no more."

That persuaded him that he should dismiss Sophy from his thoughts. He tried, but found he could not. Neither could he bring himself to ask for her hand. Useless to himself and to everyone else, Wesley grew increasingly zealous in his spiritual self-flagellation. At the same time his already-rigid demands upon members of his parish became more and more strict.

Oglethorpe was relieved to see the last of Charles Wesley. When Georgia's founder left for England in November he was keenly aware that Charles' brother was widely disliked. He had no idea, however, that the priest of whom he had entertained such high hopes would be drummed from the colony in disgrace during his absence.

Final unfolding of tangled events that erupted into the Wesley scandal was months in the future when the only Trustee ever to set foot on Georgia soil found himself facing a growing dilemma. With new settlements to be started, many forts to be built and manned, and unexplored terrain to be mapped, Oglethorpe had no time for civil administration of the colony He could and did turn much of that over to Thomas Causton, ignoring charges that had been lodged against the magistrate. With Charles Wesley gone, the preparation of reports and letters could not be delegated. His colleagues in London would simply have to trust him.

Georgia's earliest defensive force, other than charity colonists who soon showed themselves of little use as an organized militia, was made up of Yamacraw Indians plus a few rangers on loan from Carolina. Arrival of Highlanders who included seasoned veterans of European battlefields meant more than simply a better system of defense. James Oglethorpe, Esq., son and grandson of military oficers and one-time aide-de-camp to Prince Eugene, could begin taking the offensive. By now he was convinced that the Spanish, rather than the French, constituted the greatest threat to Georgia in particular and to British America in general.[3] Why wait for them to begin moving against him? Far better to show them that they now had to face a tough-minded opponent, ready and willing to take great risks to preserve — or perhaps even to extend — Georgia's territorial integrity.

During a five-year period before Georgia was chartered, soldiers of Britain had manned Fort King George on the Altamaha as the empire's southernmost early-defensive station in North America. Abandoned a few years before Oglethorpe began casting a hopeful eye upon the region, the fort had crumbled into uselessness. Now the newly-arrived Highlanders, led by Hugh Mackay,[4] could be used to erect a new fort near the old site. These professionals could also garrison the outpost.

A highly cohesive group mostly from Scotland's County Sutherland, Mackay's followers still wore Highland garb and spoke Gaelic. Men were skilled users of the broadsword. Yet even those who should have been good marksmen were handicapped by crudely-made muskets which were their only hand guns. They settled in Darien, earlier a haven for a handful of Scottish Jacobites who fled from home in order to escape punishment.[5] Soon the Highlanders managed to mount a few cannon at their outpost. That meant they had fire power beyond anything that would normally be encountered in such a wilderness.

Oglethorpe's second major new fort, Frederica, was designated for Saint Simons island at the mouth of the Altamaha. It lay very close to the southern extremity of the colony, as delineated in the charter.

Persons who were expected to establish Fort Frederica and its accompanying settlement had for the most part been recruited in London. They were far less prepared to face hardships and loneliness than were the Scots, yet began their work with zeal. To the great disappointment of the Londoners and of Oglethorpe, a band of 50 Salzburgers balked when asked to go to Frederica. Because he could do nothing else, Georgia's founder reluctantly agreed to let them join earlier German-speaking colonists. By now, these folk were well established at New Ebenezer, on the western bank of the Savannah river. Even without their aid a drab but surprisingly solid fortress, approximately 124 feet square, eventually came to dominate Frederica.

So far, Oglethorpe was within limits specified by the king and

Parliament. Even his move to establish Fort Augusta about 200 miles up the Savannah river could hardly be a subject of major controversy. Prior to taking that step he had gained the consent of Indians who claimed the rich fur-yielding region.

April 18, 1736, brought a move of quite different character. Diplomats who viewed it from the perspective of European capitals, as well as Spanish leaders in Florida and in Cuba, could only regard it as deliberately provocative.

Oglethorpe himself headed a band that included 40 Yamacraw warriors plus a party of rangers and 30 indentured Highlanders who had come to the New World because they had nowhere else to go. They moved past Georgia's boundary in order to survey a desolate island. It lay directly south of Jekyll, named for long-time Georgia supporter Sir Joseph Jekyll. Few enterprises were so thrilling as the process of putting new labels on the map in the name of one's king. Still, at Jekyll the founder of Georgia ran out of ideas. At the suggestion of Toonahowi the sandy island below Georgia was called Cumberland — in gratitude for the gold watch presented to the Indian by the youthful Duke of Cumberland.

Better than the sharpest-eyed geographer in London or in Madrid, Oglethorpe was perfectly aware that he had gone beyond his colony's territorial limit. Still he selected a site on Cumberland's only geographical feature that approached being a hill. Fort Saint Andrew must be built here, he told his followers.

In time they did construct there a fort about 65 feet deep and twice as wide. It lay about 50 miles south of Darien — slightly more than one-fourth of the distance from the Altamaha river to Spain's old and highly-developed Saint Augustine.

Oglethorpe made this move, clearly recognized as rash, in a climate of would-be appeasement by his own government. At the very moment he began making plans to build Fort Saint Andrew, special envoy Charles Dempsey was in Florida. He had been sent by British Secretary of State Thomas Pelham-Holles, Duke of Newcastle, on a mission aimed at peaceful settlement of long-standing border disputes with Spain.

Writing a lengthy dispatch to Newcastle from Frederica, soldier-of-fortune Oglethorpe acted as though he had new information that bore upon stipulations in Georgia's charter. His good friend Tomochichi, he said, had claims upon islands lying close to the mainland and extending all the way to the Saint John's river, approximately 100 miles south of Darien. Spanish Florida, Oglethorpe told Newcastle as though he had personally made the discovery, extended only to the southern bank of the Saint John's.

Georgia's charter described the colony as lying between the Savannah and Altamaha rivers. Oglethorpe wrote that Saint George's point, newly-found and named at the tip of a small island, "is the farthest part of the dominions of His Majesty on the seacoast of North America."

Later he backed this preposterous claim by declaring that the river known as Saint John's actually was a southern branch of the Altamaha. By means of forgery upon the map, at one bold stroke Oglethorpe effectively doubled the length of Georgia's coastline.

A letter dated April 17, 1736, is perhaps the most momentous one Georgia's founder ever penned. It advanced outrageous claims from which he never retreated. Simultaneously he made overtures to both Virginia and New York, asking the aid of these colonies in the event of a Spanish attack upon Georgia.

He was in communication with both the governor of Florida and the captain-general of her armed forces, Oglethorpe told the British secretary of state. In one sentence he asked for directions so that he might obey them. But that request was followed by his solemn pledge that "as I cannot deliver up a foot of ground belonging to His Majesty to a foreign power without the breach of my allegiance to His Majesty, I will alive or dead keep possession of it 'till I have His Majesty's orders."

Lands claimed by "Your Grace's most obedient and humble servant" were, he insisted, "the keys of all America." Therefore James Edward Oglethorpe, M.P., stood ready to maintain possession of them "in spite of all the force of Florida, Cuba, and Mexico."

Seldom if ever has anyone else in the western world come so close to a one-man declaration of war against a major power.

Georgia's fire-eating Trustee in residence who never became governor of the colony backed his words with deeds. He established yet another outpost, Fort Saint George, many miles south of Fort Saint Andrew. It lay within earshot of muskets that were sometimes fired from the Spanish lookout on the Saint John's river.[6]

Without authorization from his government, Oglethorpe now entered into negotiations with Spanish leaders. A "compromise" that he worked out with Florida's Governor Francisco de Moral Sanchez so angered Spanish authorities that Moral was recalled to Madrid and relieved of office. As a delaying tactic, the entire issue of the boundary of Georgia was referred to the goverments involved. While diplomats sparred across conference tables, Oglethorpe put the finishing touches upon Fort Saint George. Then he extended his patrols of the Saint John's river.

Weary but jubilant, in late October the man who once had hoped only for a haven for English debtors wrote that "All matters with the Spaniards are regulated, and the governor of Augustine contented. Therefore all being safe I shall set out immediately for Europe."

His return voyage, which began on November 23, was far from triumphant. True, in addition to outwitting Spain for the moment he had taken a giant stride toward military self-sufficiency by means of a successful conference with the Chickasaw Indians in July.

Yet it was also true that scores of settlers had left Georgia. Food was scarce and expensive in the colony. Rent for a good house in Savannah was higher than in London. Germans in particular and Europeans in general were achieving self-sufficiency. Too many English charity colonists were still dependent upon the Trust. Many who were poor but solvent when they left home had fallen deeply into debt in Georgia.

Some Trustees were furious with their colleague and representative. His letters were less frequent than ever, and often omitted vital details. Disregarding their specific instructions, he had proceeded with new settlements they did not have the money to complete. His never-ending drafts upon them had prodded them into radical action; special currency was issued for circulation only in Georgia.[7] Trustees published notices that they would no longer honor bills drawn upon them from the colony. Vexatious questions had been raised about Oglethorpe's personal New World ventures, undertaken in violation of the spirit if not the letter of Georgia's charter.

These matters were linked with international issues raised by the long-smouldering dispute over Georgia's boundary. They could not be handled from a distance of 3,000 miles. It was imperative that Oglethorpe return to London with haste. Though they never quite said so, Trustees were recalling their representative in order to question him concerning the administration of his trust.

The *Two Brothers* sailed in a season when east-bound vessels were most likely to be caught in major storms. After a rough 70-day passage the ship lay fog-bound on the English coast for nine days. When she drifted into the breakers, many sailors abandoned their posts and ran into the hold. Oglethorpe and a volunteer aide from Haslemere, young Mr. Tanner, "were obliged to jump out of bed in their Shirts to pull the ropes" abandoned by seamen.

Bone tired and acutely conscious that eight years' work would go down the drain without a great deal of money and many fighting men, James Edward Oglethorpe took inventory. At age 41 he still held the prized seat in the House of Commons, but it would be contested again soon. He had made a start at enhancing his fortune by means of New World ventures that he fervently hoped would remain fully secret.

Yet neither military rank nor real wealth had been won. His dreams concerning a utopian society of the one-time desperate of England had faded. If he had made any contributions to imperial Britain, they were by means of his stance – not through solid achievements sure to stand for decades or for centuries.

Landing at Ilfercomb, Wales, on January 2, 1737, Georgia's founder prepared to face an icy reception from fellow Trustees plus an emotion-charged and highly uncertain climate in Parliament and at the court.

Chapter 10

"THE FATE OF THE COLONY IS IN
ONE MAN'S HANDS"

January, 1737 — December, 1738

"Never meet the enemy according to his battle plan. When facing overwhelming odds, mount a surprise attack."

That strategy guided James Oglethorpe in his contest for a seat in Parliament and his conduct there. It served him well against power-conscious Trustees, jealous Carolina traders, and ambitious leaders of Spanish Florida. This was no time to adopt a different course.

Four days after landing in Wales, Oglethorpe arrived at the Old Palace Yard, London. By means of messengers he had requested a series of urgent meetings on Friday, January 7. He started the formal day by calling upon Queen Caroline. Her gracious reception encouraged him to press for an early audience with King George, himself. He promised the sovereign that he would return with maps and "all the latest intelligence concerning His Majesty's southernmost North American domain."[1]

From the palace the founder of Georgia hurried to Downing Street, to the residence of the prime minister. His meeting with the Right Hon. Sir Robert Walpole produced no tangible results. Still, it gave him an opportunity to insist that Georgia must be saved regardless of cost.

Oglethorpe was fully aware that his colleagues had met strong opposition from England's most powerful man when they went to him concerning the 1736 appropriation for Georgia. A minimum of £20,000 was urgently needed. Walpole listened briefly, then interrupted to remind petitioners that only one week earlier three Georgia Trustees had voted against a money bill. Hucks, White, and Heathcote had opposed the appropriation of £4,000 for the continuing restoration of the Chapel of King Henry VII in Westminster. Under such circumstances, how dared they apply for money?[2]

Being a man of reason, said Walpole, he would not totally oppose aid for Georgia. But he could not in conscience agree even to £15,000. Trustees settled for £10,000 — knowing that it would not fund the colony for the year ahead. Private contributions had fallen off sharply; less than 100 gifts were received during an entire twelvemonth. They'd have to do the best they could, and hope for greater success with Parliament another year.

Taking leave of Walpole, Oglethorpe went within hours to the Georgia office for a brief and less-than-cordial meeting with fellow Trustees. Many of them were fuming over unfavorable aspects of Charles Wesley's report. Others were angry that Oglethorpe had failed to obey their instructions concerning use of dwindling resources.[3] Some were ready to abandon the entire Georgia enterprise. No formal meeting was held, so no minutes were kept. At Oglethorpe's insistence a meeting of the full Trust was called for Monday, January 12, at which time he promised to present a detailed report.

By way of special preparation for that crucial meeting, Oglethorpe spent four full hours with Egmont. Before they parted the older man concluded that his colleague had done the best he could under difficult circumstances and therefore should not be censured. He was keenly interested in details of the agreement reached between Oglethorpe and Governor del Moral Sanchez of Florida, and commended his friend for having made so shrewd a bargain. Egmont remained troubled that there seemed to be no good solution to the Carolina question. So long as traders of that colony were required to take out Georgia licenses in order to do business with the Cherokees, hard feelings would remain.

January 12 saw James Vernon, Oglethorpe's most persistent critic, presiding over the meeting of the Trust. Fourteen men were present out of 21; more often than not, a gathering saw half a dozen or less on hand.

In a fashion he never fully analyzed, though he was keenly conscious that he possessed it, James Edward Oglethorpe had a rare gift of overcoming the opposition in eyeball-to-eyeball encounter.

His written reports — and the lack of them — often created tensions. His personal appearances were uniformly triumphant. When he returned from Georgia nearly two years earlier he had faced a hostile audience, but had silenced his opposition in a single session.

Much the same thing happened again. Colleagues who had been most critical of his high-handed ways, his free style of spending, and his questionable enterprises aimed at personal enrichment, didn't even mention these matters when face-to-face with the man who walked trails like an Indian and who had bested a Spanish governor in a treaty of peace.

After a meeting of unreported length in which Oglethorpe gave a detailed account of his entire second stay in Georgia, Trustees unanimously adopted a resolution "That James Oglethorpe Esqr be congratulated on his safe Return to England; And that the Thanks of the Trustees be given to him for the many and important Services done by him for the colony of Georgia."

Within two weeks London was buzzing with rumors that the member from Haslemere wanted complete and permanent government subsidization of what had started out as a charitable enterprise. All military expenses, which would be considerable and were of top priority according to Oglethorpe, should be met from the treasury. In addition, a fixed annual appropriation of no less than £7,000 was said to be needed for civil expenses of Georgia "until the colony be prosperous enough to bear this cost itself" at some undetermined time in the future.

Delicate negotiations had to be carried out with the prime minister. Earlier these discussions had been led by Egmont. But the 1734 election had brought about a permanent rift. Egmont and Walpole were no longer even speaking to one another. Oglethorpe would have to treat with the prime minister — quite a different matter from dealing with docile Georgians who owed their support to the Trust.

Sir Robert sent word to Oglethorpe that he was perplexed about the defense of the southern colonies. A scheme or plan, carefully committed to paper, would be appreciated.

If he complied with the request for a written proposal, the member from Haslemere said nothing about it when he gave Egmont a blow-by-blow account of his stormy session with the prime minister. Oglethorpe spoke his mind without using the niceties of diplomatic dialogue. Walpole said he was not accustomed to being addressed in such fashion. Georgia's founder fired at this

Spanish ship under construction

Wealth of South America had been pouring into Spain for decades. This gave Philip V virtually unlimited resources with which to expand both military and commercial fleets.

While English leaders vacillated and hoped for peace, shipyards of Spain bustled with new construction.

haughty response and replied: "Yes, he was [accustomed to being so addressed] when he was plain Mr. Walpole. But now [that he was] Sir Robert & chief Minister, he was Surrounded by Sycophants and Flatterers who will not tell him the Truth."

Walpole countered by noting that he believed there was internal friction in the Georgia Trust. It appeared that many Trustees had abandoned all thought of defending the colony.

Friction? How could anyone imagine such a thing about so united a body as that made up of men who devoted so much time and energy to Georgia? But for Oglethorpe personally, the future was uncertain. Unless fully supported by those in power, said Georgia's founder, he was ready to abandon the scheme. Why, he "had twice been over the seas to carry on the Colony, and not only ventur'd his life and health, to the neglect of his own affairs, but actually spent £3,000 of his own money."[4]

Georgia, Oglethorpe insisted, was a matter of great national concern. He personally "did not pretend to be a Don Quixote for it, and suffer in his reputation as he must do, if he continues his concern for it without a publick countenance."[5]

Go ahead and drop the colonial scheme, taunted the man who knew that he was for life under suspicion as a Jacobite less than fully loyal to the House of Hanover. Drop it! Nothing would please the Spanish more! They would, indeed, be glad to get it without a fight. But be prepared, too, to risk the loss of South Carolina and Virginia. For at the surrender of Georgia "the French would then be invited to attack those Colonies on their back, and in 27 days were able to march up to Charles Town."

Eager for peace with Spain but admitted baffled by complexities of a struggle 3,000 miles away in a land familiar to no British leader except Oglethorpe, the prime minister reverted to his original

request. He needed a written outline or plan — not too greatly detailed — which he could study at his leisure.

No plan is needed, retorted Oglethorpe; what we must have is action. Colonists have shown their inability to form a militia strong enough to defend themselves. That leaves only one alternative: station a body of professional British soldiers in Georgia. Cost of maintaining them will run to about £20,000 a year.

Entirely too much, said the prime minister.

Then raise new recruits and assign one battalion of 500 men to each colony, insisted Oglethorpe. Why, the infantry companies now in America are skeleton bodies — paper fighting forces with many vacancies. Officers are pocketing the pay of men listed on the rolls but no longer in service. Let each colony from Georgia to New England foot the cost of one battalion, fully manned.

It might work, admitted Sir Robert.

Only if all the forces are put under a single person's command, countered Oglethorpe. Without such a centralized system of authority, governors of various colonies might differ in their judgments or be so concerned about their own safety that they'd "defeat any measure that might be necessary for a defence" of British North America as a whole.

Though he was no soldier, the prime minister admitted that the proposal seemed reasonable. If it should be carried out, would the member from Haslemere accept the command of such forces?

Only if he could be named inspector general of all the forces, with full power to direct them, Oglethorpe said.

But would not such a role require the member from Haslemere to vacate his seat in Parliament?

No. That post is civil, not military. There are precedents for holding a civil and a military post, simultaneously . . .

Without committing himself to any plan, Walpole asked how much money it would take to pursue the path recommended by Oglethorpe. About £20,000 annually for the ongoing life of the colony, aside from its defense, he was told.

Then Oglethorpe took a final, decisive step — so bold that it invited total rejection of his plan. "If both the [civilian] Settlement and the [military] defence are to be provided for," he said, "there must be two distinct Estimates made." That is, Georgia must have each year a civil and a military appropriation — neither would be effective without the other, though they could be combined in a single asking.

That line of reasoning made sense to the prime minister. He did not promise to act upon it, but turned the conversation to other topics.

Hoping that he could gain assent to a 1737 appropriation of £20,000, Oglethorpe made a formal request for £30,000. Walpole was cool toward such a sum and countered by offering the governorship of South Carolina. Coupled with that post, he proposed in a later conversation, there might be a chance to get Oglethorpe named commander general of Carolina and Georgia military forces.

A colonial governorship and a military title many men with ten times his battlefield experience would covet... Plums most persons would pluck without an instant's hesitation. . . .

Oglethorpe stalled, gave excuses, and raised new questions. From the outset he realized that in order to become Governor of South Carolina he would have to relinquish his seat in Parliament. That was out of the question, though he did not say so at first. "Commander general of the fighting forces of two colonies" had a fine ring — but he wanted a formal commission as colonel of his own regiment of 700 men.

Before final negotiations began the founder of Georgia sensed what would be offered, and knew how he would respond. When he could delay no longer he refused the Carolina governorship and said concerning the military post that he "much preferred to raise a special regiment which he would command." That would give him permanent rather than temporary rank.

While discussions were under way and before Oglethorpe announced his bottom-line stand, Parliament voted on March 17 to invest another £20,000 in the Colony of Georgia.

Trustees now saw clearly that any role their colleague might play in the colony would be largely or exclusively military. Looking about for an administrator whom they could trust, they turned to Colonel William Stephens. Earlier he had made a good name for himself while working as agent for wealthy investor Colonel Samuel Horsey. In addition to holdings in Georgia, Horsey had gained a grant of 40,000 acres in Carolina.

Stephens kept a meticulous journal of his activities in taking up the Carolina land grant, and a copy of it came to the attention of Georgia leaders. After scanning it Egmont noted that "His journal is extremely well wrote, and it were to be wished it could be brought about to make him Governor of Georgia. He was in Queen Anne's reign a member of Parliament but fallen into decay."

A governor for Georgia was out of the question. Trustees had

John Wesley conversing with Indians

The Rev. John Wesley, M.A., had high hopes of success as a missionary to the Indians of Georgia. He did converse with them at every opportunity, but won no converts.

Lack of success as a missionary, coupled with an incredibly naive relationship with Sophy Hopkey, brought a disastrous end to his Georgia service.

debated that question often enough to know it need not be raised again. In order to become governor, their nominee would have to be approved both by the privy council and the king. Such a person would never be totally responsible to the Trustees. Better no governor than one whose first duty was to the crown rather than the Trust.

Though Stephens could not be governor, perhaps he could be given a title and a role that would mark him as the chief agent of Trustees in the Colony of Georgia. Negotiations proceeded quietly; Trustee records include only the most perfunctory mention of Stephens before April 18, 1737. That day leaders met briefly to hear a letter from Carolina's lieutenant-governor concerning a Spanish plot to destroy Georgia. They adjourned as a corporate body, then re-convened as its common council. Just 90 days after having voted unanimous thanks to Oglethorpe his colleagues tried to strip him of authority by creating a new post and simultaneously filling it. William Stephens was made secretary for the affairs of the Trust within the Province of Georgia. That meant he would serve as chief civil administrator.

Oglethorpe was present at the meeting of the common council, though not at the preceding session of the Trust. He knew precisely what the action meant; he felt the sting keenly. He could have objected to the broad authority given to Stephens under terms of detailed instructions filed with the board of trade. He might have abandoned the colony in anger.

James Oglethorpe neither protested the actions of his colleagues nor offered to withdraw from Georgia. At the moment he did not know that a special council of the Spanish king had been convened that very month in order to consider his — Oglethorpe's — penetration of the Saint John's river region. When the news reached him later he showed no surprise.

He was keenly attuned to talk at the British court. Gossip alleged that Sir Robert Walpole had promised some of his most intimate followers — in strict confidence, of course — that he would forbid Oglethorpe from returning to Georgia. This despite the prime minister's concurrence in actions that culminated in a brief but dramatic ceremony on June 19.

That day the son of Jacobite rebel Sir Theophilus Oglethorpe kissed the hand of King George II as a token of fidelity. Then he accepted service as "General and Commander in Chief of all and singular his Majesty's Forces employed and to be employed in his Majesty's provinces of South Carolina and Georgia in America; and likewise to be Captain of that Independent Company of Foot doing Duty in his Majesty's said Province of South Carolina."

Appointment to the military post meant a salary of £1,000 per year — more than three times the rents yielded by Oglethorpe's estate. At one stroke, a man who had never worn the uniform of any branch of Britain's armed forces was to become captain of foot, colonel of a yet-to-be-raised regiment, and general of all the forces of two colonies. As secretary to the Trust and civil administrator of Georgia, William Stephens would receive £100 per year. Oglethorpe's new military role not only brought him a handsome living; it also offered a chance for glory of the sort he never could have hoped to win as the father figure for a colony of the struggling poor.

Now it made little difference who might seek the governorship of South Carolina. With a military stipend of £1,000 per year assigned to Oglethorpe, the civil post "was not worth the while for any gentleman to apply." Georgia's founder could keep his prized seat in Parliament while savoring the juiciest financial plum at the southern tip of Britain's North American empire and exercising military authority far greater than that wielded by any previous Oglethorpe.[6]

Indian allies, of whom the member from Haslemere said little in formal discussions of his own future role, were expected to prove more potent than most Englishmen could imagine. According to Oglethorpe's optimistic calculations, he could count upon native Americans for nearly 7,000 fighting men: 400 Chickasaws, 1,500 Creeks, and 5,000 Choctaws.

Don Tomas Geraldino, Spanish minister to the Court of St. James, had a network of informants who kept him posted about developments with respect to the debated Georgia boundary. He formally repudiated the Oglethorpe-Moral agreement. Then he informed England's secretary of state that it was impossible to halt the military build-up that was taking place in Cuba.

English eagerness for peace made Geraldino bolder. He learned in June that Oglethorpe was likely to get both his commission and his regiment. Using all his powers of persuasion the Spanish diplomat set out to block Oglethorpe's return to the New World. He talked repeatedly with the prime minister, the secretary of state, and with influential Horace Walpole, brother of Sir Robert. When he sensed that some British leaders were wavering, on August 6 he delivered to Newastle the sharpest note yet sent from the king of Spain.

Robert Walpole's support of Georgia crumbled. He sent for Oglethorpe and requested him, as a gesture of conciliation, to disband the regiment that was in process of formation. In lieu of proceeding as he had earlier promised, said the prime minister, he'd see that Oglethorpe would get his own regiment in England.

August, 1737, saw the famous Oglethorpe temper flare. At the proposal made by the chief architect of British policy, Georgia's founder demanded to know what kind of man Walpole took him to be. Did the prime minister think him without a conscience, to be responsible for taking 3,000 souls to Georgia in order to abandon them?

"Tell me plainly. Say 'Yea,' or 'Nay.' Is Georgia to be given up?"

If the answer is in the affirmative, stormed Oglethorpe with more of his "very warm words," Trustees should be so informed at once. That would at least permit Georgia leaders to "write immediately over to the inhabitants to retire and save themselves in time."

As Oglethorpe reported the fiery session to Egmont, the prime minister rather limply responded that he didn't see the neccessity for notifying colonists to flee. Oglethorpe walked off in a huff and proceeded with the procurement of men in a drive to bring his regiment to full strength.[7]

In a series of conversations with Britain's leading statesmen, Georgia's founder took advantage of their ignorance. Spain had demanded, not once but repeatedly, that the British withdraw from Fort Saint George. Oglethorpe had built it, they charged, on Spanish soil at the mouth of the Saint John's river — fully aware that he was ignoring accepted international boundaries. His personal negotiations with the Spanish had included an agreement to evacuate the fort. Now they wanted assurance that he would keep his word.

Pressed by his countrymen to enumerate British fortifications in what came to be called "the debatable land," Oglethorpe resorted to a subterfuge. He said that Fort Saint George, or Fort King George

as it was often called, stood on the southermost branch of the
Altamaha river — the natural boundary stipulated in Georgia's
charter. Oglethorpe knew quite well that the Saint John's was an
independent river and not a branch of the Altamaha — but no one
in England or Spain could prove him wrong. If anyone seriously
challenged his geographical falsification, no notice was taken of the
challenge.[8]

Stephens, Georgia's newly-appointed secretary for the affairs of
the Trust, reached the colony in November. He was prepared to
face problems and difficulties but had not expected to arrive in the
middle of the most serious internal scandal yet to break in Georgia.

Exactly one year from the day she first saw the Rev. John Wesley,
Sophy Hopkey married William Williamson. She had concluded
that the clergyman never would bring himself to ask for her hand,
no matter how fervently he might yearn for it.

Surprised and shocked at the sudden marriage, Wesley began to
exercise his pastoral role more zealously than ever. After all, he was
responsible for the spiritual welfare of Mrs. Williamson. When her
spiritual ardor appeared to lag, he first warned her and then
admonished her to be more earnest about "owning her fault and
declaring her repentance."

She ignored her pastor's exhortations. One month later he
refused to admit her to the altar at a service of holy communion.

On August 8, the very day James Oglethorpe used most
undiplomatic language in a reckless challenge to England's prime
minister, Georgia's resident missionary was shocked. A bailiff
served him with a warrant charging that he was guilty of "defaming
said Sophy" and asking damages in the amount of £1,000.
Savannah storekeeper and chief magistrate Thomas Causton,
Sophy's uncle by marriage, visited the rectory and confronted
Wesley with additional charges.

Soon a grand jury of 44 males overwhelmingly voted a lengthy
true bill against the pastor. Matters went from bad to worse. Unable
to get a formal trial started, Wesley announced his plans to leave the
colony. A new court order commanded him to stay, and to post
surety of £50 cash. William Stephens made a valiant but futile
attempt to arbitrate the dispute.

Faced with almost certain conviction by what he considered to
be a rigged judicial system, the man who came as a missionary fled
in the night as "a prisoner at large." With three companions he
proceeded from Savannah to Purrysburg, S.C.[9] There he was shown
the terminus of a trail marked by "barked" trees, and leading to Port

Royal many miles away. He reached Charles Town on December 2, just one month after William Stephens took over the reins of a colony whose members were sharply divided over the Hopkey/Wesley affair. After a rough 60-day passage the clergyman landed at Deal on February 12, 1738.

Like his brother Charles, John Wesley was all but overcome by his sense of failure in Georgia. Both men indicated that they wanted to return to the colony. Neither received any encouragement from Oglethorpe or his colleagues. They were deeply influenced by their New World experiences and were so strongly attracted to their enthusiastic Moravian friends that they considered joining them. Dynamic spiritual renewal was experienced by the two Anglicans in 1738. Later they became world famous as founders of the Methodist movement. Had there been no despair at failure in Georgia, followed by their rebound, Methodism might never have been launched as an organized movement.

John Wesley presented a largely negative report about affairs of the colony from which he fled. By then Georgia's founder had ceased to be a regular participant in meetings of the Trust. He anticipated action that his colleagues made formal on March 23. For the final time they read the itemized budget for the coming fiscal year. Then they proceeded "to strike off all branches of military nature, the Parliament having given us this year's money for the settling, not the defence of the Colony."

In a move to thwart Oglethorpe if he tried to ignore the decision, they carefuly itemized expenses that their new secretary — Stephens — would be forbidden to meet: pay of provincial rangers; purchase of essential new piraguas, or small boats especially built for use on inland waterways; the garrison at Fort Saint George; the completion of the new fort at Augusta; work under way at Fort Saint Andrews; Darien and its defenses; and the previously-authorized purchase of a Carolina scout boat.

His colleagues added insult to injury by scolding Georgia's founder because of his extreme carelessness in attending meetings of the Trust. "He sees how cool many of the Trust are grown to the work," noted Egmont, "and since he is not thoroughly pleased with our proceedings, he chooses to be absent as often as he can." So did many other Trustees. It was not unusual for three or four to show up, then conduct no business because of low attendance.

Had he been pressed, Oglethorpe would have cited military needs as his excuse for non-participation in work of the Trust. Under normal circumstances Col. Oglethorpe would have had

Jenkins' pickled ear threw Sir Robert Walpole into shock

The pickled ear of mariner Thomas Jenkins triggered a violent wave of anti-Spanish feeling in Parliament and among Englishmen in general.

A satirical cartoon of the era depicts Sir Robert Walpole "swooning" when suddenly shown the famous ear by the seaman who lost it to the Spanish.

difficulty raising a regiment. These were not ordinary months, however.

Early in the year Britain was rocked by the re-appearance of English master mariner Robert Jenkins. His brig, the *Rebecca*, had been boarded by the Spanish in 1731 while he was in West Indian waters. After rifling the hold of the *Rebecca*, the Spanish commander of the coast-guard vessel had cut off one of Jenkins' ears. When he reached the Thames on June 11, Jenkins managed to get an audience with the king. Still, the matter attracted little interest at the time.

Seven years later, with many Englishmen clamoring for war with Spain, Jenkins was invited to testify before a committee of Parliament. On March 17, 1738, he repeated his story with vivid details — and displayed what he said was his pickled ear. Anger was so great that throughout Britain the public outcry for vengeance upon Spain could not be ignored.

In this climate, Oglethorpe's request for transfer of veterans from existing military units got prompt action. Recruitment of untrained men to fill out the ranks of his regiment proceeded at a rate that would have been impossible without the impact of seaman Jenkins. Though war was not declared for more than a year, when it finally came it was — almost inevitably — labelled "The War of Jenkins' Ear."[10]

April saw the House of Commons open a month-long debate "on the Depredations of the Spaniards." Strangely, the detailed report does not indicate that Oglethorpe spoke on the floor. Lords spent most of May upon the same issue.

Under terms of the Treaty of Utrecht, 1713, Britain was entitled to send only one trading ship per year to Spanish colonies in South America. British smugglers wantonly violated this restriction, and the South Sea Co. used all of its influence to press for formal

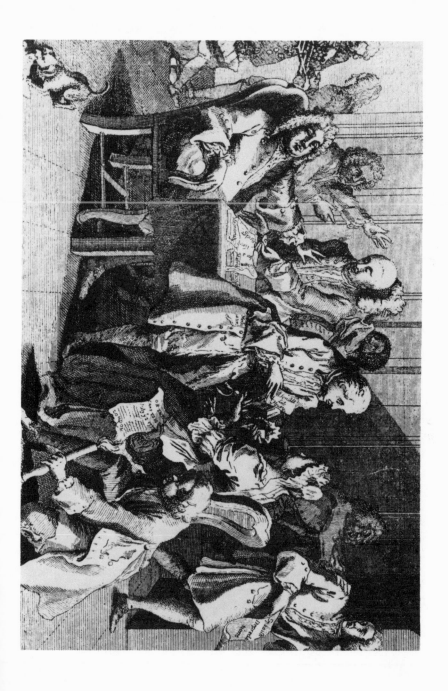

modification of the provision. Lord Carteret, who led much of the debate, cited earlier Anglo-Spanish agreements in support of his impassioned demand that all trade barriers whatever be levelled. He and others made it clear that free passage of ships and unrestricted trade — not the long-disputed boundary between Georgia and Florida — was the vital issue.

One week after military expenses were deleted from Georgia's budget, Col. Oglethorpe — as he now was most often called — invited his colleagues to see his regiment march through Holborn. For enjoyment of his friends he ordered "a very elegant dinner" at the White Hart inn.

Soldiers led by Major Cooke marched smartly by at 2:00 P.M. and impressed bystanders with their youth — all being under age 30. But there were few cheers from Georgia leaders. It was no small disappointment to Oglethorpe that only four of his 20 fellow Trustees accepted his invitation to watch and to feast.

Eleven of his colleagues responded, however, to an invitation to a farewell dinner that Oglethorpe gave on May 1. He planned to sail in about ten days. Stephens was now responsible for all civil affairs of Georgia and would administer the entire Parliamentary appropriation for the year. So the member from Haslemere could hardly stir up serious trouble. It was a civil gesture to dine with him.

Yet sparks flew before the festive evening was over. After dinner a committee of three Trustees reported to their fellows "the bad state of our cash." This they felt was partly due to poor management by Oglethorpe's deputy, Thomas Causton. Oglethorpe and Vernon got into an argument that ended in the exchange of heated words. Vernon told Oglethorpe to look after military matters and leave all other concerns of Georgia in the hands of the Trustees in London.

July saw Oglethorpe's third departure for Georgia. So many colonists wanted to go that the man-o-war *Hector* was assigned to serve as escort for the five unarmed transport vessels that made up the flotilla. Oglethorpe and part of his regiment were placed aboard the man-o-war *Blandford*. In spite of fiascos to which the brothers Wesley were central, another clergyman was in the party. The Rev. George Whitefield, soon to make a great reputation as an evangelist, had conceived a plan to erect in Savannah an orphan house. It would be the first of its sort in the New World. Land had been set aside for the project by Trustees, and all fervently hoped that money could be found to erect a building very soon.

While ships were becalmed in Plymouth Sound, Oglethorpe received a last-minute dispatch from fellow Trustees. It was a peremptory order that two seaboats earlier purchased by Georgia's founder be "immediately sent to their respective stations, to be employed for the services for which they were bought."

For his part, the member from Haslemere penned another long letter to the secretary of state. Aboard the *Blandford* at Spithead on June 6, 1738, he repeated all of his old arguments for a firm stand against Spain. This time he supported them with extracts from letters just received from South Carolina's lieutenant-governor, Col. William Bull. Oglethorpe insisted that the Duke of Newcastle personally plead the Georgia case with the king once more. It was imperative, he told the secretary of state, that artillery for his regiment be sent with haste.

"The wind is just sprung fair," he concluded, "and I hope soon to be in America where, though the odds are great, I cannot but think myself happy in having an occasion of showing the grateful sense I have of His Majesty's goodness."

Though the language of his letter was cheerful as well as bold, neither the writer nor the recipient had any delusions. Both knew that Parliament's small appropriation, coupled with Trustee action in denying funds for Georgia's military needs, left the fate of the colony in one man's hands.

Even the new regiment would soon crumble if men were not paid promptly and provided with essential gear and weapons. Because Oglethorpe's 42nd Regiment of Foot was a unit of the British Army, costs linked with its maintenance would come from the treasury — often months late, but certain to arrive. In the case of the vital colonial rangers and the equally essential program of expanding fortifications, there was no sure money either from the treasury or from Trustees.

Chapter 11

"WE MUST STRIKE FIRST;
THE BEST DEFENSE IS ATTACK".

January, 1739 — July, 1740

John Paris, attorney for the Georgia Trust, requested a hearing on Wednesday, January 10. To his chagrin he found only five men present when he went to the Georgia office. Oglethorpe's return to the colony, with severe restrictions placed upon his actions, had precipitated a colonial crisis. A letter just received from New York gave particulars about far-away events four months earlier.

Georgia's founder called a mass meeting of colonists on October 16, 1738, according to the report. He advised his followers that "it cut him to the heart to be obliged to tell them that he had the Trustees' order to shut up the stores," or put all supplies under lock and key. Ignoring the central role formally assigned to Stephens, the founder of Georgia took personal charge. No one could any longer expect to receive subsistence from the Trust, he told stunned listeners. Even worse, everyone indebted to the Trust for supplies would be required "to give bond to the Trustees for repayment."

Oglethorpe's conduct seemed cold and heartless from the distance of London. Yet the handful of Trustees who first learned of his actions could hardly criticize him. They had cut off his spending power.

Matters were sure to become worse before becoming better. With the fate of Georgia hanging in the balance during increasingly-hostile Anglo-Spanish diplomatic talks, Parliament was in no mood to continue to fund the colony. Even though Oglethorpe had been

160

present to push for it, the 1738 appropriation of £8,000 was voted with reluctance. It was barely adequate for necessities of civilian life. No one could predict whether Walpole would agree to any funds at all in 1739.

On the heels of receiving from second-hand sources a report about harsh actions by their colleague, Trustees had a letter from Oglethorpe himself. Penned in Savannah on October 19, it began on a negative note. Because storekeeper-magistrate Causton had been charged with mishandling of goods and accounts, Oglethorpe had demanded an inventory. From it, he told fellow Trustees, "You will see how small the remains of the vast stores laid in are, and how insufficient [they are for support of the colony] to midsummer."

Causton, whom Oglethorpe had trusted and to whom he had delegated much authority, remained under investigation. Threatened with arrest, he begged for mercy. Since there was no way to arrive at a quick accounting of money and goods he had handled, Georgia's founder decided to defer final action until he had more information.[1] Trustees, he suggested, should make up their minds to offer fractional payments on all debts — hoping for more money from the treasury.

"I can see nothing but destruction to the colony," said Oglethorpe's October report, "unless some assistance be immediately sent us. I support things for a while by some money I have in my hands . . . and the rest I supply with my own money."

There it was — starkly simple when reduced to a few lines of black marks upon white paper. No longer simply risking his life and giving years of unpaid leadership, the master of Westbrook manor had entered upon a course from which there was no turning back. Compared with moving toward laying his entire fortune upon the line, his initial folly in making a hasty and ill-prepared departure for Georgia was of small magnitude. This time he was being pushed into total commitment to what anyone with an ounce of sense could recognize as a hopeless cause.[2]

Before the full import of Oglethorpe's decision had been digested by fellow Trustees, they received other highly disturbing news. Many of the regulars drafted from Gibraltar into the new 42nd Regiment of Foot were malcontents. They expected extra pay and rations for the time spent on the sea. When one delay followed another, some of these men formed a plot. At Fort Saint Andrews on Cumberland island in November, they launched a full-scale mutiny.

One of the leaders took their colonel's head as his target. He fired from such short range that Oglethorpe's uniform was singed, but the bullet missed its mark and went through Oglethorpe's periwig. According to a contemporary account that circulated in Carolina, a second mutineer "presented his piece" aimed at his colonel, but powder flashed in the pan of his musket without firing. "A third drew his hanger and attempted to stab him," but Oglethorpe parried the weapon's thrust.

Captain Hugh Mackay, who had rushed to his defense, received a flesh wound. Seizing the musket that had misfired, Oglethorpe used it as a club and threatened to brain any man who stepped within reach. Then he shouted an offer to pardon every man who would disperse, and a threat to shoot any who refused to do so.

Awed by their commander who had emerged from the fray unscathed, mutineers broke ranks. A search revealed 25 loaded muskets, ready for use. Oglethorpe spent a few minutes with each mutineer on an individual basis. He promised, and — presumably from his own pocket — promptly delivered the delinquent pay. Carolina leaders attributed this near-tragedy to a villainous soldier "who had so much of a Roman Catholic spirit as to harbour an aversion to Protestant heretics." This man, they insisted, was corrupted by the Spanish. Had the mutiny succeeded, he would have led his companions in an escape to the safety of Saint Augustine.[3]

On the heels of this disturbing news Trustees received a formal petition of complaint. Drawn up in Savannah on December 9 and signed by 121 freeholders, it presented two central demands. Settlers wanted a new system of land tenure by which they'd get full title. Along with that they insisted upon "the use of Negroes with proper limitations." Both issues were crucial, declared petitioners. Because of them, during the preceding two years not more than two or three persons other than those brought on charity and servants lent to the colony by Trustees had come to Georgia either as settlers or as tradesmen. Language of the document was respectful, but its central demand was clear: Trustees must show some flexibility, or colonists would begin to think of taking matters into their own hands.[4] If soldiers could mutiny, civilians could rebel.

Along with word of Oglethorpe's near tragedy and a thinly veiled ultimatum from colonists, harried Trustees received yet another bulletin that had been dispatched months earlier. They must spare no effort to secure from Parliament a minimum of £17,000, urged Georgia's founder. Such a sum, Oglethorpe estimated, would meet a portion of the immediate pressing needs: £8,000 in debts largely run up by Causton, £5,000 for urgent civilian needs plus presents to Indians, and £12,000 for military needs.

It was in this context that the member from Haslemere voiced such confidence in Parliament that he promised to pay all essential expenses from his own pocket until a new appropriation was voted.

News from Spain reached England much more promptly than did bulletins from Georgia. Still the day-to-day progress of negotiations under way at El Pardo was not known until long afterward. Georgia Trustees asked British leaders to stand firm on the boundary question, but got no news about it. It appeared that general discussions were moving toward a peaceful solution of international issues. In this climate Oglethorpe's colleagues won Walpole's support of a bill designed to fund the colony for yet another year.

Some Trustees were suspicious. They feared that the prime minister's assent on this issue was gained at the cost of grave concessions concerning the future of Georgia. Without their knowledge, Walpole had indeed sent stern instructions to Oglethorpe. He was ordered to respect whatever boundary line might be fixed by joint commissioners from Britain and Spain.

Several Georgia leaders were tired of the struggle. At least four who were once firm supporters of the experiment concurred that surrender of the colony would be a small price to pay for peace.

As formally promulgated in March, the Convention of El Prado seemed to solve nearly all major issues except that of the Georgia-Florida boundary and the extent to which British vessels could move into Spanish waters without search and seizure. These two matters plus the British right to cut logwood in Campeachy Bay were to be settled by additional negotiations. Both England and Spain agreed to accept decisions of arbitrators as final. Spain promised to pay £95,000 in reparations for damage done to English shipping.

Spain's King Philip V, now hopelessly mad, was a figurehead only. His greedy and ambitious second wife, Elizabeth Farnese, made the major policy decisions. She saw free navigation by the British and exemption from search as possible threats to the power of her sons, so balked at approving these conditions. Soon her ministers began sending out signals indicating that the promised £95,000 might not be paid. This turn of events was sufficient to fuel the already-strong popular British sentiment for war. Newcastle, in his role as secretary of state, now put himself on record as believing "it will be pretty difficult to give up Georgia." An enthusiastic

Parliament voted a new appropriation for the colony in the amount of £20,000 — nearly three times that of the previous year.

Months were required for Parliament's action, treasury transactions, and the start of flow of funds to Georgia. During this period Oglethorpe continued to finance the colony.[5] Regardless of what others might think, he knew that tensions with the Spanish would soon lead to war. He must act decisively and spare no expense. "If we do not attack, we shall be attacked," he wrote to his friend and business associate William Bull, now lieutenant-governor of South Carolina. He had no intention of standing by and waiting for the Spanish initiative. It was imperative that British forces strike first, he told Bull.

Upon receiving word of Parliament's 1739 appropriation, he sent Trustees one of his longest and most detailed reports. Writing from Frederica on July 4, on the eve of a long-planned departure for a parley with leaders of strong Indian tribes, he explained why it was impossible fully to account for his expenditures.

He also said that he could not in honesty support changes in land tenure, for which there was growing support among Trustees. Existing titles are adequate, he insisted, "and those who made most noise about their lands are those who have taken no care to make use of them." As he frequently did, Georgia's founder signed this lengthy dispatch — wholly unsatisfactory to Trustees in London — as "Gentlemen, your most obedient, humble servant."

General of the colonial forces James Edward Oglethorpe, who was never humble and seldom obedient, consulted neither Trustees nor Britain's secretary of state concerning his next move. For practical purposes he acted as though he had never received from the secretary of state a special dispatch. In it Newcastle bluntly told Oglethorpe to cease his fretting. Both Spain and England had agreed to suspend preparations for war, he said. Peace was just around the corner.

Oglethorpe regarded this message as nonsense. War was only a matter of time. If he was to take the offensive, it was essential to use existing Indian allies and to persuade more native Americans to join his forces.

From the beginning of his New World career the man who commanded a hearing any time he spoke to bewigged English lawmakers had proved acutely sensitive to attitudes and wishes of American Indians. Tomochichi, Toonahowi, and other members of coastal tribes often accompanied him upon inland waterways. He followed Indians along forest trails and became so adept that he did not need to rely upon blazed trees to stay on the path.

Very early he began pressing to have testimony of native Americans admitted as evidence in colonial courts. Though he lost that fight, many Indians knew that it had been waged and respected him for it. In his first formal address made on Georgia soil, he urged pioneer colonists to respect native Americans. It was imperative, he insisted, that his followers conduct themselves so that "the settlement of Georgia may prove a blessing and not a curse to the native inhabitants."

In his role as commissioner for Indian affairs, he took it upon himself to speak for his king and for his empire. Runners were sent to leaders of powerful tribes whose hunting ranges lay west of the region now functioning as the Colony of Georgia. At Oglethorpe's request they agreed to meet him at Coweta. This principal town of the Lower Creeks lay on the Chattahoochee river; the overland trail to it snaked hundreds of miles from Frederica. Mary Musgrove, halfbreed wife of a trader and a minor princess who played a major role in Trustee era Georgia, was born there.

Capt. George Dunbar, Ensign John Lemon, and a hand-picked band of about 25 Europeans and Indians made the long and dangerous trip with Oglethorpe. Once they spotted smoke which was found to come from a fire made by a party of Spanish horsemen. After fording many streams, including the Ogeechee, they made contact with Creek representatives in early August. First at Coweta and then at nearby Cusseta, formal treaties of peace were proclaimed after several days spent in talking and exchanging gifts. Chislacaliche, most powerful of the Creeks, assented to every provision in the pact and put his influence behind extension of it to tribes not represented in the parley.

Oglethorpe's estimates of Indian strength had been far too high. Upper and Lower Creeks, combined, had only about 2,500 warriors. But their ties with leaders of other tribes were intimate. He could hope for some help from the Cherokees, Choctaws, and Chickasaws.

Subsidiary to his urgent military needs and almost incidental at the time, Georgia's founder asked for a formal transfer of title to vast tracts of land. Though he did not know it, long-range impact of this cession by treaty was destined to be greater than that of Indian military aid to the swashbuckling soldier-of-fortune. In a fashion unique among British colonies in North America, Georgia gained legal hold of one-time Indian land. Moreover, it was done by amicable means and not by conquest. Decades later Oglethorpe's work at Coweta proved an effective barrier to prevent Georgia from being joined to Carolina, as some British leaders wished. Had there

Oglethorpe's principal Carolina holdings

This 1757 map of part of South Carolina and Georgia was issued by Britain's surveyor-general for the colonies. Drawn to precise scale, it identifies (in a separate panel) owners of numbered lots. One small lot known to have been owned by Oglethorpe is not listed on the map.

Miniature numbers of lots that appear on the original are here enlarged for readability; sizes of lots and location of Oglethorpe's ferry have been added to the original.

been no pow-wow at Coweta, there is no certainty that a State of Georgia ever would have come into being.[6]

Though weak from fever, Oglethorpe reached Fort Augusta just ten days after concluding his treaty with the Indians. Too ill to make the most of his first visit to the post far up the Savannah river, he got up from his bed to receive a delegation of Cherokees.

Shortly afterward, on September 9, an agreeement was signed with the Cherokees. This pact may have been concluded on Oglethorpe's own land near Fort Prince George, or Palachacola. This old and important outpost lay on the Carolina side of the Savannah, and guarded the most important ford on the river.

Oglethorpe presented customary gifts to the Cherokees, promised them a substantial shipment of grain, and got from them a pledge to provide 600 fighting men. He reached Savannah in mid-September and found the town buzzing. News brought by way of Rhode Island indicated that a sudden change of policy in London had brought Britain to the verge of war with Spain. An otherwise unidentified packet, the *Tartar Pink*, said to be bearer of official tidings, was believed to be headed for Charles Town and Savannah. In this climate, problems that had created mounting internal dissension would simply have to wait. It was no longer important that Thomas Stephens, son of William, had already sailed for London in order to lodge formal complaints about Georgia's sorry state.

Unofficial word of Anglo-Spanish hostilities was good enough for Georgia's founder. After all, under date of June 15, King George II had suggested that he "annoy the Subjects of Spain" in whatever fashion he could. To Oglethorpe, the sovereign's almost-casual proposal, just received, became an order that must be obeyed.

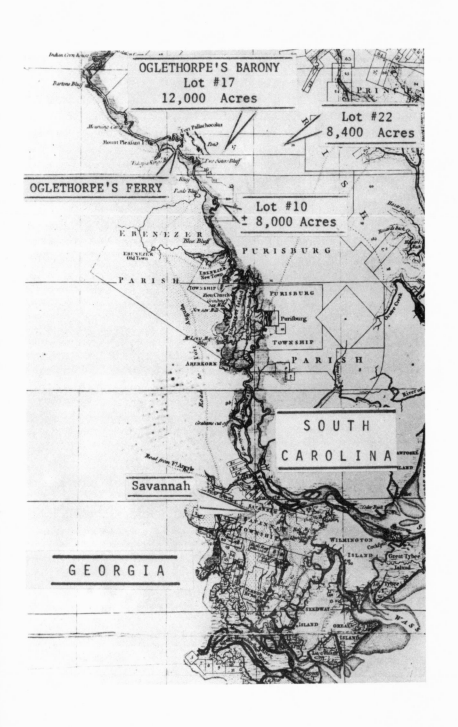

Oglethorpe estimated that 200 men in Savannah were able to bear arms. All of them plus freeholders unable to be of military service were ordered to assemble on October 3 "at beat of drum." Savannah's magistrates were told to be at the court house, in their gowns, at noon. When the hour arrived five cannon were fired; the militia "gave three handsome volleys with their small Arms," and at Oglethorpe's direction William Stephens read to the assembly a statement of declaration of war against Spain.

Meanwhile, Rhode Island's governor was said to be busy. He was signing commissions authorizing privateers to hit any Spanish targets they might choose.

In rushing toward conflict, Spanish-hater Oglethorpe had followed the dictates of his heart rather than his head. Reports about the *Tartar Pink* and her intelligence were unfounded rumors. Britain did not declare war upon Spain until 16 days after Oglethorpe's announcement. Spain's declaration of war upon Britain followed on November 28.[7] In Carolina, leaders reluctant to face the possibility of invasion from the south made no public announcement of the existence of a state of war until late in April, 1740.

Tomochichi's death, a few days after Oglethorpe's statement of intentions concerning Spain, meant the loss of one of his most trusted allies.[8] Increasing reliance was placed upon Mary Musgrove, who became a confidante as well as interpreter.

Indians were to prove more valuable as scouts and trackers than as warriors. Their most significant aid, aside from that provided by formal cession of land, came unplanned. Georgia's founder spent so much time with native Americans that he ceased to think in terms of the stiffly-formal military tactics still prevalent in Europe and began to operate as a guerilla fighter.

His plan to take the initiative against enemies to the south had Saint Augustine as a central objective. Its capture would leave his foes without a major fortified base on the North American mainland. But in order to take the city he must have help from Carolina — men, money, guns, and supplies.

Months of planning and preparation, punctuated by frequent trips to Charles Town, saw slow progress toward assembling a force strong enough to move toward Florida. Oglethorpe's initial estimate of needs from Carolina included £139,000 (colonial).[9] Repeatedly trimmed, and debated at length each time a bill was introduced into the Assembly, the request was at a standstill in March. Oglethorpe offered to lend Carolina £4,000 — equivalent to more than £30,000, colonial — at 8% interest, but the offer was rejected.[10]

While Carolina debated and wavered, Oglethorpe acted. With a small force he made a quick raid into Florida and captured two small outposts of little strategic significance. Still this was hailed as a great victory; it proved that the Spanish were not invincible. Carolina eventually provided a fraction of the men and money originally requested. They were placed at Oglethorpe's disposal so late that his original timetable for the campaign against Saint Augustine could not be followed. Delay permitted reinforcement by Spanish forces from Cuba — and made weather a major variable.

Colonial troops had no funds except those made available by Oglethorpe. Even the pay, provisions, and gear for British regulars often arrived months in arrears. Under date of April 2, Oglethorpe drew up an instrument giving accountant Harman Verelst full power of attorney. Using it, Verelst was to raise from every possible source every available pound. He could pledge all of Oglethorpe's possessions, real and intangible, to money lenders or to Sir Robert Walpole or both.

Georgia Trustee the Earl of Egmont penned a *Diary* entry that is the classic understatement of the 2400-page record. Oglethorpe's rash action, he observed, constituted "A real instance of zeal for his country!"[11]

Years afterward a disastrous fire at Westbrook manor destroyed many of Oglethorpe's personal records and papers. This loss, coupled with confiscation and chaos in the colonies during and after the American Revolution, makes it impossible precisely to determine what New World assets Oglethorpe laid on the line along with his British holdings.

Georgia's charter prohibited Trustees from owning land in the colony or deriving a profit from it. Oglethorpe seems never to have questioned this provision. In his philanthropic zeal during precharter months, it would have been completely in character for him to have drafted this stipulation.

Yet for Sir Theophilus' soldier-of-fortune youngest son, it was also in character to seek to get ahead in any way he honorably could. Clauses in Georgia's charter obviously did not apply to Carolina. That was the basis of Oglethorpe's secret agreement with Purry, whose conditional patent entitled him to four Carolina tracts of 12,000 acres each. Had he received all of these grants, his contract with Oglethorpe would have entitled Georgia's founder to 12,000 acres across the Savannah river.

Purry gained only a fraction of the land tentatively set aside for

him. But by means unknown Oglethorpe gained big tracts in
additon to at least two lots that he purchased. William Stephens was
surprised and alarmed when he discovered that Georgia's founder
held a barony of 12,000 acres in Carolina.[12] From Stephens or some
other informant, long-time Oglethorpe foe James Vernon heard of
this grant — but apparently did not know the full truth.[13]

William DeBrahm, surveyor-general of the Province of South
Carolina, issued in 1757 a map showing Oglethorpe's barony as
consisting of 12,000 acres. It lay on the north bank of the Savannah
river, just east of Purrysburg, S.C., at old Fort Prince George — or
Palachacola. An adjoining tract of 8,400 acres also belonged to
him.[14]

In addition to these large pieces of land, Oglethorpe secured by
purchase or by grant a lot of 2,060 acres "in the southernmost
extent of the Township of Purresbourgh."[15] His good friend
William Bull transferred to him a tract of 5,356 acres north of the
same settlement.[16] Probably by reason of a change of course by the
Savannah river, the last-mentioned lot measured about 8,000 acres
when DeBrahm's map was issued.

With these strategically-located holdings in Oglethorpe's hands,
he persuaded Andrew Rutledge to bring a special bill before the
South Carolina Assembly. After considerable debate, legislators
agreed to establishment of a ferry "near the Palla Chuckellas on the
land of the Honorable General James Oglethorpe." All rights in the
ferry were vested in Oglethorpe, his heirs and assigns, for a period
of 14 years.[17]

Location of the ferry was governed by the fact that it lay along a
famous old trail. An overland journey from Charles Town to Saint
Augustine required that the Savannah river be crossed precisely
here. It was the only spot within 100 miles where horses could swim
the river during some seasons.[18]

Land aside, the champion of the dispossessed and the fighter for
imperial Britain may have augmented his personal fortune from
commercial ventures. Trustee John Laroche heard that merchants
of Bristol were furious with Oglethorpe. According to reports
relayed to Laroche, Georgia's founder had "turn'd Merchant," and
had managed to gain a monopoly in the deerskin trade by paying
one shilling per hundredweight above the established price.[19] If
that accusation was valid, it meant that Oglethorpe had tremendous
potential for profit. In 1731 the annual flow of deerskins to England
from the Carolina country was estimated at 200,000.[20]

About 90% of this vast commerce flowed into Augusta, then

down the Savannah river. Deerskins usually went into big, clumsy river boats with cargo capacity of about 9,000 pounds.[21] Whether or not he actually exploited it for personal gain, Oglethorpe clearly did have the means to control this valuable trade. Each 9,000-pound shipment from Fort Augusta, valued at £12,000 to £15,000, had to pass the spot designated for Oglethorpe's ferry at Palachcola.[22]

With so many major interests holding so much promise for the future, did Georgia's founder sometimes toy with the notion of spending the rest of his life in the colonies?

One letter suggests that such might have been the case. Early in 1736 a contingent of Highlanders sent to Georgia by the Trustees included one McBane. He travelled extensively with Oglethorpe in the interior, and made one trip to Britain in an attempt to secure additional Scots as servants for the colony. A letter of March 29, 1738, from McBane to Oglethorpe, fell into the hands of Trustees. According to it the Scot had recently "been in the Cherickee nation, *where his Mr. Oglethorpe's house was going on.*"[23]

This was the more remarkable because Oglethorpe had insisted on staying in a tent in Savannah for years after houses became available. McBane's thinly-veiled implication that Oglethorpe sometimes played the role of squaw-man can neither be proved nor disproved.

Clearly, however, Oglethorpe the philanthropist had an alter-ego — a soldier-of-fortune who made the most of every opportunity whether in the colonies or in Britain. After a number of years during which he prospered in the New World, this "unknown Oglethorpe" made the most daring move of his career.

What Egmont called "a real instance of zeal for his country" was also the action of a high-stakes gambler. With no certainty that he would ever be repaid, he put everything he had on the line.[24] Earlier he had risked his life and his career.

Naturally he expected others to follow his lead, even if at a safe distance. They did not. Trustees continued to balk and to carp. England's leaders did not dispatch the naval and land forces needed for a quick victory in Florida. South Carolina trimmed her financial support and manpower.

Even Indian allies who had been eager to accept Oglethorpe's gifts failed him now. Instead of 2,000 native American warriors, his forces included only about 200. Since one-third of the men in his own regiment were needed for garrison duty in Georgia, he had less than 400 regulars with whom to attack seasoned Spanish veterans. Colonial rangers and short-term recruits from Carolina reported in

small numbers. Commanders of British warships in southern
waters had been told to heed his instructions. Yet, very early, they
bluntly informed him that their vessels would be leaving Florida
before the beginning of the hurricane season.

Under such circumstances the long-planned attack would have
been launched only by an extremely rash or a very stubborn
commander.

Oglethorpe was both.

Troop movement began in May but was sporadic from the first.
Oglethorpe himself displayed indecision not associated with him
before or afterward. After crossing the Saint John's river he and his
men spent time and energy in futile marches that were designed to
show his strength and to frighten the Spanish into easy submission.

Some officers urged an immediate assault upon Saint Augustine.
Oglethorpe shook his head. In a victory of no consequence, Fort
Mosa was captured and occupied. Meanwhile reinforcements
reached Saint Augustine from Cuba. Suddenly made bold, the
Spanish took the initiative and re-captured Fort Mosa.

British warships were unable to maintain an effective blockade;
their shelling of land bases was ineffective. Saint Augustine, Oglethorpe ruefully concluded, was too heavily fortified to make a target
for a frontal attack by land. Perhaps the city could be starved into
submission.

Besieged for about three weeks, the oldest city in North America
showed no signs of weakening. Food and water remained in good
supply, and only a few Spanish soldiers fell in combat. July 5 would
see British warships sail away in order to avoid the hurricane
season. Twenty-four hours before scheduled departure of
warships, the man who for years had itched for a show-down fight
ordered the siege abandoned.

Judged by any standard, the costly foray into Spanish Florida
was a debacle. There had been no significant military engagement,
but Oglethorpe and his forces were clearly bested. Long hostile
toward the Georgia leader, many Carolina spokesmen were now
furious at the outcome of his elaborate invasion. No more help of
any kind could be expected from the wealthy old colony.[25] Manuel
de Montiano, Governor of Florida, spoke for many in Carolina and
in Britain when he said of Oglethorpe's invasion: "I cannot arrive at
a comprehension of the conduct, or rules of this [British] General
[from Georgia]. "[26]

Now it was only a matter of time before the enemy would take
the offensive. Soon the struggle would be carried into Georgia
waters and to Georgia soil. Attacking forces would be met by

poorly-equipped fighting men whose commander -in-chief was physically ill from failure, and whose inherited fortune plus hard-won Carolina holdings appeared to be lost.

Launched under a cloud and with a series of challenges, James Oglethorpe's once-brilliant career appeared to be over, and the colony to which he had given so much seemed doomed.

Chapter 12

"THANK THE LORD, AND RAISE
ANOTHER REGIMENT!"

July, 1740 — July, 1743

Bone tired and weak from fever,[1] a listless and dis-spirited James Edward Oglethorpe retired to his cottage on Saint Simons island. His only home in Georgia, complete with a garden and 50 acres of land, it belonged to the Trust but he had the use of it as long as he wished. At least for now, he preferred it to his Savannah refuge. Widow Overend's home at #1 Jekyll Tithing had been a frequent haven as late as February.[2] To use it now would require him to receive a stream of visitors — who would be about as welcome as swarms of gnats and mosquitoes.

Defeat weighed even more heavily upon him than did physical effects of the disastrous Florida campaign. As he was prone to do whenever he entered a period of enforced idleness, Georgia's founder planned, plotted, schemed, took stock . . . and remembered. Some nights he paced the floor for· hours at a time, pausing at intervals in order nervously to wipe the persiration from his face.

He had dreamed big dreams. England's dispossessed would find a haven in the colony that, more than any other man, he had planned and shaped. While lifting themselves by their own boostraps, they would enrich Britain.

Now many of the English charity colonists had given up the struggle. More were restless, hoping to flee before the start of certain invasion from the south. From a peak population of about

174

5,000 Georgia had dwindled to little more than 500 civilians. Only the Germans were quiet, determined, prosperous, and dependable. They made poor militiamen, but ideal settlers. Thank God for the Germans!

Savannah, once constantly echoing to the sounds of saws and hammers, was virtually deserted. John Wesley's bitter prophecy was impossible to forget. Had not the clergyman prophesied that the town would revert to its pre-Oglethorpe status as "a settlement of oppossums, raccoons, and like inhabitants"?

Partly because of the manner in which Oglethorpe's physical presence caused followers to converge upon any place he stayed, Frederica was now half as large as Savannah. But once-powerful Darien's population had dropped well below 100. When the Spanish came — as come, they surely would — they would find few flourishing farms to ravage. Most of the houses they would seize would be empty, with their doors swaying idly in the wind.

Even in the decimated colony, radicals, malcontents, and trouble-makers were plentiful enough. Thomas Stephens, son of the Trustee-appointed chief civil officer of the colony, was ring-leader among them. Whenever a mental image of Stephens' face appeared in imagination, Oglethorpe's eyes blazed with indignaion. Dr. Patrick Tailfer and his cohorts were little if any better. Individually and collectively, they were determined to make trouble for Georgia in general and for Oglethorpe in particular. To compound the problem, these were not soft-spined charity colonists; most of them were men of substance and education, who would not quickly quit their carping.

There was one remaining bright spot in the Georgia picture. Very early, the Rev. George Whitefield had envisioned an institution to care for destitute and homeless children. He announced plans for an orphan house when he had no assets except a plot of ground assigned by Trustees. Yet he managed to lay a cornerstone in March, 1740.

Destined to become America's first orphanage, Bethesda was funded by means of Whitefield's whirlwind visits to New York, Philadelphia, and other long-established centers. Under the golden tongue of the impassioned evangelist, even tough old Benjamin Franklin had softened and had emptied his pockets into the passing hat. Whitefield had renewed Oglethorpe's faith in the clergy — faith so badly battered by his dealings with the brothers Wesley.

For more than 60 days Oglethorpe remained in seclusion. He received few visitors and brooded constantly.

Bethesda orphanage, Savannah

Money collected by George Whitefield in northern cities funded the erection of America's first orphanage, Bethesda. The first brick was laid on March 25, 1740.

Time after time, he took stock of his personal situation. No wonder his enemies had openly called him a fool, and his closest friends had used the label behind his back. Look at the investment... Most of his time and energy during a full decade dedicated to planning, launching, and then trying to defend Georgia... Not just once, but several times, he had narrowly escaped death ... no real military advancement of permanent significance; though habitually addressed both in person and in writing as "General," the title would mean nothing when he quit the colony ... His all-important seat in Parliament was becoming harder and harder to retain, and much more expensive. From a distance of 3,000 miles it was difficult to hold even those voters who resided in his own properties, where rents were deliberately kept at a low level.

Remembering his youthful vision of amassing a great fortune in order to restore splendor to the family name, Oglethorpe sometimes gave a dry audible laugh that echoed through the empty house. When he pledged everything in order to fund Georgia's military build-up, he expected easy victory and quick reimbursement. Now, sick from failure as much as from fever, he knew that he had no choice. If he expected ever to recoup anything, he'd have to win. That would not be possible without continuing pay for rangers, purchase of more boats, tons of provisions for fighting men, and presents plus weapons for Indians.

Already he was at least £15,000 in debt — perhaps £25,000.[3] Never good at keeping accounts, he didn't know precisely how much he owed. Even if he'd had exact details at his fingertips, he wouldn't have dared to commit everything to a letter — there was too much danger of interception by foes. But the very thought of trying to retain possession of Westbrook manor while staving off creditors brought beads of cold sweat to his feverish forehead. Often his hands and feet tingled in a fashion that no medicine would relieve. If he didn't borrow another shilling, interest on his debt would be an intolerable burden for the rest of his life.

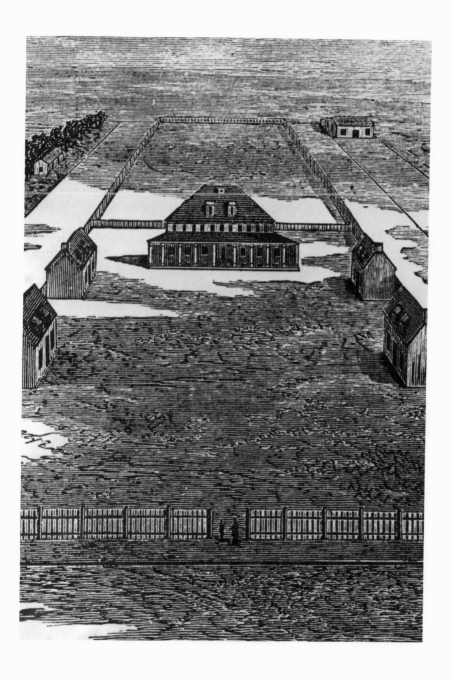

In his least lucid intervals he remembered suspicions voiced by
Col. Cecil, one of his agents. Prior to 1740 Cecil had wondered
whether Britain's leaders might want his employer to stay in
Georgia because "it was designed to sacrifice him."[4] Could that now
be true?

There was but one hope of redeeming his folly: accleration of his
pace on the path to ruin. Spain must be stopped, whatever the cost.

In occasional tranquil hours, Oglethorpe realized that he was
bordering upon lunacy. He knew, intellectually, that it was not
rational for him to spot a Spaniard under every bush — yet he
couldn't avoid seeing them. Beyond a shadow of a doubt, one of
their agents had gotten to Thomas Stephens and had corrupted
him. Catastrophic fires in New York and in Charles Town were
clearly the work of malcontents who had gone over to the Spanish
cause. Philip V and his minions were plotting, Oglethorpe was sure,
to trigger new and more violent revolts among the blacks of
Carolina. Savannah's mutinous temper, fomented by the unseen
but ever-present enemy, represented but one phase of Spain's
"scheme for raising a general disturbance through all North
America."[5]

Near-paranoid though Georgia's founder was, there were
plenty of sound reasons to fear the future. Swarming northward
from Caribbean bases, Spanish privateers terrorized colonists from
Georgia to New York. Captured vessels were taken to Spanish
waters at an incredible rate. More than 30 English prizes went to
Saint Augustine, alone, during the year that ended in August, 1741.
Even plantations well removed from sea lanes were not safe. Some
distance inland from Jekyll island, Carr's holdings — though
protected by soldiers — were overrun and sacked. Other known
forays upon the mainland included bloody assaults upon several
North Carolina villages.[6]

Bulletins plus rumors from overseas overshadowed domestic
news that otherwise would have been of first importance. Long-
smoldering resentment had finally led to a determined move to oust
Britain's prime minister. Though he was a weak supporter of
Georgia and had shown himself ready to make peace at any price,
Walpole at least represented stability. No one was sure who was
most likely to be his successor, or what positions a new prime
minister would take on heated issues.

Stung by criticism from Parliament, Georgia Trustees had
prepared a formal report. In the propaganda warfare that was
mounting in intensity, critics of Oglethorpe and of Georgia were

issuing booklets like mad. Prominent Georgia settlers who had fled to Charles Town already had in the printing press a polemic entitled *A True and Historical Narrative of the Colony of Georgia in America.* Thomas Stephens was at work on *The Hard Case of the Distressed People of Georgia,* while preparing to take his case to London and the king.

Printed counter-blasts included Benjamin Martyn's *An Impartial Enquiry into the State and Utility of the Province of Georgia* — ostensibly a private undertaking by one Trustee, who was anything but impartial. Decidedly more official in nature but still not bearing Trustee imprint, *An Account Shewing the Progress of the Colony of Georgia in America from its First Establishment* was years out of date when issued. It stopped with the arrival of the *Ann* in Georgia, and did not so much as mention internal or external troubles of the colony in turbulent months of the early 1740's.

Beseeching Trustees to support his pleas to Britain's ministry, Oglethorpe had in June warned that "without any new succors from Europe we are ravaged." It was too early to expect even a reply, to say nothing of action. No one could predict what might happen in the volatile political climate at home. Many members of Parliament had nodded vigorous assent when Sir John Cotton had urged that for the sake of peace, Port Royal in the Carolina colony should be made the southern boundary of Britain's domains in North America.

At the risk of being ravaged, Oglethorpe intended to make his weight felt. Spain might indeed conquer if help did not come soon — but he could make her victory costly. At his own expense Oglethorpe doubled his rate of purchase of arms, ammunition, stores of war, and naval stores. Again from his pocket, he paid to triple the size of garrisons at Fort Augusta, Mount Pleasant, Fort Argyll, and other outposts. Not knowing when or even whether he would be repaid, he boosted the flow of purchases for Indians plus soldiers on active duty from £2,516 per year to £6,979.

His fears were well founded; his actions were taken just in time. October, 1741, brought secret orders from Madrid to Havana. Cuba's governor was commanded to assemble a mighty fleet and a powerful land force for an invasion designed to crush Georgia quickly, then move leisurely into Carolina.

Some of Britain's leaders were sure that Oglethorpe exaggerated wildly. Others half believed him but thought Georgia's loss would be a small price to pay for peace. As chancellor of the exchequer, Walpole had authorized Oglethorpe to draw upon the treasury for military expenses — a policy he subsequently changed without

A typical 18th-century battle

European warfare was stiffly formal, and followed unwritten but elaborate rules

As late as the closing decades of the 18th century, civilized soldiers fought according to unwritten but elaborate codes.

A typical battle of the era was as carefully orchestrated as a ballet — to whose movements it bore some resemblance. Depicted here is the battle of Dvina, in 1701.

notifying the Georgia leader. Domestic cost of the colony was becoming intolerable; to fund a sinking ship was to throw good money after bad.

That is why Parliament's 1741 appropriation for Georgia was sliced to £10,000. In 1742, for the first time since lawmakers had assumed partial responsibility for the colony, there was no appropriation at all.[7]

Yet the southernmost of Britain's North American holdings had already received more money from the treasury than any other colony. Charles Town suffered a catastrophic fire on November 18, 1740, with losses estimated at £250,000. Pleas from Carolina leaders and staunch friends at home brought Georgia's neighbor a mere £20,000 in relief funds.

Oglethorpe found it hard to comprehend that military aid was as difficult to get as was financial aid. To imperial Britain, the southern colonies and their defense was inconsequential — when viewed against the background of Anglo-Spanish conflict in many waters. Admiral Edward Vernon's already-powerful force was augmented by 12,500 additional troops. He assembled a fleet such as the New World had seldom seen. After an initial victory in Jamaica, he failed even to attempt to capture Havana. Vernon turned aside from Havana in order to attack a secondary target, Santiago, where he suffered a humiliating defeat. That left the Caribbean a safe haven for Spanish warships and privateers, a logical staging-point for the long-awaited assault upon the mainland.

Governor Manuel de Montiano of Florida commanded the invading forces. In size and fire power his vessels ranged from men-o-war to piraguas and other small boats. His force of at least 3,000 men included a regiment of dragoons — equipped with bridles and saddles for use upon British horses they expected to capture.

Except for a small band of horsemen recruited in Virginia at his expense, Oglethorpe got no help. Still angry over the Saint Augustine fiasco and absorbed with her merchants' attempts to gain indemnification for their losses linked with that campaign, Carolina ignored Oglethorpe's pleas. His long-time ally William Bull, now at the head of the colony in the role of lieutenant-governor, reported to the Duke of Newcastle that " 'Tis not expected that he [Oglethorpe] can long hold out against so great a force [as Spain has dispatched]."

Judged by objective military standards, Oglethorpe's subsequent actions were no longer foolhardy; they were suicidal. Not a single British man-o-war was at his disposal. His fighting force had dwindled below 1,000 — including Indians. He had only a few pieces of small artillery. Knowing himself to be vastly outnumbered, Georgia's founder slowly withdrew and destroyed his bases behind him. Saint Simons island was chosen for a stand. Here they would fight until the last man dropped.

Montiano effected a landing early in the evening of July 5, 1742. Meanwhile, Oglethorpe retreated to Frederica. About ten o'clock on July 7 scouts raced to the fortress with a warning that foes were within a mile of it. Georgia's defender reacted as though he did, indeed, harbor the "repressed death wish" that has been attributed to far more celebrated commanders.

According to an account penned at the time, Oglethorpe "leaped on the first horse" and personally led the Highland Company plus 60 guards and a few Indians in a suicidal attack. During hand-to-hand conflict in which he reveled "The General took two Spaniards with his own hands." When the Spanish advance-guard turned tail and fled, Oglethorpe "pursued the chase for near a mile."[8] Then he took action wholly out of character for a veteran of campaigns directed by the great strategist, Eugene of Savoy.

Long-established protocol of European conflict on land dictated that opposing commanders select a great open space upon which to deploy their troops in well-ordered ranks. After completing their preparations in full sight of their foes, men marched stiffly to the line of fire. Always maintaining the most precise formation possible, they fired, knelt for comrades in the next rank to fire, then wheeled and turned and fired again until the regiments of one body were thinned beyond further resistance.

Oglethorpe threw European military manuals out of the window. About five miles from Frederica he posted guards to the right and to the left of a narrow roadway that led along the side of a marshy savannah, or meadow. Then he deployed every man he could muster, sending them into the thick forest that bordered the meadow. In order to reach the Georgia advance guards, foes would have to make their way over a rough causeway of brush-plus-logs that swayed at every footstep.

Following tracks left by the English who were presumed to be in flight, Spanish troops were forced to defile at the edge of the marsh. A narrow column moved awkwardly forward. Suddenly Oglethorpe's sharpshooters opened fire. Concealed by brush and trees, only flashes from their weapons suggested their approximate positions. After pressing forward bravely for a few minutes the Spanish turned tail and fled. They withdrew too rapidly to stop for their own dead and wounded.

Measured by any standard, this was a minor skirmish. Yet it soon became fabled as the battle of Bloody Marsh. Very little Spanish and no English blood was shed; there were only a handful of casualties.[9] Yet the resort to guerilla warfare in lieu of fighting in traditional battle formation had done to Montiano what Saint Augustine's sturdy defenses had done to Oglethorpe. Unwilling to press forward, the Spanish commander considered giving up the campaign; he was under orders to return home with his command as nearly intact as possible.

While Montiano hesitated a French soldier slipped from Oglethorpe's ranks and deserted to the enemy. He had detailed information about troop strength and deployment, hence threatened to do the British cause much harm. So Oglethorpe, the perennial gambler, tried a risky stroke. He forged a letter that contained news of the impending arrival of relief forces, including ships of the line, and addressed it to the deserter. Then he released a Spanish prisoner on his oath that he would deliver the letter to the Frenchman, and no one else.

Oglethorpe had rightly counted upon the Spanish to search the man who was released. They found and read the fake letter and apparently believed it. Six days after Bloody Marsh their lookouts caught a glimpse of masts advancing at a distance. They belonged to the man-o-war *Flamborough*, which was accompanied only by two sloops and a galley. But sight of the approaching vessels confirmed the worst fears of Montiano — a major fleet of heavily-armed British warships was just over the horizon. In near panic he ordered hasty evacuation of Saint Simons island and a return to home bases in Florida and Cuba.

When the Rev. George Whitefield heard of what had happened, he marvelled. This great deliverance, he exulted, was like one of the mighty rescues described in the Old Testament. Others might credit luck or misunderstanding on the part of the Spanish; Whitefield and Oglethorpe were convinced that Almighty God had taken the side of the English.

Over and over, variations of the phrase, "God hath been our deliverance," ring through Oglethorpe's letters of the post-invasion period. Georgia's founder was deeply religious in a non-institutional fashion. While he voiced thanks to the Almighty, he interspersed these expressions with importunate cries to raise another regiment in order to be ready for the next encounter with foes of Georgia and of Britain.[10]

By January, 1743, there were subtle but significant changes in Oglethorpe's written pleas for more guns, new fighting units, and additional money with which to pay for defense. Writing to the Duke of Newcastle from Frederica, Georgia's founder asked the secretary of state to intercede with King George II, himself.

It was urgent, said Oglethorpe, that His Majesty be apprised of "the dangerous situation of these provinces." He must be made fully aware that all British North America, not merely young and weak Georgia, faced an impending "second Invasion from the Spaniards which is to be supported by the French." As an absolute minimum, Georgia's founder begged, "let a second Battalion be added to the [42nd] Regiment [of foot]."[11]

Acting without authorization, Oglethorpe stepped up the pace of his recruitment drive outside Georgia. For the year that began with victory at Bloody March, his out-of-pocket outlay for "levying men in Virginia, and of their Subsistence until Orders are given relating to them" sky-rocketed to £2,394.[12]

During periods of reverie, the founder of Georgia had for years envisioned himself as an 18th-century Sir Walter Raleigh. His copy of Raleigh's *Journal*, worn from frequent handling, gave no hint that the greatest of English colonizers had ever visited Georgia. But one thing that immediately attracted Oglethorpe to old Tomochichi was the Indian's chief's remarkable store of orally-transmitted lore. According to it, a Yamacraw who must have been an ancestor of Tomochichi had watched in awe as a very large vessel entered the Savannah river. A "great white Man with a red Beard" alighted from the vessel. He visited the Yamacraw village and delighted native Americans by demonstrating the use of talking leaves that transmitted messages.

Studious calculations by Oglethorpe, made within weeks of first setting foot on Yamacraw bluff, led him to conclude that Admiral Sir Walter Raleigh had spent some time on Georgia soil in 1584.[13]

Now he had no time to revel in past glory of Britain and her heroes. Neither could he devote attention to future advancement of his personal interests. Even the laws of Georgia, shaped by him, could not claim his full defense. When he learned that changes were in the air he fought to the bitter end. But he lost no sleep when he discovered that men he once called friends had made fundamental revisions in the colony's code. They repealed laws forbidding the importation of rum. They revised regulations dealing with the land system. They divided Georgia into two counties.

No matter. Existence of Georgia — and of all British North America — was teetering in the balance. Unless help came soon, combined Spanish-French forces would wipe Oglethorpe's colony from the map.

Goings-on in London by Thomas Stephens, reported in Georgia after many weeks, got little of Oglethorpe's time and interest. Supported by Robert Williams and Andrew Grant, the son of Georgia's chief civil administrator brought a humble petition to His Majesty. From the crown it soon reached Parliament, where the lawmaking body resolved itself into a committee of the whole in order to ponder testimony.

For a day or so it appeared that Parliament would take Georgia out of the hands of her Trustees. Testimony against Oglethorpe was particularly vitriolic and left him, in Egmont's words, "much bespattered." It was as a result of these hearings that Trustees made radical changes in land laws and relaxed restrictions upon use of rum. They did not, however, yield on the vital issue of slavery. This despite young Stephens' importunate insistence that "Nothing but Negroes will do to make this colony like Carolina."

Walpole put up a struggle but eventually fell from power. That left commons speaker Sir Arthur Onslow — re-chosen for the post in 1742 — temporarily the most influential man in Britain. His long-time friendship with Oglethorpe proved decisive. Largely through his personal influence, members who sat through days of blistering testimony ended by castigating Stephens. Oglethorpe's accuser was required, as an act of contrition, to come before the assembled house in June, 1743. Stephens bent upon one knee. "Both knees!" demanded Onslow, who forced him to remain in this position for a full half hour.[14]

Official vindication did nothing to strengthen Oglethorpe's

military position or to salve his wounds. But King George II, apparently without consulting his ministers, permanently altered the status of Georgia's founder. On February 17, 1743, he made Oglethorpe a brigadier-general in gratitude for "good service in repulsing the Spaniards."[15] Unlike the colonial commission, this one gave Sir Theophilus' son permanent military rank.

All who knew him well had come to realize that the philanthropic founder of a colony had long ago been displaced by the military commander. His unexpected boost in rank in the aftermath of Bloody Marsh put him in this respect, if in no other, above every earlier member of the Oglethorpe family.

Instead of improving, financial affairs of the member from Haslemere became more involved. In 1741 when his indebtedness incurred for the sake of Georgia was beginning to mount by the week, the son of his closest British friend chose to make a contest for the seat in Parliament long held by Oglethorpe.

Young Lord Percival estimated that the pocket borough represented by Oglethorpe had only 69 votes — of which Percival claimed 43 in advance. Perhaps without the knowledge of his father, the Earl of Egmont, Percival set out to buy the seat. He claimed that two attorneys who represented Oglethorpe's interests had been in the practice of "hawking the borough," or offering it for sale. Oglethorpe's agents and friends made a frantic last-ditch effort and managed to hold the seat for him — at a cost of £1,200, practically an entire year's income from all sources.[16] Even worse than the catastrophic bills run up by Oglethorpe's fourth political contest, it brought a permanent rift with Egmont — most influential Trustee who never saw Georgia.

Even before the election of 1741, Oglethorpe had been eager to return home to look after his personal affairs. Weighing alternatives, he had concluded that he must remain in the colony no matter how great the cost. Within a short time after learning of his military promotion, the question whether to go or to stay was taken out of his hands.

Lieutenant-Colonel William Cooke, for a time the officer next-in-command in Oglethorpe's regiment, had become extremely hostile during the Saint Augustine campaign. Pleading ill health, he got a 12-month leave of absence and used it to go to London. There he preferred 19 formal charges against his chief. High on the list was the allegation that Oglethorpe habitually defrauded his men "by making them pay for the provisions the Government sent them over gratis." In order to answer Cooke's charges, ruled the war office, it would be necessary for Oglethorpe to appear and testify in person.

About the same time the lords commissioners of the treasury received a deluge of complaints concerning bills of exchange drawn upon the government by Oglethorpe. Eventually, about £12,000 in such bills was disallowed. That meant he stood to lose the principal of these bills plus accrued interest, fees, and commissions. Had there been no preliminary preparation for a court-martial, Oglethorpe's own interests would have demanded that he quit Georgia once more in order to represent himself before the king, Parliament, and agencies of the government.

He had much unfinished business in the colony. Among other major items, he hoped soon to perfect his "grand scheme to unite all American Indians" on the side of the British. So he boarded his vessel on July 22, 1743, with great reluctance.

A handful of staunch supporters and long-time friends, with Germans predominant, were on hand to see him off. One admirer, often-married Mary Musgrove Matthews, later testified (as Mrs. Bosomworth) that he must have had a premonition that he would never see Georgia again. For said the more than ordinarily comely half-breed with whom Oglethorpe had frequently been linked in gossip, "on parting he gave me a diamond ring of £1,000 value."

As "Empress and Queen of both the Upper and the Lower Creeks," as well as official interpreter for the colony, her services to Georgia had been vital. Whether or not these official roles prompted the removal from Oglethorpe's finger of a ring that cost a year of his salary as colonial general, Mary Musgrove vowed that he wanted her to have it so she would never forget him.

On the long voyage home the patron of an American Indian princess endured another period of enforced idleness. He couldn't banish the Spanish and the French from his thoughts, yet they were seldom dominant. Now he must prepare to deal with formal charges brought by a veteran military officer. In Parliament, documents dealing with the Saint Augustine campaign had been laid on the table in March, waiting for Oglethorpe's personal appearance. His colleagues would require him to give full particulars concerning the ill-fated invasion of Spanish territory.

He could not predict what the lords of the treasury, the prime minister, the king, the war department and Parliament would do about his incredibly large expenditures made in a desperate bid to save Georgia. He could only hope for reimbursement on a scale that would enable him to retire at least a part of his debts.

To some enthusiastic admirers, Oglethorpe returned home a national hero — a victor over Spain. A spontaneous outpouring of gratitude, expressed in letters from every colonial governor from New York through North Carolina, more than made up for South Carolina's sullen silence.

To his critics and his foes, Oglethorpe returned home under a cloud of suspicion blacker even than that which surrounded his Jacobite father in his darkest hours.

Chapter 13

BITTERSWEET YEARS

July, 1743 — June, 1752

Two trans-Atlantic voyages took Georgia's founder through life-threatening storms. Three others were rough and uncomfortable. Though by no means fast, this 60-day crossing — destined to be his last — was tranquil and actually pleasant. His vessel's name, *Success*, was a source of great comfort. Before landfall it was elevated into a symbol.

Once more confident of success in the varied challenges that confronted him, the member from Haslemere was so rested and refreshed from his voyage that he could not wait for action. Governor James Glen of Carolina was understandably jealous of Oglethorpe's military post and salary. He had been an outspoken critic of the Saint Augustine expedition. He had lent his name and authority to a lengthy set of charges that were suppressed, for the moment, only through influence of the accused man's sister and friends.

Immediately after landing on September 28, according to a letter written the following week by Dr. Thomas Birch, Oglethorpe went to Glen's residence. He demanded a retraction and an apology, but got neither. According to Birch he brought the confrontation to a climax by severely caning the colonial governor in his own house. His blood properly warmed by having trounced Glen, Georgia's founder was impatient for military leaders and lawmakers to be about the business for which they had called him home.

Some matters — notably his letters to Newcastle of July, 1741 —

189

had been presented to the House of Commons in March, 1743. Lawmakers laid them upon the table and for a full year did nothing except to issue a demand that Oglethorpe present himself in person to answer for his actions. Back home in response to that demand, he cooled his heels at Westbrook and in London for six months. Then colleagues got around to the urgent matters that had altered all of his personal plans.

March 21, 1744, saw a series of documents presented to the House of Commons. Especially significant items included: Oglethorpe's letters to Newcastle of April 28 and May 12, 1741, plus an October 19, 1741, letter of instructions to Oglethorpe from the lords justices.[1] At the same time the war office offered a summary of "extraordinary Services incurred in *Georgia*, for the Preservation and Defence of his Majesty's Dominions on the Continent of *North America*, from 22nd *September* 1738, to 22nd *July* 1743, when General *Oglethorpe* sailed for England." Monies claimed to have been provided by Oglethorpe from his own pocket, plus deductions for provisions issued to him and for treasury remittances at irregular intervals, were summarized in some detail.[2]

While colleagues pondered evidence and prepared to decide his financial fate, military leaders called upon the veteran of New World action. All signs pointed to an impending attempt at invasion by forces under the command of Bonnie Prince Charlie, The Young Pretender. Despite the virtual certainty that such a force would include one or more of his close relatives, Oglethorpe was asked to help prepare to face it. Earlier conversations were brought to a satisfactory conclusion in March. He was formally commissioned to raise a regiment of Hussars in order to aid in defending his German sovereign from the armies of the Stuarts.

As yet, there was no indication when he would be called before a military tribunal in order to answer charges leveled against him by Lieutenant-colonel Cooke.

March 21 saw the Commons, guided by astute Arthur Onslow, refer the war office estimate of Oglethorpe's expenses to the committee of the whole. On the following day the committee of the whole recommended, without a head count of "yes" and "no" votes, that £66,109 13 shillings 10 pence "be granted to His Majesty, on Account of extraordinary Services incurred in *Georgia* . . . and not provided for by Parliament."[3] Except for interest, fees, commissions, and costs incurred after September 29, 1743, Parliament's action meant full and immediate reimbursement to Oglethorpe for his out-of-pocket expenditures on behalf of Georgia.[4]

Nearly as important even as his personal financial rescue, the soldier-of-fortune who put his total resources behind his colony had the satisfaction of seeing that his time and effort had not been wasted. For the year 1744 Parliament voted a grant of £19,168 for Georgia's military needs — about 60% of what Oglethorpe had spent in each of the two preceding years. This sum was expected to provide for two troops of rangers, one Highland company, half galleys, schooners, sailors, and boatmen.[5] Such a committment to the colony left behind by Oglethorpe meant — at least for now — that Parliament suddenly considered Georgia to be valuable. There was no more talk of abandoning the colony, except by a few loose-tongued men such as Sir John Cotton,[6] whose voice was loud but whose followers were few.

Against incredible odds in London and in America, the charitable enterprise had evolved into a military buffer powerful enough to turn back Spanish forces sent against it. Many stronger and better-financed colonial experiments had failed. Oglethorpe's had succeeded. Though still far from self-sufficient and still torn by internal strife, a weak-kneed shadow of the utopia originally envisioned, Georgia endured. It was a triumph with no counterpart in British colonial history.

Victory in Parliament was due in part to events for which Georgia's founder was not responsible. Had Sir Robert Walpole not fallen from power, there is no certainty that Parliament would have acted as it did. In the power vacuum created by Walpole's surrender of leadership, no individual even came close to taking his place. Henry Pelham, born in the same year as Oglethorpe and already chancellor of the exchequer, became prime minister — but never exercised Walpole's power. Pelham's brother, the powerful Duke of Newcastle who served as secretary of state for 30 years, had consented to many of Oglethorpe's actions if he did not, indeed, suggest them. John Carteret, Lord Granville, one-time part owner of Georgia, was briefly England's most influential statesman.

Carteret, the secretary of state, the prime minister, and the speaker of the house momentarily put their differences aside in order to unite behind Oglethorpe. As a result Georgia's founder handily trounced those who questioned his military decisions or challenged his incredibly daring unauthorized expenditures. Those who wondered how on earth he managed to persuade creditors to extend to him the vast sums he spent[7] kept their questions to themselves.

Having been voted reimbursement, it was now up to Oglethorpe to justify the total. For months much of his time and energy went into a methodical search for bills, receipts, memoranda, and invoices — anything and everything bearing upon his claimed expenditures in Georgia. Some items were necessarily reconstructed from memory.

Oglethorpe's "Accompt," somehow generally overlooked until now or pushed aside because regarded as unimportant, has been lying in the Pulic Record Office for generations. Yet it is second only to Georgia's charter in significance and is rich in details found nowhere else. British officials received a copy on August 2, 1745 — more than a year after partial reimbursement of Oglethorpe's expenses. Hundreds of widely varied items are listed; they range from quite large to very small expenditures such as:[8]

	£	s.	d.
To Captain Hugh Mackay for 10 Boatchains, padlocks, Staples and 45 Feet of Chain -------------	5	4	0
To Harman Verelst for 16 empty half Firkins -----	15	8	0
To John Tuckwell for 1800 Gun Worms --------	4	10	0
To [same] for 425 Pair of Men's Shoes ------------	85	7	0
To Edward Rush for mending and cleaning 67 Indian guns--	1	2	6
To 5 Soldiers for assisting to put out a fire-----	0	10	0
To David Thomson and 3 men assisting to bring in a ship --	0	7	6
To Samuel Williams for killing an Allegator------	0	5	0
To Thomas Hucks Esqr and William West for 15 Tons of Strong Beer in 8 Barrels with 2 Iron Hoops each ---	119	8	0
To Thomas Marriott for Pipes and Tobacco for the Indians---	0	2	0
To Francis Moore which he paid over to Sergeants Cook and Bailey and some others and to 7 Soldiers being a Gift to them on St. George's Day ----	2	7	6
To Captain Cuthbert for 3 month pay for Rangers ---	36	0	0
To Thomas Summer for fitting the Cutter's Oars and making 2 Rammers for the great Guns --------	0	4	6
To Sam Davison for carrying Shells & Lyme---	2	10	6
To Michael Martin for taking a Deserter --------	5	0	0
To Mary [Musgrove] Matthews for her being Interpreter to the Chiefs of the Creek Indians -----	20	0	0
To Captain Wm. Thomson for Sundrys for the			

	£	s.	d.
Boats used in December 1739 on the Expedition to Florida, part of his account for £606 - 16 - --------	70	20	0½
For sundry utensils for John Saller's Scout Boat--	4	17	1½
For 7 pounds of meats and 7 pounds of bread each week for each [of 100] privates, Highland Independent Company, 2 May 1740 to 2 September following £6,092 (Carolina Currency)-----------------	761	10	0
To the Trustees for Georgia for the Rent of the Storehouse at Frederica Fort built by Them and Charged on General Oglethorpe in his Account with ye Trust ---	20	0	0
To John Robertson for setting up a Furnace for John Calwell---	1	0	0
To Thomas Walker in full for a Roof to the Arsenal ---	10	0	0
For leather Harnesses, the use of an House for a Hospital, and for several Works -----------------------	24	9	1
To Thomas Loop for mending wheelbarrows----	0	6	0
To Mr. Cardogan on his going to Charles Town to prosecute Deane as per Major Cook's Account----	20	0	0
To John Brownfield for making 27 Shirts for Indians ---	1	13	9
To Samuel Becks for his discovering where some of the Clothing for the King's service were sold ---	2	10	0
To John Brownfield for Arms and Stores -------	178	2	3

On October 27, 1747 — more than two years after it had been lodged with authorities, Oglethorpe appeared before Charles Clarke to make oath as to the accuracy of his "Accompt" and to sign it. At this accounting, he showed an overage of £6,563 — 18 —3¾. Parliament had made no provision for repayment of this or any other charges not included in the 1744 war office estimate.

Only now was it possible to proceed with the formal audit of the sworn statement. A few relatively small changes, insignificant with respect to the total, had been made in the account as presented in August, 1745. To the eternal regret of Georgia's founder, large additional sums — chiefly fees, interest, and commissions — were found still owing to his creditors.

Lawmakers were no longer keenly interested in Oglethorpe's personal affairs — or, indeed, in other matters that had seemed

urgent a year or so earlier. Now they were preoccupied with issues
raised by the mounting threat of armed invasion.

On the heels of a Commons debate over estimated cost of
raising and maintaining mercenary troops from Germany, there
came a demand for better intelligence about anticipated sailing of a
French fleet. Both houses of Parliament sat through lengthy
sessions that dealt with the intended invasion by The Pretender. In
an attempt to deal with civil chaos that such an invasion would
surely bring, there was a spirited move to suspend the habeas
corpus bill. At the same time it was made high treason to hold
correspondence with the sons of The Pretender.[9]

Nearly nine months after acting upon the directive of the war
office that required him to leave Georgia, the colony's founder got
his long-awaited hearing. Nineteen charges by Cooke were heavily
weighted with allegations that Oglethorpe had pocketed military
money. Separate specifications dealt with regimental sea-pay,
provisions, bedding, food, ammunition, and building of fortifications.
Collectively, these allegations spelled embezzlement, with other
charges of purely personal nature attached. Even the issue of sexual
involvement was not overlooked. Cooke alleged that when there
was no food in the camp, his commanding officer supported several
women who were lying-in after childbirth.

When these charges were compiled and presented to the war
office, Cooke's grievances were directed at a man just one grade
above him in permanent rank. By the time a hearing was scheduled
in June, 1744, general officers — who did not constitute a formal
court-martial — merely had to decide whether to believe a
lieutenant-colonel or a brigadier-general.

It took only a few hours to reach a verdict. With Lord Mark Kerr presiding, seven generals ruled that every article of complaint was "either frivolous, vexatious, or malicious, and without foundation." As part of their report, assembled general officers recommended the dismissal of Lieutenant-Colonel William Cooke. There are no records from which to form a conclusion concerning whether or not action of Oglethorpe's peers constituted the whitewashing of questionable financial dealings.

Reaction of the Member from Haslemere was characteristic. He was glad to have a cloud of doubt dispelled, but was impatient at the lack of action in his military assignment at home. So he addressed to the secretary of state a fresh offer to return to Georgia in order to renew the fight against the Spanish and the French. When his petition was ignored, he began fitting out another vessel and prepared to send it to the colony at his own expense. Meanwhile he was busy raising a new regiment that he intended to take to Georgia.

He could afford to be mangnanimous. Long-awaited vindication of his conduct in the New World had finally come. Now he was ready to take the single most certain upward step open to members of the minor gentry. A frequent subject of London gossip, his stated intention to marry evoked at least one false report. He was prematurely and incorrectly said to have taken as his bride wealthy Lady Elizabeth Sambrooke.

That story surfaced as a result of Oglethorpe's financial dealings with her.[10] He chose, however, to marry a commoner of child-bearing age. Elizabeth Wright, daughter of a baronet, had in her own right an annual income of about £1,500 — substantially more than that of her bridegroom. In addition, she stood to inherit the extensive estate of her bachelor brother.

Elizabeth Wright became Oglethorpe's wife in the King Henry VII Chapel at Westminster Abbey on September 15, 1744. If he should outlive his brother-in-law and his bride, Brigadier-General James Edward Oglethorpe stood to enter the lower ranks of Britain's great landlords. One after another, his youthful ambitions had been fulfilled.

No record has been found concerning Mrs. Oglethorpe's reaction to their honeymoon. Part of it was spent at Westbrook manor, where she found herself required to play hostess to a Chickasaw Indian chief who had accompanied her husband to England.

Six months after their marriage, while Oglethorpe was occupied with preliminary discussions about possible purchase of Puttenham manor in Surrey, he was promoted to the rank of Major-General. At once the founder of Georgia got the opportunity he had been wanting — a chance again to command men in battle. Led by Bonnie Prince Charlie, troops had affected a landing in Scotland and were preparing to strike at England's heart. Oglethorpe's regiment, intended for Georgia, was sent to Yorkshire to help repel the invaders.

Georgia's founder had been outfitting the ship *Success* for service in the colony. Now England needed the men and arms aboard the vessel. While the *Success* was being unloaded at Hull by his orders, Oglethorpe set about shaping a group of Yorkshire gentry into a volunteer cavalry unit. He became, of course, Colonel of the Royal Regiment of Hunters in addition to holding his other posts.

December, 1745, brought the first significant bloodshed of the Jacobite uprising still remembered throughout Britain as The Forty-Five. Soon defeated, Charles Stuart made a hasty retreat. Oglethorpe's troops were in a position to hamper or even thwart that withdrawal, but they did not. A final and decisive victory of the Hanoverian forces came at the battle of Culloden, Scotland, on April 16, 1746. No Stuart would ever again offer a serious military threat to the stability of Britain.

But the commander of British forces was not satisfied with a sweeping victory. So many wounded and defeated Highlanders were slaughtered on the field that the Duke of Cumberland came to be called "Butcher."

Third son of King George II, Butcher Cumberland had always nourished a fierce hatred for everyone and everything having even the slightest Jacobite tinge. Major-General Oglethorpe, he now insisted, had acted in strangely indecisive fashion. Was he not the son and grandson of notorious Jacobites? Did not the forces of The Young Pretender include at least one of Oglethorpe's own nephews? Had not Georgia's founder been intimately linked with Scots who formed the backbone of The Forty-Five? Why had he encouraged the flow of Scottish colonists to Georgia, and why had he relied upon the Independent Highland Company for defense of the region? Could anyone with half his wits about him fail to discover the answer to such questions?

For Cumberland, guilt by association was enough. Oglethorpe was relieved of his command shortly before Culloden. Rumor had it that he would immediately return to Georgia, but military authorities knew better. He had already been served preliminary notice of fresh charges against him. This time, accusations gathered

Westbrook manor, mortgaged to the hilt for the sake of Georgia

Oglethorpe's home, Westbrook manor, fell into disrepair in decades after his death. This view represents a reconstruction by Joseph N. Smith, Fellow of the American Institute of Architects.

With all surrounding real property included, the value of Westbrook was below £15,000. Had Parliament not voted partial reimbursement for his expenses incurred in the defense of Georgia, Oglethorpe would have lost Westbrook — and everything else he had.

by Cumberland would require nothing less than a full-dress court-martial.

While evidence was being gathered and witnesses were being selected to testify against Georgia's founder, authorities proceeded with other trials. Lord Simon Lovat, chief of the clan Fraser, was so old and fat that he could neither walk nor ride a horse. So he was brought to London in a litter. There he was given a summary hearing and executed shortly after heads of two other high-born Jacobites rolled.

Major-General Oglethorpe went on trial late in September, 1746. He was charged with "having disobey'd or neglected his orders," thereby permitting rebel forces to escape. This time he came before the tribunal under arrest, for a verdict of guilty would have been tantamount to conviction of treason.

In spite of the great influence of the Duke of Cumberland, James Oglethorpe was acquitted. There was no evidence of an offense more serious than indecisive leadership. Yet his name was permanently blackened. After The Forty-Five he never again got an active command and was forced for life to remain "a half-pay general."

Oglethorpe remained on the list of general officers and in time was promoted to Lieutenant-General and then to General. He held that rank for so many years that in old age he was the senior ranking officer of the entire British Army.

Like her founder, Georgia surivived by a miracle — but fared no better than did Oglethorpe. Both in Parliament and in the Georgia office, interest in civil affairs of the colony waned. Had no other

"Butcher" Cumberland, victor over the Jacobites

The Duke of Cumberland gained his nickname "Butcher" because of the fury with which he slaughtered wounded Jacobites. His zeal in bringing action against Oglethorpe stemmed in part from his life-long conviction that Georgia's founder always was a secret sympathizer with the Jacobite cause.

evidence been available, the flow of both financial support and of new Georgians would have revealed the sad state of affairs there.

During the eight years that followed Oglethorpe's victory at Bloody Marsh, Parliament provided only £16,608 for non-military needs of the colony. Yet lawmakers voted £23,961 to fund Georgia's military defense for a 14-month period.

After the first great wave of popular interest and support during the early 1730's, charitable contributions fell off sharply. A high point was reached in 1736-37 when hundreds of enthusiastic supporters of the colony that promised to solve so many of Britain's social and economic problems poured £3,627 into the hands of Trustees. Such gifts amounted to only £909 in the following year. By 1741-42 the annual total from this source of support was just £10. After Oglethorpe left the colony, all private contributions plus treasury payments to settle long-standing imperial accounts amounted, collectively, to just £1,022.

An equally abrupt change took place in the colony's Indian affairs and in her relationship with Carolina. With Oglethorpe gone, the long-contested Georgia monopoly in the skin trade was relinquished. By informal agreement, Georgia kept her hold upon the trade with the Upper Creeks. South Carolina resumed her pre-Oglethorpe dominance in dealing with other tribes. Reporting upon the matter in 1750, Governor Glen — whose back may still have smarted, in memory, from Oglethorpe's furious personal assault upon him in 1743 — stressed that the long-simmering feud between the two southernmost colonies was now "buried in oblivion."[11]

If the few remaining Trustees who had a genuine interest in Georgia knew what was taking place 3,000 miles away, they kept their reactions to themselves. Meetings of the Trust and of its

common council became increasingly sporadic, with attendance low. In the aftermath of Oglethorpe's vote of confidence from Parliament, the common council went for seven months without a session. From the time of active military movements in The Forty-Five until the dissolution of the Georgia Trust, minutes of the common council occupy just 57 printed pages — as opposed to 468 pages for the period from issuance of the charter until The Forty-Five.

A dramatic change in the type of settlers took place during the eight years that followed Oglethorpe's return to Britain. His colleagues sent just seven small groups of persons to Georgia on the charity. During each of four annual periods, the number of new settlers of this class was zero.

Yet the stream of adventurers and tradesmen and petty gentry who — with their flocks of servants — went at their own expense, took a dramatic upturn. During three periods (1748-49, 1749-50, and 1751-52) the number of new Georgians of this sort far exceeded the number of charity colonists who went to the colony in its banner years (1733-34, 1735-36, and 1741-42).

Radical transformation between Oglethorpe's Georgia and the post-Oglethorpe colony is indicated by stark statistics. After her founder left, only 172 charity colonists went to Georgia during the remaining years of the Trust. But during the same period privately-financed voyages took 2,499 adventurers and their servants to Georgia.[12]

Victory over Spain was a crucial factor in this transformation of colonial character. Almost as important were changes in the land system and relaxation of the law of 1734 against spiritous liquors. Self-financed settlers demanded a sure hold upon land and a ready supply of rum.

Many if not most of them also wanted one thing they failed to get as long as James Edward Oglethorpe played even a nominal role in the affairs of his colony. Absolute prohibition of slavery in Georgia, under the law of 1734-35, made the colony the first (and only) British outpost in the New World where ownership of humans was forbidden.[13] From the outset of the experiment this statute was a source of constant bickering and complaint. Hickory-hard Oglethorpe turned a deaf ear to whining of colonists who looked to him and to the Trust for everything they had.

By 1738 pro-slavery forces made up of self-financed settlers were strong enough, under the leadership of Robert Williams, to get a formal protest before the Georgia Trustees. Williams later testified before a parliamentary committee. But Oglethorpe's powerful hand easily prevailed with Trustees and lawmakers alike. Even the heavily pro-slavery petition of grievance framed and presented by Thomas Stephens ended in the abject humiliation of William Stephens' son.

After 1745 the founder of Georgia rarely attended a meeting of the Georgia Trust. His long-time friend and supporter, Egmont, now turned political foe as a result of his son's attempt to seize the seat Oglethorpe held in Parliament, had abandoned the Georgia enterprise in disgust. Of the charter members of the Trust whose voice carried weight, only two remained active in its affairs.

James Vernon, who so often challenged and crossed Oglethorpe during years when Georgia's founder spent most of his time in the colony or on the seas, dominated the Trust after The Forty-Five. His presence in a meeting was enough to persuade Oglethorpe to present himself less and less frequently. The Rev. Stephen Hales was articulate and persuasive, so enamored of the power of the printed word that he collected thousands of books for distribution in Georgia. He attended most of the infrequent meetings of the Trust, but never had a dominant role in policy-making.

Vernon long favored relaxation of the law that absolutely forbade slavery in Georgia. His views got strong support in 1748, when William Stephens sent a plaintive report to his superiors in London. Great numbers of persons from colonies to the north had applied to Georgia's governing body for grants of land, said Stephens. This influx of a new kind of settler — an American on the move, rather than a European seeking a refuge — had led to the introduction of "Numbers of Negroes into the Province."

According to the report, Stephens and his colleagues had taken every possible step to drive "the said negroes" out of Georgia, but without effect. To continue this futile rear-guard action, declared Stephens, would do nothing but "dispeople the Colony." Stephens ventured to hope that Trustees would establish restrictions and regulations under which slavery would be permitted in Georgia.

In May, 1749, Vernon presided over a meeting at which only three other members of the Trust were present. Since the only three official laws ever enacted for Georgia had been approved by the king in council, Trustees had no authority to alter them. Solemnly the four men who at that moment governed Georgia from England voted to ask the nation's leaders to repel "The act for rendering the Colony of Georgia more defensible by prohibiting the Importation and Use of black Slaves or Negro's."

On August 9, 1750, the common seal of the Trust was affixed to an act repealing the anti-slavery statute enacted in Georgia's infancy. That day, the last distinctive feature of the Oglethorpe era vanished. Georgia endured, but it had no major characteristic in common with the haven for the oppressed and the wealth-generating empire based upon silk and wine that had been envisioned in dim, far-away days of the early 1730's.

Yet members of the Trust who had never seen big tracts of Georgia land totally bare of mulberry trees (with Oglethorpe's knowledge and unwritten consent) continued to nourish a fading dream. As revised, the law relating to slaveholding was hedged about with qualifications. For every five black males brought into the colony, owners were required to bring one black female "who would be taught the winding of silk from the cocoons." Toothless though it was, the stipulation calling for 1,000 white mulberry trees to be planted on each 500-acre tract remained in effect.

For the protection of slaves it was stipulated that an owner who endangered the life of a black by means of corporal punishment would be fined £5. Should an owner fail to require his slaves to attend a service of divine worship held contiguous to their abodes, he would forfeit twice that sum. In order better to fund the all-important Established Church, Trustees created a new excise tax. It would cost a planter 15 shillings in duty to bring into Georgia a black of age 12 or above — plus annual duty of one shilling per black in subsequent years. Money raised by this means was to be applied to "maintenance of ministers of the gospel" plus building and repair of churches — and support of officers of the government.[14]

With the termination of the 21-year period of Trusteeship not far in the future, London leaders finally gave reluctant assent to a semblance of self-government by Georgians. They were partly motivated by fear that if no mechanism for token self-government existed at expiration of the charter, Carolina might be tempted to annex her sister colony. Long infirm, highly-respected and trusted William Stephens — who never made trouble for the Trustees — had become incompetent to carry out London's instructions. So provision was made for a provincial assembly to meet in 1751. Formal authorization for it came a few weeks before proposed revision of the slavery code was approved by the king in council.

Sixteen elected deputies who gathered in Savannah on January 15, 1751, had no real power. During two weeks of conversation and debate they did, however formulate a list of 11 grievances for which they asked immediate redress. Most of their complaints resulted in action.

Yet these first elected representatives of Georgians could not establish by-laws of even the most temporary sort. Final and absolute authority still centered in offices of the Georgia Trust in London. Success of the provincial assembly was sufficient, however, to persuade Trustees to make the experimental body a permanent one. They took that action when already deeply involved in the process of seeking an early surrender of the charter for which pioneer leaders had struggled so long and hard.

James Edward Oglethorpe played no role in the final events of the Trustee era. He attended no session of the common council of the Trust after January 19, 1749. March 16 saw his last participation in a meeting of the Trust itself. He wanted no part in the radical changes that were about to take place. His beloved regiment was formally disbanded in June, but 151 of its men elected to remain in Georgia as civilians.

With Georgia's charter due to expire in June, 1753, Trustees clung firmly to the reins of government. At their instruction, advertisements were placed in the *London Gazette* notifying the public that land in the colony was now granted "with free inheritance." That is, restrictions and barriers that had discouraged self-supporting tradesmen and adventurers from going to Georgia were finally abolished.

By April, 1753, civilian population of the nearly-decimated colony had jumped to 2,381whites and 1,066 blacks.[15]

In a never-say-die spirit a handful of Trustees made a fresh — but futile — application to Parliament for a grant in aid. To support their plea they stressed "the promising state of trials with indigo."

On July 6, 1751, a three-man Trustee session ruefully took stock of the financial situation. They found that they still faced considerable expenses "without any Fund to answer them, except the Money due from Gen¹ Oglethorpe to the Trust." So they instructed their accountant to present Georgia's founder with a bill for "One thousand four hundred and twelve Pounds and two pence half Penny."

Instead of flying into a rage, Oglethorpe conferred with Harman Verelst and informed him that his last financial report to Trustees showed them indebted to him. What's more, he sent word to startled Trustees, he was holding still another account of expenses incurred by him for the Trust but not mentioned earlier. January, 1749, had seen him present what was supposed to be his final accounting to his colleagues; unfortunately, records since discovered indicated that he was due yet more reimbursement.[16]

Bickering between Oglethorpe and other Trustees continued for two months, with no yielding on either side. This stand-off was the last personal involvement of Geogia's founder in affairs of the colony or of the Trust.

By November, members of the Trust — now led by the Earl of Shaftesbury — had shaped a document to be presented to the privy council. In it they indicated their readiness "for the service of the Crown, to surrender their Trust for granting the Lands" in the colony for which they once had such high hopes. They did, however, stress their concern that the Colony of Georgia "be confirmed a separate and independent Province." Whether this played any part in the establishment of Georgia as a royal colony is doubtful. Indian treaties made long ago by Oglethorpe virtually guaranteed this result.

Members of the privy council studied the Trustee resolution and presented it to the solicitor general for a legal opinion. While surrender of the charter was pending, Parliament granted Georgia leaders a final £4,000 to enable them to settle outstanding obligations. Papers, books, and the seal of the Georgia Corporation were placed in safekeeping on May 6, 1752. Final formalities were completed in June, and the charter was surrendered a full year before its expiration.

Born of enthusiasm, sustained by the reckless daring of one man, and incredibly successful by dent of sheer survival against impossible odds, Oglethorpe's Folly moved smoothly through a transitional period and became the Crown Colony of Georgia in North America. When that step was accomplished, the future of the once-experimental society was assured.

Chapter 14

LION OF LONDON

June, 1752 — June, 1785

Some Americans tend to view James Edward Oglethorpe's post-Georgia life as a minor appendage to an epoch-making era. British analysts who look only at large-scale events having long-range effects upon lives of multitudes do the same thing. So regarded, the 30+ years that followed Parliament's vindication of a one-man war against Spain are minimized if not ignored.

Lieutenant-General Oglethorpe, husband of Elizabeth Wright and Member of Parliament, saw matters in a different light. Having no Saint Augustine to assault and no Savannah to defend, he remained sometimes wholeheartedly enthusiastic, sometimes belligerent with respect to widely-varied objectives.

While still awaiting court-martial on charges brought by the hated Duke of Cumberland, Oglethorpe started expanding his holdings near his inherited manor. Vineyards and gardens of Westbrook, plus its leather mill and textile mill, had long served as training grounds for would-be Georgia colonists. Now that the crown had assumed total responsibility for the New World enterprise, it was time to devote his enormous energy to his own interests plus selected philanthropic causes.

Puttenham, a few miles north-east of Westbrook and adjacent to the Hog's Back, lay outside the pocket borough upon which Oglethorpe depended for his seat in Parliament. Yet the manors of Puttenham Bury and Puttenham Priory with about 300 acres under cultivation, an equal number in pasture, and some 4,000 unimproved acres seemed an exceptionally good buy at £4,400.

207

Jasper Jones, who sold the property, was more astute than he appeared. Before the new owner could get a clear title, he was forced by the Court of Chancery to pay £1,200 in quit claims and releases. Oglethorpe fought these every inch of the way, as doggedly if not as gleefully as he had fought Trustees at the Georgia office, the king in council, South Carolina, and the Spanish. In the end, he paid. That made him master of lands in Bramley, Elstead, Tongham, and Compton in addition to Puttenham and his earlier holdings.

Clearly speculative, purchase of the new estates was followed very soon by mortgaging them for £2,500. By 1757 the holder of instruments relating to these properties was none other than Dame Elizabeth Sambrooke — who lent £5,796 upon them. She was more pliant or less astute than Oglethorpe, for when the property was sold in 1761 it brought only £5,200.

A purchase on High Street in Haslemere was made for career considerations rather than potential profit. His friend John Tanner offered the Town House, to which a vote in Parliamentary elections was attached. With his long-standing edge over challengers beginning to erode a bit, Oglethorpe snapped up the property even though it entailed a small drop in his annual cash flow. Every vote was important, and the more he could put in his pocket the better.

Votes attached to properties he owned would become increasingly vital, since his marriage made him an absentee landlord. After a honeymoon spent largely at Westbrook manor and a stay during the following Christmas season, General and Mrs. Oglethorpe never came back except on business. Cranham Hall, center of her extensive estates in Essex, was their official home. During some years, however, the general spent eight months in London. Initially he resided in an elegant mansion in Whitehall and later in a more modest establishment on Lower Grosvenor Street that was just big enough for gracious entertaining.

Sir Hans Sloane and six distinguished friends sponsored Oglethorpe's application to become a Fellow of the Royal Society. Elected by acclamation on April 6, 1749, he seems to have regarded the clearing of the high hurdle of admission as bearing its own reward. Never an active participant in the society, after nearly a decade had passed he was expelled from membership for nonpayment of dues — then owing just over £18.

Sloane, a physician by vocation and a naturalist by passion, had served at the sick-bed of King George II. During the visit of Tomochichi and other Georgia Indians to Britain, it was Sloane

who rushed to the aid of a stricken native and made a futile attempt
to save his life.

At least as much as any other individual and perhaps more, it
was Sloane who persuaded his friend Oglethorpe to lay great stress
upon botanical affairs in Georgia. During the year that preceded the
sailing of the *Ann*, leaders of the colonial enterprise established a
special restricted fund "to be applied for Encouraging and improving
Botany and Agriculture." Early gifts were not numerous, but were
impressive for their source and size: Sir Hans Sloane, £20; the Duke
of Richmond, £30; the Earl of Derby, £50; Charles DuBois, £10;
James Oglethorpe, £5.

Sloane had in 1702 inherited the library of naturalist William
Courten. From this nucleus, during half a century he built up one of
the world's outstanding specialized libraries — about 50,000
volumes plus thousands of manuscripts. Coins, pictures, and
curiosities were also accumulated. For years Oglethorpe urged him
to make sure that the unique collection would never be scattered to
the wind. Sloane toyed with the idea of leaving it to the nation as a
gift. Oglethorpe dissented. From personal experience he was
convinced that no one really appreciates anything gained without
cost or effort.

Oglethorpe agreed to serve as a trustee of his friend's estate and
as pall-bearer at his funeral — assuming that he would outlive the
colleague nearly 40 years his senior. Sloan's will was published in
January, 1753. Under its terms his renowned collection was offered
to the king and Parliament for £20,000. Even those persons who
were eager to meet terms of the document realized that Sloane's
treasures would become a liability unless properly housed.

Here was a challenge to which the founder of Georgia could
apply his boundless energy.

He immediately proposed a national lottery, and evoked a
storm of protest. Questionable practices linked with this method of
fiancing governmental projects had caused many persons to vow
they'd never again sanction a lottery. Spirited debate in the House of
Commons led to the appointment of a committee charged with
establishing and conducting a lottery. In order to gain votes of
lawmakers, backers of the plan had agreed, in advance, to purchase
two other collections and to place these, with Sloane's, in "a worthy
receptacle." Oglethorpe and two colleagues were named to take
charge of the project.

It was one thing to gain reluctant approval of yet another great
lottery; it was quite another thing to attend to countless details

Mrs. James Edward Oglethorpe

Elizabeth Wright, who became the wife of James Oglethorpe, held property valued at
several times that of her husband. In addition, she expected to inherit the assets of her
unmarried brother.

Though her husband spent much of his time at her estate rather than his own, Mrs.
Oglethorpe kept a firm hand upon her holdings.

involved in organizing and executing the scheme. For two years
Oglethorpe devoted much of his time and energy to the lottery plus
development of plans for a permanent national collection of
literary and other treasures.

Unfortunately, "the Sloane lottery" was relegated to a professional agent, Peter Lehuep. He was selected because he made bold
promises that, in the judgment of Oglethorpe and his colleagues,
outweighed the impact of his unsavory reputation.

Lehuep employed all of his accumulated skills in manipulation.
He arranged that the ticket office should be open just six hours for
the sale of 100,000 tickets — then siphoned off the bulk of them to
be distributed by scalpers at a personal profit believed to exceed
£40,000.

Parliament devoted weeks to an inquiry into the conduct of this
lottery.[1]

In spite of mis-management in raising funds, Trustees of the
newly-created British Museum began business with a capital of
£95,194 derived from Oglethorpe's lottery. When all purchases of
initial collections had been completed and all obligations had been
paid, the trust had about £44,000 on hand for investment.

Later, Montague House in Bloomsbury was purchased with
£300,000 from yet another lottery. Extensively remodelled, it was
opened in 1759. Jealous colleagues succeeded in blocking Oglethorpe's
appointment to the post of Trustee of the new institution. Those
persons close to the British Museum realized, however, that it was
largely due to his enthusiasm and persistence that the world-
famous institution came into being.

Other noble enterprises got their share of Oglethorpe's attention, too. Though no longer serving as one of its governors, he maintained keen personal interest in Westminster Infirmary. Whenever possible he visited and inspected the Foundlings Hospital, of which he was a faithful Trustee. He was chief spokesman for a special petition presented to Commons by the Moravians. He rose to second Sir John Barnard's motion that the poor be relieved of some of their onerous taxes. He served as a member of a council, headed by the Duke of Bedford, whose goal was the maintenance and education of exposed and deserted children.

Britain's all-important fishing industry got a share of his time as a member of Parliamentary committees. He did more than attend meetings and speak on the floor of Commons. With characteristic zeal he ordered stock in the Free British Fishery — but failed to pay for at least two purchases, so the certificates were never issued.

Still a staunch supporter of the military service, he introduced a number of reform bills and supported others. Especially in the heated debate on the Mutiny Bill, he spoke earnestly in support of clauses that promised to make the condition of enlisted men a bit better. Even the social ills that had triggered development of the first phase of the Georgia scheme — prisons and treatment of their inmates — were again attacked by the Member from Haslemere.

Nearly a decade spent in Georgia, followed by years as an absentee landlord, made Oglethorpe increasingly insecure in his hold upon a seat in Parliament. In 1754 he took advantage of long-standing laws and customs in order to offer in two boroughs simultaneously: Haslemere, plus Westminster in London. In the capital city he trailed a field of four candidates led by Charles Cornwallis. In Haslemere a member of the Molyneaux family, long-time rivals, trounced him. Defeat was more than he could stomach; he never offered again.

To his growing frustration, the founder of Georgia discovered that it would take years to gain reimbursement for the last of his out-of-pocket expenditures made for the sake of holding Georgia against the Spanish.

When Oglethorpe's "Accompt" was formally submitted for audit in October, 1747, a supplementary statement attached to it indicated that his total outlay for Georgia — with interest, fees, and commissions computed to that date — then amounted to £103,395 — 16 — 1¾. Of this total, £2,464 had been paid to men levied in Virginia for service after Michaelmmas, 1743 — close of the period used for the war office estimate to Parliament. Much of the remaining portion of the £12,690 balance consisted of interest, commission owed to Harman Verelst, and unpaid accounts of merchants who had sent supplies to Georgia. This 1747 balance was very close to the total worth of Oglethorpe's extensive properties. At 5% interest on that sum he still owed, charges that continued to accumulate from expenditures not reimbursed came to nearly twice his net income from all rental properties in Britain.

Oral tradition, lacking documentation, offers the plausible assertion that the financially-pressed veteran warrior with no opportunity to gain an active command, went to the Continent under an assumed name and fought as a mercenary in at least one campaign. Another oral tradition, equally vague and less plausible, holds that after having been promoted to the rank of general in 1765 he was offered the command of British land forces in North America, but refused it. Though he did take an active part in attempts to prevent a permanent rupture between the colonies and the home government, his debts plus his love of a fight almost certainly would have persuaded him to take any British post offered.

Not getting an offer, the ex-lawmaker who was now the senior general officer of the entire British army returned to earlier interests. During his entire career he was a small-scale patron of struggling and aspiring writers. His long-standing ties with the Wesley family stemmed in part from his generosity in subscribing to expensive books issued by The Rev. Samuel Wesley, father of Charles and John. A similar link with architect Robert Castell brought him face-to-face with the horrors of debtors' prisons.

When the Colony of Georgia was less than a decade old, on one of his trips home Oglethorpe had subscribed to a poem called "London." Its author was then-unknown Samuel Johnson, age 29, and already thinking of a daring new approach to the making of a dictionary. Aging but in no sense mellow, General Oglethorpe became the patriarch of the literary circle that revolved about now-famous Johnson. Everyday life of Georgia's founder became a constant circle of entertaining and being entertained by celebrities to whom he was The Lion of London.

Oliver Goldsmith, Sir Joshua Reynolds, Hannah More, Edmund Burke, David Garrick, and dozens of lesser notables sought Oglethorpe's company. His one-time political rival Horace Walpole, brother of Sir Robert, joined the circle of ardent and vocal admirers. William Pitt never forgot that the Member from Haslemere had remained true to his father during a long up-and-down career. As

James Boswell recorded Oglethorpe's conversation

A number of significant anecdotes concerning the career and temperament of
Oglethorpe would have been lost had not James Boswell made notes of conversations in
which Samuel Johnson was involved.

A single colorful tale, doubtless embroidered by time and shared with Johnson,
provides the only specifics known about Oglethorpe's military exploits in Europe as a
youth.

chancellor of the exchequer, first lord of the treasury, and prime
minister, "the Younger Pitt" took every opportunity to express his
admiration for Oglethorpe as law-maker and as colonial administrator. In less public fashion he made it clear that he intended to
have the treasury complete its reimbursement of military expenses
long ago claimed by Georgia's founder and still under audit or
challenge.[2]

With Boswell perennially in the process of making notes or
poised with pen in hand, the old warrior recalled with relish and
enthusiasm nearly-forgotten exploits of long ago. Sometimes he
bragged about actions of the moment — such as the occasion when
he challenged a neighboring gentleman to a duel because the fellow
had trespassed upon Oglethorpe's property.

Emotions of the aging general were kindled when someone —
perhaps Oliver Goldsmith — ventured to suggest that now-
outlawed resort to pistols at dawn might be inconsistent with
morality. "Undoubtedly," observed the aging social lion whose
youth had been marked by periodic resorts to violence, "a man has
a right to defend his honour." Listeners may have questioned his
verdict, but if so they remained silent out of respect for his great
prestige and his advanced years.

Women half his age boasted of having flirted with Oglethorpe.
Hannah More termed him "perhaps the most remarkable man of
his time . . . heroic, romantic, and full of the old gallantry." He
figured in the intimate correspondence of Mrs. Elizabeth Carter,
Mrs. David Garrick, Mrs. Elizabeth Montague, and others whose
names were constantly on the lips of those who moved in the
highest social circles. Horace Walpole marvelled that though his

teeth were gone, his spirits remained in full bloom and "his eyes, ears, articulation, limbs, and memory would suit a boy."

Edmund Burke spoke for half the notables of London when he lauded James Oglethorpe as "the most extraordinary person I have ever known." Alexander Pope's *Essay on Man,* completed in the year Georgia was founded, is better known but hardly more stirring than lines that laud the man who launched England's last American colony:

> Hail, Oglethorpe, with triumphs crowned
> That ever were in camps or sieges found, —
> Thy great example shall through ages shine,
> A favorite theme with poet and divine.
> People unborn thy merits shall proclaim,
> And add new luster to thy deathless name.

Oglethorpe ate it up. He positively reveled in his role as darling of the ladies and mentor of Britain's most renowned political and literary leaders.

Why shouldn't he? After all, as he frequently reminded himself with glee, he had reached one by one all of the high personal goals set in early manhood. Long ago, he had ceased to fret even that his branch of the Oglethorpe family would die with him and that the century-old estates in Surrey would pass into other hands.[3] It didn't matter that his wealthy wife kept a firm hand upon her extensive estates. He had everything. For him, there literally were no more worlds to conquer.

Wisely, he was careful not to become involved in debates or disputes involving the colony that owed its exitence to his one man effort. He kept abreast of news but stayed out of controversy — a stance that was altogether uncharacteristic of him.

It took the lords commissioners of trade and plantations, to whom Georgia was consigned upon surrender of her charter, nearly two years to complete the transition by which a royal colony came into existence. Veteran navy commander John Reynolds was put in charge late in 1754. Since neither Oglethorpe nor Stephens ever held a comparable post, Reynolds became Georgia's first governor.

Oglethorpe long ago came to terms with reality and for practical purposes abandoned the attempt to produce silk in Georgia, though interest of London-based Trustees remained keen. Numerous colonists who had gone as self-supporting adventurers had sent reports asserting that the climate was not right for the enterprise.

Yet officials in Whitehall never got the message. When a new seal was designed for the new royal colony, it bore a design in which Georgia was represented as a young woman delivering a skein of silk to King George.

August, 1756, brought a formal letter of complaint against Governor Reynolds. Oglethorpe laughed aloud when he heard of it. Some of his peers in Parliament had always been ready to receive such complaints during the Trustee era. Now they faced the prospect of a bitter fight over the guilt or innocence of a royal governor who held office by virtue of a commission from the king in council. Reynolds left Georgia on *The Charming Martha* early in 1756, but never got a full-dress hearing. French privateers captured his vessel and seized papers that were vital to the case.

Henry Ellis, whose official role was that of lieutenant-governor,[4] took charge of the colony upon Reynolds' departure. He inherited not only the animosity that had resulted in Reynolds' recall — but also the most emotion-charged legal quarrel that erupted in early Georgia.

Mary Musgrove, the influential half-Indian who had played a crucial role in Oglethorpe's public life in the colony, seems to have been promised £100 per year for her service as interpreter. That was precisely the salary granted to William Stephens in his capacity as chief civil administrator of the colony.

John Musgrove,[5] Mary's first husband, ignored Oglethorpe's attempt to enforce the ban upon rum and stayed drunk much of the time. He came very close to disgracing the entire Georgia enterprise when, as interpreter with the band led to London by Tomochichi, he was once too befuddled to function. Returning to Georgia he died. His widow soon married one of her servants, Jacob Matthews. After Matthews' death in 1742 she accepted comfort from The Rev. Thomas Bosomworth, who came to the colony in 1743 as chaplain to Oglethorpe's regiment.[6]

Early in his relationship with the woman whose name was often linked in salacious gossip with that of the colony's founder, Bosomworth saw a golden opportunity. He married Matthews' widow and took charge of presenting her claims against the Colony of Georgia. In a long deposition drawn up in 1747 he declared that his wife, whose native name was sometimes spelled Cowsaponckesa,[7] had been the most influential single person in delicate negotiations with leaders of various tribes.

According to Bosomworth's claims, Oglethorpe paid his all-important interpreter only £200 during his stay in Georgia.[8]

Because of the fatigue she had undergone in frequently travelling several hundred miles by water in open boats "plus the losses sustained in her own private affairs by the neglect thereof on his Majesty's service," husband #3 felt that she was due exactly £5,714.

For weeks the Bosomworth affair was the chief talk of Savannah. London was deeply involved, but was too far removed from the scene of action to keep abreast of fast-moving developments. Failing to get satisfaction, Bosomworth led a band of natives to Frederica and issued a demand that all Europeans immediately evacuate the entire region south of the Savannah river. Splendid-appearing in his most colorful clerical vestments, Bosomworth brought his queen and her native allies into Savannah on July 20, 1747. Failing to get satisfaction from colonial authorities, the Bosomworths five years later spent a period in London pursuing their claim. A dozen years after litigation began, in 1759 the harrassed government paid Mrs. Bosomworth £2,100 and gave her a deed to Saint Catherines island.

Oglethorpe laughed until his sides ached when he learned the final outcome of the long-drawn struggle. Throughout, he remained aloof and refused even to say what promises he had made or what payments she had received from him. If he did in fact regularly pay her for her services during his decade of leadership, as government witnesses testified but were unable to prove,[9] he kept discreet silence and let Georgia's new leaders come to terms with Mary. Partly because his own claims for reimbursement were contested in such detail and at such length, it pleased him mightily to see his New World friend get the best of the treasury.

He approved, too, when a man with personal knowledge of the New World became Georgia's governor in 1760. For far too long the important decisions had been made from a distance by persons who had no first-hand understanding of colonial conditions.

Son of a South Carolina chief justice, James Wright lived in that colony until he went to London to study law. Back in Carolina, he served as attorney-general for nearly 25 years before accepting the more lucrative post of colonial agent, with residence in England. King George II, fast aproaching his death-bed, named Wright to take over affairs in fast-growing but still largely unsettled Georgia. Except for Oglethorpe himself, no man in England was better acquainted with the region, its opportunities and its problems.

Interrupted only by a brief period during which patriots controlled the colony during the American Revolution, James Wright served as Governor of Georgia for 22 years. Astute in looking after his own interests, he acquired about 25,000 acres of Georgia land that was divided into 11 plantations which produced an estimated 3,000 barrels of rice per year.[10]

Rapid rise in property values had accompanied a surge in population. In the pre-revolutionary era the colony boasted an estimated 33,000 persons — more than six times the population at the height of Oglethorpe's leadership. Reflecting on this rapid growth, the aged general glowed in the knowledge that many national leaders were fully aware that Georgia owed her existence to him.

Strangely, for a life-long champion of imperial Britain, Oglethorpe's sympathies were divided during the American Revolution. Years earlier he had joined William Pitt and a minority of eloquent orators in seeking for the American colonies a set of policies that would foster reconciliation instead of armed rebellion. During actual British-American hostilities the founder of Georgia maintained discreet silence.

June 1, 1785, saw an event unparalleled in British history. His Majesty King George III formally received John Adams, who came as the first minister to the Court of Saint James from the United States of America. Just three days later General James Oglethorpe, 88 but straight as a ramrod, called upon Adams and gave him a hearty welcome. Britain's press could not ignore the fact that, alone among the nation's great colonial leaders, the founder of Georgia had lived to see his once-weak and struggling enterprise gain its independence.

Oglethorpe's courtesy to Adams, hailed by Edmund Burke as one of the most thrilling gestures of the century, was a fitting climax to a long and eventful life. After a very brief illness, Georgia's founder died on June 30, 1785. Five months later the last royal governor of the colony — Wright — who had been on the ground for the transition to a free and independent state, followed Oglethorpe to the grave.

When Parliament's Member from Haslemere led a band of 114 followers up Yamacraw bluff, then laid everything on the line for what seemed a foolish and quixotic enterprise, England was a contestant for first place among world powers. At first a tiny coastal outpost, Georgia expanded again and again until she became substantially larger than England. After a mere 250 years the population of the experiment that began as Oglethorpe's Folly substantially exceeds that of Trustee-era England.[11]

During the century following Oglethorpe's death, upland

cotton — believed first propagated in the Trustees' Garden in Savannah — became to Georgia what her founder and his contemporaries
had hoped silk would be. Partly because England prohibited the
export of manufactrured goods from her colonies, those who framed
the Georgia scheme had expected the colony's economic bonanza to
come from the soil. Today, total value of goods and services produced in Georgia is more than $61,900,000,000 per year with manu-
factured goods being exported — at a rate of almost five billion dol-
lars annually.

A grateful nation rewarded Georgia Governor James Wright with
knighthood and burial in Westminster Abbey. Remains of James
Edward Oglethorpe went into an obscure grave at Cranham. Long
neglected and then lost for decades, it was re-discovered in 1923 by
Oglethorpe University President Thornwell Jacobs.

In stark contrast with the last resting place of James Wright,
baronet, that of Georgia's founder was given no splendid marker. It
needed none of bronze or marble.

Now a world center of transportation and manufacturing on a
scale never dimly envisioned by any Georgia Trustee, the Empire
State of the South is James Edward Oglethorpe's living memorial.

SOURCES AND NOTES

JEO = James Edward Oglethorpe

Major sources used in preparation of several chapters or providing an overall perspective are listed here, with brief descriptions where advisable. They are supplemented by lists of sources consulted in the preparation of individual chapters.

Notes have been held to a minimum: explanatory material plus citations of sources not readily available in standard works dealing with JEO and Trustee era Georgia. Citations are abbreviated to the simplest and most readable form.

An asterisk (*) indicates primary source material, while articles that appeared in serials are placed between slanted bars / /. For those listings that were consulted frequently, abbreviations are shown in brackets [ ].

Abstract of British Historical Statistics. Cambridge: University Press, 1962. [ABHS].

*An Account, Shewing the Progress of the Colony of Georgia in America, from its First Establishment. London, 1741. [Account]. Reprinted in Force.

**Acts of the Privy Council, Colonial Series, 1720-1745.* Hereford: H.M's Stationery office, 1910. [APC].

/Anderson, Jefferson R., "The Genesis of Georgia," GHQ 1929, 13:229-84./ [Anderson].

**Arredondo's Historical Proof of Spain's Title to Georgia*; edited by Herbert E. Bolton. Berkeley: Univ. of Cal. Press, 1925. [Arredondo].

Bolton, Herbert E. and Mary Ross, *The Debatable Land*: a sketch of the Anglo-Spanish contest for the Georgia country. Berkeley: Univ. of Cal. Press, 1925. [Bolton].

**A Brief Account of the Establishment of the Colony of Georgia under Gen. James Oglethorpe.* Washington: Peter Force, 1835. *[Brief Account]*. Reprinted in Force.

* *Calendar of State Papers; Colonial Series: America and West Indies, 1732-38*; 7 vols. London: H.M's Stationery Office, 1939-68. Original documents reproduced or condensed here are preserved in the Public Record Office. Volumes are individually indexed by document numbers rather than page numbers. [CSP].

*Carroll, Bartholomew R., *Historical Collections of South Carolina*; embracing many rare and valuable pamphlets, and other documents, relating to the history of that State, from its first discovery to its independence, in the year 1776; 2 vols. N.Y.: Harper and Bros., 1836. [Carroll].

*Causton, Thomas, *Journal* (1737). Reprinted in Reese, *First*.

Chatelaine, Verne E., *The Defenses of Spanish Florida, 1565-1763*, Washington; Carnegie Institute, 1941. [Chatelaine].

221

Church, Leslie F., *Oglethorpe*: a study of philanthropy in England and Georgia. London: Epworth Press, 1932. [Church]. A fellow of the Royal Historical Society, Church spent years with original documents in the Public Record Officce. His meticulous research for a Ph.D. thesis, University of London, uncovered no significant variations between manuscripts and then-existing published versions.

Profusely documeñted, this biography is essential to the serious student of JEO. It suffers, however, from the author's absorption with JEO the philanthropist — almost, but not quite, to the exclusion of other emphases. Immense quantities of material then available only in manuscript form have since been published and may be found in major U.S. libraries.

*Cobbett, W., *Parliamentary History of England*; 12 vols. Edinburgh, 1811. [Cobbett].

Colonial Records of Georgia; Allan Candler, *et. al.* editors; 29 vols. [CRG]. Publication, which began in 1904, is still in progress. Note that some volumes are not indexed, and that where indices are included they are useful but not definitive. Exact citations listing volumes and pages and/or dates are usually available in Church, Ettinger, Ivers, Spalding, or Temple.

Corry, John P., *Indian Affairs in Georgia, 1732-1756*. Philadelphia: George S. Ferguson, 1936. [Corry].

*/Coulter, E. Merton, editor, "A list of the first shipload of Georgia settlers," in GHQ 1947, 31:282-88./ [Coulter, "List"].

/Crane, Verner W., "Dr. Thomas Bray and the charitable colony project, 1730," *William and Mary Quarterly* 1962, 19:49-63./

/Crane, Verner, W., "The origin of Georgia," GHQ 1930, 14:93-110./ [Crane, "Origin"].

/Crane, Verner W., "The philanthropists and the genesis of Georgia," *American Historical Review* 1921, 27:63-69./ [Crane, "Genesis"].

Crane, Verner W., *The Promotion Literature of Georgia*. Cambridge: Harvard Univ. Press, 1924. [Crane].

Crane, Verner W., *The Southern Frontier, 1670-1732*. Durham: Univ. of N.C. Press, 1928. [Crane, *Frontier*].

Davis, Harold E., *The Fledgling Province*: social and cultural life in colonial Georgia, 1733-1760. Chapel Hill: Univ. of N.C. Press, 1976. [Davis]. Because the treatment is topical, it is difficult to locate from the index material dealing specifically with the Trustee era of the colony.

DeBrahm's Report of the General Survey in the Southern District of North America; Louis de Vorsey, Jr., ed. Columbia: Univ. of S.C. Press, 1971. [DeBrahm].

A Description of Georgia, by a gentleman who has resided there upwards of seven years, and was one of the first settlers. London: 1741. Reprinted in Force.

A Description of the Golden Isles; 1720. Reprinted in Reese, *First*.

A Description of the Province of South Carolina, drawn up at Charles Town, in September, 1731. Translated from Mr. Purry's original treatise in French, and published in the *Gentleman's Magazine* for August, September, and October, 1732. Reprinted in Force.

Dictionary of National Biography. Oxford: Univ. Press, 1917.

/Dunn, Richard S., "The Trustees of Georgia and the House of Commons, 1733-52" The William and Mary Quarterly 1954, 11:551-65./ [Dunn].

*Egmont, *Diary of Viscount Percival, First Earl of Egmont*; 3 vols. London: H.M's Stationery Office, 1920-23. [Egmont, *Diary*]. Essential for any comprehensive study of JEO and Georgia during the Trustee era. Comprehensive index is helpful, but in order to locate specific references, volume and page numbers and/or dates are often necessary. See Church, Ettinger, Reese, Spalding, and Temple for such citations.

*Egmont, *The Journal of the Earl of Egmont*: abstract of the Trustees proceedings for establishing the colony of Georgia, 1732-38; Robert G. McPherson, ed. Athens, Univ. of Ga. Press, 1962. [Egmont, *Journal*]. The time span here covered precedes CRG 5, and supplements Egmont, *Diary*, of the same period.

*Egmont, *The Journal of the Earl of Egmont, 1738-44*. [Egmont, *Journal* #2]. Found in CRG 5.

Ettinger, Amos E., *James Edward Oglethorpe*: imperial idealist. Oxford: Clarendon Press, 1936. [Ettinger]. Detailed documentation fills approximately 30% of this volume; unfortunately, many notes include multiple listings and hence are difficult to follow. Generally regarded as the definitive biography of JEO. Note, however, that Ettinger fails to deal with some primary materials, and that Taylor was not available to him.

/Fant, H.B., "Picturesque Thomas Coram, projector of two Georgias and father of the London Foundling Hospital," GHQ 1948, 32?77-104./ [Fant].

*Fleming, Berry, *Autobiography of a Colony*: the first half-century of Augusta, Georgia. Athens: Univ. of Ga. Press, 1957. [Fleming].

*Force, Peter, *Tracts* and other papers relating principally to the origin, settlement and progress of the colonies in North America from the discovery of the country to the year 1774; 4 vols. Washington: Peter Force, 1836-46. [Force].

General Account of all Monies and Effects Received and Expended by the Trustees, 1732-52. [CRG 3]. Appended to this record of receipts and expenditures, itemized throughout, is "An account showing the progress of the colony of Georgia in America from its first establishment," issued by the Trustees in 1751; reprinted in Force.

General Oglethorpe's Georgia: Colonial letters, 1733-37; 2 vols. Savannah: Beehive Press, 1975. [GOG].

*/The *Gentleman's Magazine* 1731-88, vols. 1-58. London, 1731-88./ [*Gentleman's*].

/Georgia Historical Quarterly; 66 vols. to date, 1917-82 [GHQ]. Edited by E. Merton Coulter for half a century, this publication gives genealogy only a fraction of the attention devoted to it by many journals of state historical associations. For specific topics treated, consult Rowland and Dorsey, plus indices of individual volumes.

*Georgia Historical Society *Collections*. Savannah, 1873 —. [GHS *Collections*].

Gipson, Lawrence H., *The British Empire Before the American Revolution*; 15 vls. Caldwell, Idaho, 1936-70. [Gipson]. Especially pertinent material, treated from the British point of view, is included in vols. 1 and 2.

*Gordon, Peter, *Journal of Peter Gordon, 1732-35*. Reprinted in Reese, *First*. [Gordon].

*Hacklyt, Richard, *Virginia Richly Valued*. London, 1609. Reprinted in Force. [Hacklyt].

*Hilton, William, *A Relation of a discovery lately made on the Coast of Florida*. London; Simon Miller, 1664. Reprinted in Force.

*Ingham, Benjamin, *Journal of Benjamin Ingham, 1735-35*. Reprinted in Reese, *First*. [Ingham].

Ivers, Larry E., *British Drums on the Southern Frontier*: the military colonization of Georgia, 1733-49. Chapel Hill: Univ. of N.C. Press, 1974. [Ivers]. Widely accepted as the definitive study of the military aspect of Georgia during the Trustee era.

The Jacobite Attempt of 1719 — Letters of James Butler, Second Duke of Ormonde, relating to Cardinal Alberoni's project for the invasion of Great Britain on behalf of the Stuarts, and to the Landing of a Spanish expedition in Scotland; William K. Kickson, ed. Edinburgh: Univ. Press, 1895. [*Jacobite*].

*Jesse, John H., *Memoirs of the Pretenders and Their Adherents*; 3 vols. Boston: Francis A. Niccols, n.d. [Jesse].

Jones, Charles C., *The History of Georgia*; 3 vols. Boston: Houghton Mifflin, 1883. [Jones].

Journals of the House of Commons, 1722-88. [JHC]. Not indexed.

Journal of the Trustees [of Georgia] *1732-52* [CRG 1]. Not indexed.

King, Horace M., *James Edward Oglethorpe's Parliamentary Career*. Milledgeville: Georgia College, 1968. [King]. A former speaker of the House of Commons, King deals with a single aspect of JEO's career and here adds to contributions made earlier by Church and Ettinger.

*King, Spencer B., *Georgia Voices*: a documentary history to 1872; comp. by Spencer B. King. Athens: Univ. of Ga. Press, 1966. [King, *Voices*].

Knight, Lucian L., *Georgia's Landmarks, Memorials, and Legends* 2 vols. Atlanta: Byrd Ptg. Co., 1913. [Knight]. Because it is not a reliable source of specific data this work is often bypassed by academicians. It is, however, valuable as a source of insights into value-judgments and attitudes on the part of 20th-century Georgians.

Lanning, John T., *The Diplomatic History of Georgia*: a study of the epoch of Jenkins' ear. Chapel Hill: Univ. of N.C. Press, 1936. [Lanning]. Based upon archival material of Spain, England, and France, this volume treats the War of Jenkins' Ear from the persepctive of Georgia's involvement. Alone among analysts of JEO, Lanning labels him a "buccaneer."

McCain, James R., *Georgia as a Proprietary Province*: the execution of a trust. Boston: Richard G. Badger, 1917. [McCain].

McCrady, Edward, *The History of South Carolina under the Royal Government, 1719-76*. N.Y.: Macmillian, 1899. [McCrady].

*Martyn, Benjamin, *Reasons for Establishing the Colony of Georgia*. London, 1733. Reprinted in Reese. [Martyn].

Meriwether, Robert L., *Expansion of South Carolina, 1729-65*. Kingsport: Southern Publishers, 1940. [Meriwether].

/Miller, Randall M., "The failure of the Colony of Georgia under the Trustees," GHQ 1969, 53:1-17./ [Miller].

Minutes, Common Council of the Trustees [of Georgia], *1733-52*. [CRG 2]. Not indexed.

Miscellaneous Papers: Trustees [of Georgia] and others. [CRG 29].

*Montgomery, Sir Robert, and Colonel John Barnwell, *The Most Delightful Golden Isles*: Being a proposal for the establishment of a colony in the country to the south of Carolina. Int. by Kenneth Coleman. Atlanta, 1969. [Montgomery].

*Montgomery, Robert A., *A Discourse concerning . . . the Most Delightful Country of the Universe*; 1717. Reprinted in Reese.

*Moore, Frances, *A Voyage to Georgia* (1735). London, 1744. Reprinted in Reese, *First*. [Moore].

A Narrative of the Proceedings of the People of South-Carolina, in the Year 1719. London, 1726. Reprinted in Force. [*Narrative*].

*Newman, Henry, *Henry Newman's Salzburger Letterbooks*; transcribed and edited by George F. Jones. Athens: Univ. of Ga. Press, 1966. [Newman].

*Oglethorpe, James, "The ACCOMPT of James Oglethorpe Esqr, General and Commander in Chief of His Majesty's Forces in South Carolina and Georgia for Extraordinary Services incurr'd for His Majesty's Service in Georgia and Florida in America from the 22nd of September 1738 to the 22 of July, 1745, when General Oglethorpe sailed for England." [JEO, *Accompt*]. Sworn to and subscribed by James Oglethorpe, October 27, 1747. ("Accompt" is an archaic form of a term for "a money reckoning," or account.) Audit Office: "Colonial expenses in Georgia, West Florida, & the Carolinas from ca. 173- through 178-. A.O. 3-119. Microfilm, Univ. of Ga., E303/C55.

*Oglethorpe, James, *A New and Accurate Account of the Provinces of South Carolina in Georgia*. London, 1732. [JEO, *New*]. Reprinted in Reese.

Original Papers, correspondence; Trustees, General Oglethorpe and Others. 1735-37 [CRG 21]; 1737-39 [CRG 22 pt. 1]; 1737-40 [CRG 22 pt. 2]; 1741-42 [CRG 23]; 1742-45 [CRG 24]; 1745-50 [CRG 25].

*Patrick, J. Max, ed., *Azilia*: a discourse by Sir Robert Montgomery projecting a settlement in the colony known as Georgia. Atlanta: Emory Univ. Sources and Reprints, Series 4, No. 3, 1948. [Patrick].

*Proceedings of the President and Assistants, Savannah, 1741-54. [CRG 6].

*Purry, Jean Pierre, Memorial . . . to the Duke of Newcastle; 1724. [Pury]. Reprinted in Reese.

*Purry, Jean Pierre, Memoire sur le Pais des Cafres, et la Terre de Nuyts; par raport a l'utilite que la Compagnie des Indes Orientales en pourrait retirer pour son commerce. Amsterdam, 1718.

*Purry, Jean Pierre, A Method for Determining the Best Climate of the Earth; trans. from the French. London, 1744. [Purry, Method].

*Rand, Benjamin, Berkeley and Percival: the correspondence of George Berkeley, afterwards Bishop of Cloyne, and Sir John Percival, afterwards Earl of Egmont. Cambridge: Univ. Press, 1914. [Rand].

/Ready, Milton, "The Georgia concept: an eighteenth century experiment in colonization," GHQ 1971, 55:157-75./ [Ready]. A brief rebuttal of Ready's thesis is included.

Reese, Trevor R., Colonial Georgia: a study in British imperial policy in the eighteenth century. [Reese, Colonial]. Athens: Univ. of Ga. Press, 1963.

Reese, Trevor R., The Most Delightful Country of the Universe: promotional literature of the colony of Georgia 1717-34; int. by Trevor R. Reese. Savannah: Beehive Press, 1972. [Reese].

Reese, Trevor R., Our First Visit in America: early reports from the Colony of Georgia, 1732-40; int. by Trevor R. Reese, Savannah: Beehive Press, 1974. [Reese, First].

/Roberts, R.A., "The birth of an American state: Georgia," Transactions of the Royal Historical Society 1924; 4th series 6:23-49. [Roberts].

Rowland, Arthur R. and James E. Dorsey, A Bibliography of the Writings on Georgia History, 1900-70. Spartanburg: Reprint Co., 1978. 5080 books, articles, graduate and unpublished research papers are listed. Topical index provides quickest generally-accessible aid to location of 20th-century writings dealing with specific topics.

*Rudle, T., Sermon . . . to recommend the charity for establishing the new Colony of Georgia. London, 1734. Reprinted in Reese.

*The Saint Augustine Expedition of 1740 Columbia: S. C. Archives Dept., 1954. Reprint of the Carolina assembly's investigation of the campaign, with an introduction by John T. Lanning. [SAE].

/Saye, Albert B., "The Genesis of Georgia: merchants as well as ministers," GHQ 1940, 24:191-206./ [Saye, "Genesis"].

/Saye, Albert B., "The Genesis of Georgia reviewed," GHQ 1966, 50:153-61./

Saye, Albert B., New Viewpoints in Georgia History. Athens: Univ. of Ga. Press, 1943. [Saye].

/Saye, Albert B., "Was Georgia a debtor colony?" GHQ 1940, 24:323-41./ [Saye, "Debtor"].

*Select Tracts Relating to Colonies: 1732. Reprinted in Reese.

Sherman, Richard P., Robert Johnson: Proprietary and Royal Governor of South Carolina. Columbia: Univ. of S.C. Press, 1966. [Sherman].

Sirmans, M. Eugene, Colonial South Carolina: a political history, 1663-1763. Chapel Hill: Univ. of N.C. Press, 1966. [Sirmans].

/Smith, Henry A.M., "Purrysburgh," South Carolina Historical and Genealogical Magazine 1909, 19:187-219./ [Smith].

*Some Account of the Designs of the Trustees for Establishing the Colony of Georgia in America; 1732. Reprinted in Reese. [Some Account].

*South Carolina; Carolina Records of South Carolina — the Journal of the Commons House of Assembly, 1736-49; 10 vols. to date. [SCCR]. Set includes no volume numbers.

South Carolina Historical and Genealogical Magazine, 1900-82; vols. 1-83; 3 vols. of indices. [SCG&H].

Spalding, Phinizy, Oglethorpe in America. Chicago: Univ. of Chicago Press, 1977. [Spalding].

*A State of the Province of Georgia, attested upon oath in the Court of Savannah, November 10, 1740. London, 1742. Reprinted in Force.

*Stephens, William, Journal, 1734-41. [CRG 4, supplement].

*Stephens, William, The Journal of William Stephens 1741-43; E. Merton Coulter, ed. Athens:

Univ. of Ga. Press, 1958-59. [Stephens]. Supplements CRG 4 and CRG 4, supplement.

*Tailfer, Pat., M.D., *et.al., A True and Historical Narrative of the Colony of Georgia, in America*. Charles Town, 1741. Reprinted in Force. [Tailfer].

Taylor, G. Stirling, *Robert Walpole and His Age*. London: Jonathan Cape, 1933. [Taylor, *Walpole*].

Taylor, Paul S., *Georgia Plan, 1732-1752*. Berkeley: Graduate School of Business Administration, 1972. [Taylor]. Using computers and research facilities plus clerical help from the school, Taylor explored a neglected facet of Trustee era Georgia.

Trustees kept meticulous records about persons sent on the charity, but except for notations about land grants they viturally ignored the flood of self-supporting adventurers who, with their servants, went to Georgia to take up tracts ten times as large as those assigned to charity colonists. Though findings are not exact, this relatively obscure work corrects a serious imbalance in most analyses of JEO and his colony.

/Temperley, Harold W.V., "The causes of the war of Jenkins' ear, 1739," in *Transactions of the Royal Historical Society* 1909; 3rd Series, 3:197-236./ [Temperley].

Temple, Sarah B.G. and Kenneth Coleman, *Georgia Journeys*: being an account of the lives of Georgia's original settlers and many other early settlers from the founding of the colony in 1732 until the institution of Royal Government in 1754. Athens: Univ. of Ga. Press, 1961. [Temple].

*Thompson, Mrs., *Memoirs of the Jacobites*; 3 vols. London: Richard Bentley, 1845. Vignettes of individual Jacobites.

*Urlsperger, Samuel, ed., *Detailed Reports of the Salzburger Emigrants who Settled in America*; 5 vols. Univ. of Ga. Press, 1968-80. [Urlsperger].

*Von Reck, *An Extract of the Journals of Mr. Commissary Von Reck*. London, 1734. Reprinted in Force; extracts reprinted in Reese, *First*.

*/"The Voyage of the Anne — a daily record," edited by Robert G. McPherson; GHQ 1960, 44:220-30. ["Voyage"]. Detailed daily log kept by Thomas Christie.

*Wesley, John, *Extract . . . Rev. John Wesley's Journal (1735-37)*. London, 1739. Reprinted in Reese, *First*.

Westbrook, by Frances Harrold *et. al.* Atlanta: Ass'n of the Amer. Inst. of Architects, 1977. [Westbrook].

*Whitefield, George, *Journal (1738-40)*. London, 1739-41. Reprinted in Reese, *First*.

Wright, Robert, *A Memoir of General James Oglethorpe*. London: Chapman and Hall, 1867. [Wright]. Less than fully reliable, but influential because used as a source by numerous Oglethorpe biographers.

Chapter 1. A HERITAGE OF GLORY AND SHAME

SOURCES — Church; Cobbett; Ettinger; JHC; King; *Westwood*; plus

Hill, Patricia K., *The Oglethorpe Ladies*. Atlanta: Cherokee Pub. Co., 1977. Primary focus is upon JEO's sisters who were most active in the Jacobite cause; helps to establish the climate in which JEO grew to maturity.

Oxford English Dictionary.

/Spalding, Phinizy, "The death of James Edward Oglethorpe," GHQ 1973, 57:227-34./ [Spalding, "Death"].

NOTES — 1. By the time James II reached the throne in 1685, English was rapidly displacing Latin even in the realms of diplomacy, science, and religion. Still the long-established usage according to which the sovereign was designated by a Latin rather than an English name remained pervasive. As late as the era of JEO's Parliamentary career, numerous official documents used "Georgii IIdi" to indicate the king.

"Jacobite" was not employed as a label for a follower of James II and/or his male descendants prior to 1689. Once the term became current it was universally used and understood. True Jacobites — among whom the Oglethorpes were notable — made clear distictions between the House of Stuart in its totality (including William III and Queen Anne) and the male line stemming from the deposed James II. A·ːkward as the label is for use by 20th-century Americans, employment of it in its full 18th-century British meaning is essential for understanding the development and career of JEO.

2. King, 1. In many instances voting rights attached to property rather than to persons. This meant that a landlord normally had control over votes linked with his holdings. With only 100-125 votes assigned to Haslemere, this borough was almost (but not quite) literally "in the pocket" of its landlords. Oglethorpe holdings were not so extensive as those of the Molyneux family, however. Rivalry between the two principal landowners meant a spirited contest for each of the seats assigned to Haslemere.

3. Following an error in newspaper obituaries, many early biographers of JEO listed his birth date as June 1, 1689. This mistake stemmed from failure to distinguish between James Oglethorpe, d. 6-15-1690, and JEO. See Spalding, "Death."

Sir Theophilus and Lady Eleanor Oglethorpe named their first three sons, in order of birth, Lewis, Theophilus, and Sutton. Use of James in 1689 (the very year in which "Jacobite" gained currency) can hardly have been casual. Nor can the significance of again using James (with Edward added) for the son of a 46-year-old father be overlooked. During childhood and youth JEO was constantly reminded of the symbolic significance of the name given him to bear in lieu of his brother who had died at age one.

4. See King.

5. Peter Burrell, a wealthy merchant in the Portugal trade, was generally counted as a Whig — a member of the party long in control of Parliament. Oglethorpe, a Tory, remained true to the party widely regarded as suspect because of its links with leaders of the Jacobite uprising in 1715. Burrell had gained ownership of several Haslemere properties by the time JEO was ready to stand for Parliament. He and JEO became long-time allies, each channelling those votes he controlled toward his colleague as well as himself. See *Westbrook*, 16ff.

6. Cobbett, 8:216. English law of the era made it a crime to report Parliamentary debates. Though no verbatim reports were issued, many subterfuges were employed to publish abbreviated and interpreted versions of debates. Writing for *Gentleman's*, Samuel Johnson used the thinly-disguised label, "Debates in the Parliament of Lilliput." Strictures upon visitors were so great that when the mother of the first Pitt wished to hear her son speak, she slipped into the gallery disguised as a male. See JHC for detailed regulations, published at the beginning of each session.

Chapter 2: A RISE TO PROMINENCE IN AN ERA OF GRANDIOSE DESIGNS

SOURCES — APC; Boswell; Church; Cobbett; Crane, "Genesis;" Egmont, *Diary*; Ettinger; JHC; King; Rand; plus
Babington, Anthony, *The English Bastille*. London: MacDonald, 1971.
Bayne-Powell, Rosamond, *Eighteenth-century London Life*. New York: E.P. Dutton, 1938.
Besant, Walter, *London in the Eighteenth Century*. London: A. & C. Black, 1925.
Bruce, James, *Life of General Oglethorpe*. 1890.
Carswell, John, *The South Sea Bubble*. London: Cresset, 1960.
Fox, Lionel W., *The English Prison and Borstal Systems*. London: Routledge and Kegan Paul, 1952.

Hinde, R.S.E., *The English Penal System*. London: Duckworth, 1951.

Langford, Paul, *The Eighteenth Century*. New York: Saint Martin's Press, 1976.

Lecky, W.E.H., *A History of England in the Eighteenth Century*; 8 vols. London, 1878.

Maccoby, Simon, *Eighteenth Century England*. London: Longmans, 1931.

Mackay, Charles, *Memoirs of Extraordinary Popular Delusions*. London: National Illustrated Library, 1852.

Marlow, Joyce, *The Life and Times of George I*. London: Weidenfeld and Nicolson, 1973.

Melville, Lewis, *The South Sea Bubble*. New York: Burt Franklin, 1968.

Mowat, R.R., *England in the Eighteenth Century*. New York: McBride, n.d.

Owen, John B., *The Eighteenth Century, 1714-1815*. Totowa, N.J.: Rowman and Littlefield, 1975. [Owen].

/Pennington, Edgar L., "Thomas Bray's Associates," *American Antiquarian* Society 1938; vol. 48 n.s./

/Saye, Albert B., "The genesis of Georgia," *Georgia Review* 1947, 1:117-25./

NOTES — 1. *The Sailor's Advocate*, 1777, bears imprint "Seventh Edition." No copies of editions #2 through #6 have been found. See critical commentary in Sarah C. Hills, "A New Appraisal of James Edward Oglethorpe," abstract of unpublished master's thesis, Emory University, 1959, pp. 80ff.

2. A copy is held by The American Institute of Architects, Washington, D.C. The volume includes no city plans. But Castell's plates that depict formal gardens are strikingly suggestive of the plan of Savannah.

3. JEO's own estimate of April 1, 1730. See Egmont, *Diary*, 1:90. Writing to George Berkeley in May, JEO put the number at 6,000; see Rand, 275ff. Despite general silence of the press there were some public expressions of praise. Samuel Wesley, Jr., brother of Charles and John Wesley, penned and published an extravagant eulogy that he called "The Prisons Open'd — A Poem occasioned by the late glorious Proceedings of the Committee Appointed to inquire into the State of the Gaols of this Kingdon" (London, 1729).

4. Utrecht serves as an omnibus title for a series of treaties effected during the period 1713-15. At Utrecht the crucial War of the Spanish Succession ended; hence, this agreement's name attached to subsidiary treaties.

5. At the time JEO's British properties were placed on the market in 1788, gross annual rental amounted to £353. Land taxes ranged from 10% to 20%, with additional war taxes levied on houses, windows, carriages, servants, and even dogs. Net rental income from the entire holdings in and about Godalming, Surrey, ranged just above or below £300 per year. See *Westbrook*, 12-13.

6. According to I.S. Leadam, *The Political History of England*, 6:295, this bizarre proposal netted the promoter some £2,000. It is strangely like some advanced a few years later to Georgia Trustees; see Egmont, *Journal*. In the latter cases, the mysterious offers proved to be Trustee-sponsored lotteries.

7. Owen, 24.

8. First issued in London in 1717, the *Discourse* has been reprinted many times. The complete text is readily available in Reese.

9. Despite his long-time service as a Trustee for Georgia, Egmont never made more than token contributions to the colony.

10. JEO entered into litigation about King's estate and won a favorable verdict. Yet there is no record that the eagerly-awaited £5,000 — springboard for the entire Georgia scheme — was ever received.

Chapter 3: CONCEPTION, GESTATION, AND BIRTH OF A GRAND UTOPIAN SCHEME

SOURCES — APC; Church; Cobbett, Egmont, *Diary* 1; JHC; King; Rand; Ready; Saye; Saye, "Debtor;" plus

Cobbett, W., et. al., ed's., *A Complete Collection of State Trials*. London: 1809-29; 17:616-7, 562ff.

Cumming, William P., *The Southeast in Early Maps*. Chapel Hill: Univ. of N.C. Press, 1962. See #158, pp. 181-3. Indiana University's Eli Lilly Library holds a copy of #158, complete with insets.

Davies, Kenneth G., *The Royal African Company*, N.Y. Longman, Green, 1957.

NOTES — 1. "Scheme" is the term used over and over in primary sources that deal with JEO's proposals, modified in rapid-fire fashion almost as soon as they were advanced.

2. This approach to financing the scheme was received with great enthusiasm. As a result, just ten days after it was made, Egmont presented Walpole with names of 20 persons "who we of the Carolina Company desired tickets in the intended lottery for each 100 tickets."

3. During this phase of pre-planning, geographical terms were used loosely and interchangeably: Carolina, South Carolina, the Indies, the Colonies, and — finally — Georgia.

4. Until the Glorious Revolution of 1688 the British sovereign was all but absolute. A central effect of the revolution was the change by which the crown came to rest "with the king in Parliament." Walpole strongly objected to the propsal that Parliament pass an act enabling the sovereign to grant the charter. He preferred that the charter come directly from the king, so that there would be no financial responsibility on the part of Parliament. See Saye, 47-49.

5. Egmont, *Diary*, describes the £20 gift as coming from "an unknown person by Mr. Oglethorpe's hands." This phrase and variants of it occur repeatedly in records of Georgia's founding. Were some such gifts anonymous contributions from JEO? Possibly, but not positively. During 20 years collective cash gifts of Georgia's Trustees, as reported, did not total £2,000. This despite the fact that Egmont and Hucks plus at least ten others who served as Trustees for a long or a short time were men of substantial or great wealth.

6. JEO held the post for only one year. He gives no hint concerning his decision to abandon it, but upon becoming acquainted with the inner workings of the corporation he quickly discovered that it long ago passed the peak of its profit-making period.

7. Purry's *Memorial . . . to the Duke of Newcastle* painted an idyllic picture. More than any other early publication, it was responsible for the naive notion that Georgia had a climate perfect for humans, animals, and exotic plants of every variety.

8. An English-language translation of this contract is held by the University of Georgia Library, Athens. JEO seems to have been of some service to Purry; see Egmont, *Diary*, 1:286. If JEO realized a profit from this secret agreement, it was never mentioned. Yet his Carolina holdings (see Chapter 11, below) were geographically close to those of Purry. Nowhere in the voluminous JEO papers are there even terse references to his success in his attempt to gain possession of extensive New World tracts.

9. No published map included the name "Georgia" before 1732. In that year, rivals of noted Dutch-born geographer Hammond Moll, recently deceased, pirated and re-issued his "New and Exact Map of the Dominions of the King of Great Britain on ye Continent of North America" (London, 1715). Moll's map included several insets, of which #1, six by seven inches, showed "the South Part of Carolina, and the East Part of Florida, posses'd since 1712 by the French and called Louisiana; together with some of the principal Indian settlements and the Number of Fighting Men." In the pirated re-issue "350 men" was burnished from a spot just under "Yamasee" in order to have "Georgia" inscribed there. Because 1715 still appears on the map proper, this version (1732) issued concurrently with Georgia's charter

has led to the mistaken interpretation that the region was originally named in honor of King George I.

10. The full text of Georgia's charter has been reprinted many times and is readily available. A curious notation appears only in the Public Record Office copy (the original). Here it is recorded that the manuscript of the charter delivered to the Trustees occupied five skins. On Nov. 8 it was "examd. and compar'd" with the original before being handed over to JEO. See SCP 1732 #258 (p. 146).

Chapter 4. A RASH DECISION, MADE IN HASTE

SOURCES — ACP; Anderson; *Brief Account;* CSP; Church; Cobbett; Crane, "Origin;" Crane, "Genesis;" Egmont, *Diary*; Egmont, *Journal*; Ettinger; Force; CRG 3; *Gentleman's*; JHC; CRG 1; Martyn; CRG 2; Montgomery; Rand; Reese; Roberts; Saye, "Genesis;" Saye, "Debtor;" 07. [Osgood].

Osgood, H.L., *The American Colonies in the Eighteenth Century*; 3 vols. London: Macmillan, 1904-07. [Osgood].

NOTES — 1. Fant, 90ff.

2. Manuscripts Division, Library of Congress.

3. Egmont, *Diary*, 1:292. Payments sometimes fell below subscriptions. In the case of the Bank of England, the actual remittance was only £252 (CRG 1:75).

4. Egmont, *Diary*, 1:287-8; cf. Egmont, *Journal* #1, 4.

5. Osgood 3:37.

6. See detailed listing in Saye, "Debtor," 332-334.

7. JEO's extreme interest in aged persons (including Tomochichi and himself as The Lion of London, when he steadfastly refused to divulge his age) may account for his having included what seems on the surface to be an incredibly naive report.

8. CRG 3:407-11. This list was entered into the record in 1735, by which time it had become standard.

9. "Anniversary" sermons, preached on February 23 or 24 annually for many years, began in 1732.

10. Egmont, *Diary*, 1:260.

11. Lady Oglethorpe died on June 19, 1732; brief notices appeared in six periodicals.

Chapter 5. SEVENTY-NINE DAYS: ENGLAND TO GEORGIA

SOURCES — *Brief Account*; Church; Coulter, "List;" Crane, "Origin;" Egmont, *Diary* Egmont, *Journal*; Ettinger; CRG 3; *Gentleman's*; Gordon; Jones; CRG 1; CRG 2; Roberts; Saye, "Debtor;" Spalding; Taylor; Temple; "Voyage."

NOTES — 1. Several secondary accounts plus such primary source material as Christie's log list the vessel as the *Anne*.

2. 91 heads versus 114 persons.

3. "Voyage."

4. This aspect of the ship's provisioning has led to misunderstanding on the part of some analysts, who have considered the quantity of beer remarkable. "Ton" was a variant of "tun," a special type of cask which, if standard, held 252 gallons; see OED. Usage "ton" occurs repeatedly in JEO, *Accompt*. Beer and wine did not spoil so readily as did water, which could become foul in a very few weeks.

5. More books brought by Hale on November 8 arrived too late for any portion of them to go aboard the *Ann*.

6. Saye, "Debtor," presents the results of an exhaustive inquiry, according to which "having been imprisoned for debt was not the determining factor in the selection of a single colonist" and "not more than a dozen debtors were ever sent to Georgia."

7. Coulter, "List," 282-88; cf. Temple, 295ff, where the listing is alphabetical and does not precisely correspond with that of Egmont.

8. If a settler died, a male heir of 16 was eligible to inherit his improvements. But at least in theory, land tenure involved forfeiting all rights if stipulations were not met. Every part of a grant was supposed to be cleared, cultivated, and enclosed with a six-foot worm fence within 18 years — or title was lost. Failure to plant ten white mulberry trees per acre was also a legal cause for forfeiting rights in land. In practice, JEO relaxed these and other requirements quite early, but did so without Trustee authorization or knowledge.

9. Named for Julius Caesar, the Julian calendar that was followed in the western world for many centuries was in error by more than 11 minutes per year. As a result there was a gradual shift of the equinox. In a bull of March 1, 1582, Pope Gregory XIII ordered corrections by which the civil year would be brought into harmony with the astronomical year. Some Catholic nations grumbled but most agreed to the change. As a result, in these countries the day that would otherwise have been October 5, 1582 (Julian style), became October 15, (Gregorian style).

Strong anti-Catholic sentiment in England delayed adoption of the revised calendar for many years. When by act of Parliament it finally became the legal standard in 1752, eleven days were dropped in September. At the same time New Year's Day, formerly observed on March 25, was shifted to January 1. Properly and accurately to change Julian or Old Style (O.S.) dates to Gregorian or New Style (N.S.) dates, it is necessary to add one to the number of any O.S. year for periods between January 1 and March 25; i.e., 1732 O.S. becomes 1733 N.S. during these three months only. In order accurately to adjust days and months it is necessary to add eleven to the number of every day up to and including September 2, 1752.

In practice this procedure is so cumbersome that most adjustments deal only with the year — not the day of the month on which a given event occurred. So treated, January 11, 1745 (O.S.) becomes January 11, 1746 (N.S.)

American colonies resisted the new calendar much more vigorously than did even the British. Hence some pivotal dates (such as the birthday of George Washington) were long observed O.S. even though the N.S. calendar was legally in effect.

Eventual adoption of N.S. dates for virtually all purposes created a special dilemma. Such events as Washington's birthday and the founding of Georgia were advanced one year plus 11 days over corresponding O.S. dates. For example, by JEO's reckoning colonists landed at Yamacraw Bluff on February 1, 1732 (corresponding with February 12, 1733, N.S.).

Since central events in the crucial first three months of 1732/33 are now universally treated as having occurred according to the N.S. calendar, for the purposes of this study the N.S. correction for that year (only) includes addition of 11 days to dated events in the period January-March.

10. Actual time that transpired. Gregorian calendar adjustments for the first three months of 1732/33 make the journey appear to be 11 days longer than it actually was.

Chapter 6. THE WORLD TURNED UPSIDE DOWN: OGLETHORPE IN GEORGIA

SOURCES — *Account*; APC; *Brief Account*; CSP; Church; Coulter, "List;" Davis; Ettinger; CRG 3; GOG; Gipson; Gordon; Ivers; CRG 1; King, *Voices*; McCain; Newman; Roberts; Saye, Spalding; Taylor; Temple; Von Reck; plus
/Hart, Bertha S., "The first garden of Georgia," GHQ 1933, 29:325-32./
Knight, Lucian L., *Georgia and Georgians*, vol. 1. Chicago: Lewis Pub. Co., 1917.

NOTES — 1. At the Mariners Museum, Newport News, Virginia, a careful search was made for prints or paintings depicting vessels without which there would have been no Georgia. All were privately owned and most were small. Even their names appear in no standard sources other than the Georgia records.

A water color attributed to Charles T. Warren and/or his son Alfred William Warren depicts the frigate *Pearl* as she was believed to have appeared in 1780, capturing the French merchant frigate *Esperance*. It is possible, but improbable, that the merchant ship which reached Savannah on the day land was first allocated to settlers was later converted to a 32-gun frigate.

Except for this less-than-satisfactory reference, librarians at the Mariners Museum found no hint offering any details whatever about the ships that made the England-to-Georgia run during Oglethorpe's first stay in the colony.

2. Taylor, Table V, 308.

3. JEO, letter of 2-21-33, GOG 1:4. Unlike many later letters, the entire tone of this one marks it as a straightforward report — making no effort to say what recipients wanted to hear. JEO reported, for example, almost casually that ten of his company were already ill with the bloody flux. Tomochichi did attend divine services with some frequency, but never became a convert.

4. Germans settled in the region selected by Von Reck and in May erected a chapel —their first building. Soon they began finding fault with the site of their town. Their protests, made collectively rather than individually, were more effective than those of charity colonists or even of gentleman adventurers who didn't like their alloted land. Permission to move a few miles to the junction of Ebenezer creek and the Savannah river was gained in 1736, against the strong objections of JEO.

Salzburgers abandoned the site they now began to call Old Ebenezer and transferred the name Ebenezer to the new community. When additional large groups of these European Protestants arrived, almost all of them went to Ebenezer rather than settling in Savannah or other outpost towns.

December 27, 1734, brought 65 additional Salzburgers and 63 followed two months later. That made the Germans the largest and most cohesive non-British group in Trustee era Georgia. In a fashion different from that of persons in any English-speaking town or settlement, these hard-working colonists — many of whom had experience in farming — achieved self-sufficiency plus a degree of success in producing silk.

Chapter 7. OGLETHORPE'S COMRADES BEGIN TO FLEX THEIR MUSCLES

SOURCES — APC; CSP; Church; Egmont, *Diary*; Egmont, *Journal*; Ettinger; Force; CRG 3; GOC; *Gentleman's*; Jones; JHC; CRG 1; McCain; CRG 2; Roberts; plus

Clark-Kennedy, A.E., *Stephen Hales*; an eighteenth-century biography. Cambridge: University Press, 1929. [Hales].

Stevens, William B., *A History of Georgia*. Savannah: Beehive Press reprint; 2 vols., 1972. [Stevens].

NOTES — 1. Stevens, 1:463-75, gives a complete 21-year list, with brief summaries of individual accomplishments. See also McCain, who deals only with the ten most active Trustees.

2. Nineteen years older than JEO, Hales never became really prominent in the Anglican Church. He is credited with having launched the science of plant physiology, and won more than local renown as an inventor of mechanical devices. See CRG 3: 21, 24, 61, 94, *et. seq.*, for itemized lists of books collected by Hales for Georgia.

3. Taylor, 34. Here the periodic totals are: first six years, £23,280 next eight years, £9,060; final six years, £27,120.

4. Money lent to artisans and tradesmen to enable them to establish their "different callings" was both advanced by and underwritten by "Father Oglethorpe." See GOG for numerous references to this and related practices by JEO.

5. JEO refers to these Irish convicts as "indentured servants." Full details of his disposition of their services may be found in GOG 1:29ff.

Chapter 8. A LONG LEVER AND A FULCRUM ON WHICH TO REST IT

SOURCES — APC; Church; Davis; Egmont, *Diary*; Egmont, *Journal*; Fant; CRG 1; CRG 2; CRG 3; McCain; Roberts; Spalding; Temple; plus
Arkell, R.L., *Caroline of Ansbach*. Oxford: Univ. Press, 1939.
Brockett, L.P., *The Silk Industry in America*. Philadelphia: Silk Assn. of America, 1876.
Shaw, W.A., ed., *Calendar of Treasury Books and Papers*. London, 1898.

NOTES — 1. Though all of the dried plants were "exotic," only contrayerva had any known use. British adventurers in Jamaica found this New World plant being used by natives as an antidote to snake-bite, as well as a tonic and stimulant. It never had any economic significance, however.

2. An English law, effective 1731, prohibited the Colonial manufacture and exportation of merchandise that could be produced in England. Georgia's pioneer potash maker hoped to sell his product in other North American colonies. Small shipments of potash — sent as samples to demonstrate that the industry was in operations — went to London during 1734-36.

3. Raw silk came from Georgia at irregular intervals: eight pounds in 1735, 20 pounds in 1739, 45 pounds in 1741, 19 pounds in 1743, 23 pounds in 1745, and 34 pounds in 1747. Each shipment, however small, fanned the smoldering fires of hope according to which this commodity, alone, would make Georgia — and Britain — rich. Unlike deerskins, silk was not normally placed on the market. Trustees waited — in vain — for the year in which the crop would be of such spectacular size that its sale would rivet the eyes of the nation upon the distant source of wealth.

4. More Molyneux, defeated by JEO in their contest for the House of Commons in 1722, eventually despaired of collecting by honorable means and in 1727 took legal action to get the past-due rent.

5. Legally no more than a corporation with severely limited powers, the Georgia Trust when created was expected eventually to have a large number of members. Hence the charter provided that a common council — originally made up of 15 Trustees, with expansion to 24 expected — would be empowered to handle much business of the Trust.

A person who wished to do so could resign from the common council, but there was no provision for resignation from the parent Trust. Members of the common council took an oath to perform faithfully; no such oath was required of Trustees not named to the council. In order to transact business the council was required to have at least eight members present; in the case of the corporation, no quorum was specified.

This clumsy and complicated system produced a paradoxical climate in which to transact business. When the common council assembled it could take no action if seven or fewer members were present. But the parent body, the corporation proper, could convene and transact any and all business with only three members present. In practice, many of the affairs of the Trust were handled by a quorum of three Trustees. See McCain, 98-115.

6. During a period of 40 years, Carolina currency had only minor fluctuations in the rate of exchange — approximately seven pounds (Carolina) for £1, sterling. Many transactions of Trustee era Georgia were conducted in Carolina currency, but for such matters as JEO's all-

important salary as general of the army (from 1737) and his personal "Accompt" for expenditures, it was the pound, sterling, that was used.

7. According to Roberts, reticence about religion stemmed from the fact that in spite of treatment by Sir Hans Sloane, their stricken comrade had already died of smallpox. This tragedy, they believed, stemmed from their having talked too freely about sacred matters.

8. Though the original by Verelst was subsequently lost, at least two well-known artists (Faber and Kleinschmidt) had already made engravings from it. As reconstructed from these engravings, the Verelst study depicts a stalwart Tomochichi no more than 60 years old and perhaps as young as 45. This is the only bit of evidence from the era by which to arrive at an estimate of Tomochichi's age. If the portrait was in any sense realistic, the man who sat for it was decades away from the 90-year mark that JEO accepted without question and skillfully exploited in the triumphant English visit of "the venerable American sovereign."

9. As late as 1737 Trustees still tried, ineffectively, to frame laws that would go into force upon privy council approval. Some of the affairs they hoped in vain to regulate in this way were: "the manner of private Persons giving Credit to One Another and of their suing for Debts; the Watch and the Militia; the Use of Gold and Silver in Apparel and furniture in Georgia, and prevention of Extravagance and Luxury;" plus establishment of a port duty for both the Savannah and Altamaha rivers of "a Pound of Pistol Powder per Ton according to their Tonnage." See CRG 1:280-81.

10. Any lingering questions concerning the basic viewpoint of JEO are dispelled by a careful reading of his *A New and Accurate Account*. Here he dangles bait before prospective settlers in Georgia by telling them that adjoining Carolina has "above Forty Thousand Negroe Slaves, worth at least a Million of Pounds Sterling."

11. It is not clear why Parliament followed this procedure. Money earlier provided by the crown and Parliament had been designated for specific purposes. Fortunately, Trustees were super-conscious of restrictions and were careful not to apply designated funds to general uses — even when there was a surplus of money for the former and a lack of cash for the latter.

12. General funds of the treasury were involved in the 1735 appropriation. Earlier monies (£10,000 from Parliament in 1733 and £3,161 from the crown the following year) came from restricted accounts not available either to Parliament or the crown for use at will.

13. Appropriations made to Georgia Trustees amounted to £136,608; for itemized list see Fant, 29; Dunn, 553; Church, 278. Direct expenditures for military purposes plus reimbursement of expenses incurred by JEO involved £91,705 for the period September 22, 1738, through July 22, 1743, only. For a summary of items included in the latter total see JHC 17 Geo. II, 615. Georgia's military defense cost Britain, in direct appropriations, £153,344 for the period 1744-51. A grant of £2,632 was made to Trustees to enable them to meet outstanding obligations that remained after surrender of the charter. A grant of February 21, 1754, went to satisfy claims of merchants, arising from the Saint Augustine expedition and the Spanish invasion of Georgia. Finally, Mary Musgrove Matthews Bosomworth received a cash settlement of £2,100 in 1759. Direct expenditures by Britain, not including the cost of maintaining regular British military units, brought the Trustee era cost of Georgia to the king and Parliament to a total of £401,886.

Chapter 9. UNEXPECTED STORMS — THE SECOND VOYAGE TO GEORGIA

SOURCES — APC; Church; Corry; CSP; Davis; Egmont, *Diary*; CRG 1; CRG 2; CRG 3; Ettinger; Fant; Fleming; GOG; Gordon; Lanning; McCain; Reese; Saye, "Debtor;" Spalding; Temple; plus
/Barnwell, John, "Fort King George, Journal of Col. John Barnwell," SCH&G 1926, 27:189-203./

Callaway, James E., *The Early Settlement of Georgia*. Athens: Univ. of Ga. Press, 1948.
Clowes, William Laird, *et. al., The Royal Navy*, a history; 7 vols. London, 1897-1903.
/Heath, William E., "The early colonial money system of Georgia," GHQ 1935, 19:145-60./
"The Spanish Official Account of the Attack on the Colony of Georgia," GHS *Collections* 1840,
    1:80-152.

NOTES — 1. Internal dissension caused Georgia's Moravian community to dwindle from 30
to 12 persons. Some returned to Europe; others went to Pennsylvania. At the time the
Spanish were expected to invade Georgia, all able-bodied males of the colony were called
upon to bear arms. Because they were conscientious objectors, the remaining Moravians
refused to obey this order and left, in a group, for Pennsylvania.

2. In addition to written reports, Wesley gave a detailed oral account to Egmont. As noted
in the *Journal* of the latter, it involved 27 separate items. Both favorable and unfavorable
verdicts were included. Wesley's estimate, based largely upon hearsay because he was not in
Georgia long enough to accumulate specific personal data, indicated that 700 settlers had
abandoned the colony. According to the priest these persons were "seduced away by
Carolina." If Wesley's count was approximately accurate, total deserters up to this time
approximately equalled the 1735 population of Savannah. See Egmont, *Journal*, 214-19.

3. This argument represented a decided shift in position from that taken in the successful
effort to win a huge appropriation with which to make ready to resist the French. Was the
change in viewpoint a result of having received new intelligence from Indian allies? Perhaps,
yet it must be remembered that Anglo-French relations were for the moment improving
somewhat, while Anglo-Spanish relations were deteriorating rapidly. JEO both responded
to this deterioration and contributed to it. From this point he never wavered in his conviction
that Spain represented the paramount threat to Georgia, and that if Georgia should fall, all of
British American would follow.

4. Mackays abounded in Trustee era Georgia. There were two Charles Mackays, two
James Mackays, and three Hugh Mackays. Capt. Hugh Mackay, Sr., reached the colony in
1733. He was a veteran soldier who for a time held the rank of lieutenant in the British army.
His nephew was Hugh Mackay, Jr., who rose from the rank of ensign to captain under JEO.
Both Hugh Mackays were in the party that surveyed Cumberland island for the first time;
Mackay, Sr., was (next to JEO) the ranking officer of the party.

5. Scottish Jacobites, who must have been sure that they would find a haven in the colony
led by the son of famous English Jacobites, soon settled at New Inverness. It later became
Darien.

6. This northernmost Spanish site was not continuously manned. At his first visit JEO
found it deserted. From time to time it housed companies of soldiers, however, and even
when unmanned it was clearly and unequivocally Spanish.

7. Trustees, desperately trying to control JEO's expenditures without totally alienating
him, decided on July 24, 1735, to issue currency for use in the colony. Because this currency
was designed solely for Georgia circulation, the term "sola bills" was customarily used to
designate it. Actually a limited bill of exchange, the sola bill was not legal tender. When an
effort was made to pay bills of the colony with sola bills, the rate of exchange fluctuated in the
range of £8 sola to £1 sterling. During the period 1735-61 sola bills in the amount of £33,510
were issued. This clumsy form of colonial currency added to administrative problems of
Georgia, rather than reducing them.

Chapter 10. "THE FATE OF THE COLONY IS IN ONE MAN'S HANDS"

SOURCES — APC; Arredondo; Bolton; Corry; CSP; Davis, Egmont, *Diary*; Ettinger; Fant;

Gipson; Ivers; JHC; King; Lanning; McCain; Reese; Roberts; Taylor; Temperley; plus British Public Record Office, Board of Trade, *Georgia*; vols. 12-13. Entry book of instructions, powers, commissions and leases issued by the Georgia Trustees. [PRO/BT].

Jackson, Thomas, *The Life of the Rev. Charles Wesley, M.A.*; 2 vols. London: John Mason, 1841.

Wesley, John, *The Journal of the Rev. John Wesley, A.M.*; Nehemiah Curnock, ed.; vol. 1. London: Robert Culley, 1909.

NOTES — 1. This was not a new tactic. Immediately after his return from his first voyage to Georgia, JEO called upon the sovereign. A surprised aide discovered the king and the Member of Parliament "poring over military maps."

2. There is no evidence that Georgia Trustees constituted a voting bloc in Parliament. Some of them did sometimes oppose the prime minister's measures, but as a body they were not consistently aligned for or against Walpole. Some individuals — notably Egmont — became bitter enemies of the prime minister. In one of his furious encounters with Walpole, JEO twitted him about his fears (genuine and valid, as it proved) that his ministry might soon be overthrown.

3. As usual, much of the blame was heaped upon JEO. Trustees learned on January 18 that on October 22, 1736, he drew six bills against them for a total of £475. This action was taken by Georgia's founder 27 days after their notice prohibiting such bills was published in the South Carolina *Gazette*. JEO, who was present when the matter was heatedly discussed, explained that the bills were drawn for essential provisions.

He was at Frederica at the time, he said. He had not yet been notified that his authority to purchase in the usual manner had been rescinded. A bill for £500, drawn in May, had been refused by the Trustees. JEO told them that the money was needed "to prevent the Spaniard being supplied with Guns and Duffils for the Indians." After discussion and grumbling, these and other bills drawn by JEO were honored — interest being added to the bill Trustees had earlier refused to pay.

4. Almost from the beginning of colonization, JEO began dipping into his own pocket for cash needed in emergencies. Most such early advances of personal funds were repaid without interest from funds of the Georgia Trust. That was not the case with later and much larger sums that JEO gambled — with no assurance of repayment — upon Georgia's military establishment.

5. Here, JEO himself refutes the label, "Paladin of Philanthropy," later bestowed upon him by early biographer Henry Bruce. JEO did, indeed, risk years of hard work, his life, and his fortune — but he did it upon his own terms. There was always a chance, however slim, that he would emerge from the long struggle a victor upon many fronts.

6. "General of the Forces of South Carolina and Georgia" was a title, not a rank. His signed orders were issued on June 20, 1737. Elevation to the rank of General of the Army did not come until years later. His commission as colonel was issued on August 25, meaning that he held this rank throughout the empire. In spite of this somewhat ambiguous situation, appointment as head of colonial forces effectively transferred to his pockets the only significant stipend attached to the office of Governor of South Carolina. For a detailed listing of Oglethorpe's commission(s) see "British-Amrican Officers, 1720-1763," compiled by W.R. Williams, SCH&G 1932, 33:183-87.

7. Authorized strength of 684 officers and men was never reached. Approximately 200 professionals, mostly Irish, were drafted from a unit stationed at Gibraltar. Overseas, Carolina's Independent Company of Foot, formed in 1720, was regimented into JEO's 42nd Regiment. Many men were recruited in England and a few transferred from other outfits.

Typically, a commander released his least effective men when faced with a "draft order" requiring him to provide a contingent for new service. This meant that JEO had a regiment comprised of potential trouble-makers plus green recruits. Most men re-assigned from Gibraltar went directly to Georgia and arrived well ahead of JEO and his recruits.

8. JEO seems to have forged a map that supported his claim. Purportedly, this map depicted "the southern branch of the Altamaha" as debouching very near the Saint Mary's. See Bolton, 73. A very early French map associated with the 1562 voyage of Jean Ribault to Florida [the entire southeastern part of North America] depicts a double-branched Altamaha river. It is doubtful, however, that Oglethorpe was familiar with this map.

9. According to the report sent to Trustees by William Stephens, loss to the colony was considerable. Not only did their missionary flee in disgrace he took with him a constable named Coates plus a barber named Campbell and even a tithingman, Gough. Though Stephens castigated the fugitives as "obnoxious," they had many sympathizers. Causton, long supported by JEO and then by Stephens, who had not been in the colony long enough to understand the complex issue, wielded considerable influence. But scores of colonists were perplexed and angry at the events that took place. Savannah was never again even close to being "of one mind" until Georgia became a Crown Colony.

10. Years later it was suggested that Jenkins was a charlatan who actually lost his ear in the pillory. Though widely circulated, this charge is not supported by firm evidence. Rear-Admiral Charles Stewart entered a formal protest about treatment of Jenkins to the Governor of Havana in September, 1731. See *The English Historical Review* 1889, 4:743, for the text of this protest. Editors of the DNB accepted the story of the ear as authentic.

Chapter 11. "WE MUST STRIKE FIRST; THE BEST DEFENSE IS ATTACK"

SOURCES — Arrendondo; Carroll; Chatelain; Church; Corry; Crane, *Frontier*; Davis; Ettinger; Fleming; Force; CRG 1; CRG 2; GOG; *Gentleman's*; Gipson; Ivers; Jones; King, *Voices*; night; Lanning; McCain; McCrady; Meriwether; Miller; *Narrative*; Newman; CRG 22; CRG 23; Reese, *Colonial* SAE; Saye; Sherman; Sirmans; Spalding; CRG 4; CRG 4, supplement; Stephens; Tailfer; Temperley; Temple; Urlsperger; plus
/Lodge, Richard, "Sir Benjamin Keene, K.B." a study in Anglo-Spanish relations."
  Transactions of the Royal Historical Society; 4th series 1932, 15:1-43./
Naval and Military Memoirs of Great Britain from 1727 to 1783, by Robert Beatson; 3 vols. Int. and
  preface to vol. 1 by George A. Billias. Reprint edition; Boston: Gregg Press, 1972. [*Naval*].

NOTES — 1. Under a heavy cloud of suspicion and charged with misuse of funds, Causton sailed for England. His announced purpose was to clear his name. But when he reached London he said that the wartime atmosphere made it impossible for him to risk transporting all of his ledgers and vouchers. At the order of Trustees he later set out for Georgia to secure these documents. His ship went down at sea and he was lost.

There was no authoritative conclusion concerning his innocence or guilt, or the extent of his embezzlement if guilty.

2. For the full text of this all-important letter see GOG 2:359-62.

3. According to Jones, 1:264, some mutineers "were shipped and drummed out of the service." No more than five men, all of whom were branded as ringleaders, were punished. Others received full pardons and served with distinction in later campaigns against the Spanish. See Ivers, 83-5.

4. For the text of this petition see GOG 2:371-8. Aggrieved settlers exaggerated somewhat. Though the flow of adventurers and their servants declined from the peak of 1735-36 (139 private adventurers and family members, 40 servants) it did not cease entirely until 1738-39. During the period indicated in the petition, adventurers plus family members and servants swelled Georgia's population by 56. See Taylor, Table V, p. 308.

5. By the summer of 1739 JEO's personal unsecured loans to Georgia, relatively small in earlier periods, were beginning to mount. He had used the whole of a personal capital fund of about £2,000. Many bills of exchange he sent to London were now drawn upon him

personally, rather than upon the Trust. He had made arrangements for his military salary and perquisites plus his income from rental property and investments to be handled by Harman Verelst, accountant for the Georgia Trust. With a five-month accumulation of funds on hand, Verelst was instructed to use any or all available cash to meet bills forwarded from the colony. Verelst always charged full commission for transactions in which he was involved.

6. For depositions concerning the Coweta treaty, plus texts of the agreements made, see GHQ 1920, 4:3-16. Knight, 1:69-72, calls Coweta "a death-blow to France on the Mississippi." Though his estimate of its effect is exaggerated ("a treaty of friendship the ultimate effect of which was to give an Anglo-Saxon character to the whole subsequent history of North America"), he is correct in stressing its paramount importance. Because it was far less dramatic than events that soon followed, the signing of the treaty is often overlooked as a prime example of a JEO success that had far-reaching effects.

See DeBrahm, p. 30, for brief mention of the boundary congress of 1763 — first of the sort between leaders of four southern colonies and Indian chieftains, and an outgrowth of Coweta. Spalding, p. 97, sees Oglethorpe's genius as being responsible for "the decision to keep Georgia as a distinct and separate province." According to this analyst, had JEO not been preoccupied with other matters "he might well have emerged as one of the eighteenth century's best scholars of Indian lore" (p. 96).

7. For the complete texts of the two declarations of war, see *Naval*, 1:10-16. Neither document gives significant emphasis to the contested Georgia-Florida boundary. Both deal largely with commercial interests — the paramount insoluble issues that precipitated the conflict which merged into the War of the Austrian Succession.

8. As reported in London, Tomochichi's death occurred at age 97 after a lingering illness. "He expressed the greatest tenderness for General Oglethorpe," who gave him a military funeral and buried him in a town square. Notice of his death was accompanied by a summary of preparations already made for an attack upon the Spanish. In Savannah it was hoped — vainly as events proved — that numerous privateers operating in North American waters would sail to join and support JEO's land forces. See *Gentleman's* 10:128.

9. South Carolina records are here much more detailed than are those of Georgia. JEO's initial estimate of "forces, provisions, presents for Indians & etc." requested from Carolina is itemized in SSCR — *Commons Journal, March 26, 1741-December 1, 1741*, pp. 168ff. In addition to money and manpower, he wanted from his wealthy neighbor 1,000 pounds of beef per day for 182 days. Among estimates of basic supplies for Indians were blankets, guns, and hatchets —one each for every warrior — at a cost of £11,000 (colonial).

10. Some secondary authorities indicate that the £4,000 JEO-Carolina loan was made. Still being debated in September, 1740, the issue is reported at great length in *Commons Journal*, March-December, 1741. Here the law actually passed is reported as authorizing special commissioners "to borrow of General Oglethorpe, or from any other Person willling to furnish the same, a loan of 2,000 Pounds Sterling." There is no certainty that JEO ever consummated this loan.

11. Egmont, *Diary*, 3:146.

12. See Stephens, 1:236-7 and Appendix A.

13. Egmont, *Journal*, 10 November 1736, p. 212. Only in colonial South Carolina did "barony" have the general meaning of "a tract of 12,000 acres." Though South Carolina archives include no documents concerning a direct grant of a barony to JEO, legal notices concerning other properties adjoining "the barony of General Oglethorpe" are sprinkled through incomplete records of land holdings and transfers of title. See, for example, mss. in S.C. *Memorials* 7:309 (re Edward Cavanaugh, 1759); *Memorials* 14:83 (re Thomas Noble, 1759); and *Memorials* 10:449 (re John Stafford, 1764). These and other allusions focus upon "John Peter Pury's land, which is called Oglethorpe's barony," in what was then Granville County.

14. "A Map of South Carolina and a Part of Georgia," by William DeBrahm; published November 20, 1757, by Thomas Jefferys, geographer to the Prince of Wales. Oglethorpe's Barony is indicated by lot #17 (square Nf), adjacent to which is lot #22 (square Ng), also owned by JEO. A full-scale copy of this map is held by the University of Georgia, with a photographic copy being held by the office of Georgia's surveyor-general.

In 1780 William Faden re-published the DeBrahm map (reduced in scale) "with additions made from surveys of John Stuart, Superintendent of Indian Affairs." Here the JEO holdings are shown unchanged. Because the 1780 map does not take into account changes effected by the American Revolution, it cannot be regarded as authoritative. A copy is held by the office of Georgia's surveyor-general. Cf. Ivers, pp. 26, 88.

15. *S.C. Colonial Plats*, 1:289 (copy); *S.C. Colonial Grants*, 1:216 (copy).

16. Records of the Public Register, S.C., *Conveyances, 1719-1776*, Vol. S, pp. 442-44; Auditor General, S.C., *Memorials* 3:532 (copy); S.C. *Colonial Grants*, 3:102; S.C. *Colonial Plats*, 2:111.

This tract is shown as lot #10 (square O-f) on the DeBrahm and the Faden map. See note 13, above. Original size of this purchase, 5,365 acres, was substantially increased by the time of the DeBrahm survey. This could have come about either by means of the more accurate survey or by a shift in the course of the Savannah river.

17. Bill #5, S.C. Assembly, November 10, 1739. See SSCR, where there are 17 references to this ferry before ratification of the bill that established it.

18. CRG 22:236.

19. Egmont, *Journal*, 212; Egmont, *Diary*, 2:307. Note, however, that though Trustees undoubtedly discussed JEO's personal ventures among themselves, they never took a formal stand about them. Neither the common council nor the Trust proper preserved any record of allegations about land or deerskins. Indeed, in the very week that Egmont first mentioned these matters, he and his colleagues gave routine approval to ten separate bills of exchange drawn by JEO.

20. Force, 7.

21. CRG 3:389; CRG 26:337.

22. CRG 4:666.

23. Egmont, *Diary*, 3:492; italics in original — extremely rare in this source. McBane further reports to JEO that he has in his charge 27 of 52 servants brought over in a group. Since the original of the letter was not preserved, the accuracy of Egmont's memory about its contents cannot be established.

24. Presumably, but not positively, this included his extensive Carolina holdings. JEO's heirs had only vague knowledge of property he acquired in the New World. When his British real properties were offered for sale in 1688 the heirs addressed an inquiry to George Washington. But they mistakenly asked for information about JEO's holdings in Georgia, rather than in Carolina. In 1789 Washington reported, accurately, that no record could be found that JEO owned any tracts in the colony he established.

JEO's Carolina lands could have been mortgaged, along with Westbrook manor and properties attached to it, to help finance the attack on Saint Augustine and the defense of Georgia against the Spanish. Even if that was done and titles were later cleared, these properties of an absentee owner could have been lost during the general confiscation of Tory assets after the American Revolution.

25. For a comprehensive account of the campaign see SSCR *Commons Journal* 1739-41, 78-247. Available in reprint form; SAE. Working through Carolina's British agent, Peregrine Fury, JEO's sister Anne succeeded for a time in suppressing the devastating summary issued by Georgia's sister colony. Egmont, *Diary*, 3:238 (Jan. 10, 1742), incorrectly identifies her as "Mrs. Oglethorpe."

26. Letter of July 28, 1740, Montiano writing to Don Juan Francisco de Guemes y Horcasitas.

Chapter 12. "THANK THE LORD, AND RAISE ANOTHER REGIMENT!"

SOURCES — Arredondo; Carroll; Chatelain; Cobbett; Corry; Crane, *Frontier*; Davis; Dunn; Ettinger; Fant; Fleming; Force; GOG; CRG 1; CRG 2; CRG 3; *Gentleman's*; Gipson; Ivers; Jones; JHC; King; Lanning; McCain; McCrady; Meriwether; Miller; *Narrative*; Newman; Reese, *Colonial*; Saye; Sirmans; Spalding; Taylor, *Walpole*; Temple; Wright; plus
/Cate, Margaret Davis, "Fort Frederica and the battle of Bloody Marsh," GHQ 1943, 27:111-74./ [Cate].

NOTES — 1. A recurrent motif in JEO's correspondence from 1739 onward, "fever" is a general term for illness plus fatigue. Said he: "A bearskin for a bed, and a cloak for a tent, bad weather and violent rains" constitute "ill remedies for distemper." See GOG 2:535.

2. CRG 25:174. Mary Overend came to Savannah on the *Georgia Pink* in August, 1733. Until she arrived, she did not know that her husband, Joshua, had died in June.

3. JHC 17 Geo. II 615. For the period September 22, 1738, through September 29, 1741, JEO's out-of-pocket expenditures totalled £30,849. For the same period, deductions for provisions supplied to his men amounted to £1,818 and treasury remittances totalled £18,397. Lengthy delays were occasioned by trans-Atlantic shipment of accounts, bills of exchange, and remittances. At the time he lay in his cottage licking his wounds, JEO's cash-flow outlay was in the range of £20,000 (including interest and charges). There was no assurance that any part of this would ever be recovered.

4. Egmont, *Diary*, 3:142.

5. GOG 2:601, 612, 659; CHS *Collections* 3:112, 120, 126.

6. William Stephens, *Journal* (CRG 4), supplement, pp. 117, 223-24. Cf Bolton, 90; and Egmont, *Journal* (CRG 5), 484, 529.

7. Georgia's initial £10,000 grant, in 1733, came from restricted funds over which the sovereign exercised discretionary power. Until 1735, all requests for Parliamentary support were denied. From 1735 through 1741, total governmental support — much of it designated to civil needs only — amounted to £72,000. Unlike JEO, who had gone too far to turn back, many members of Parliament would have settled for the loss of everything invested in Georgia, in preference to risking additional funds that also might be wasted.

8. Francis Moore came to Georgia in 1736. He became storekeeper and recorder at Frederica, but resigned his office after the Saint Augustine campaign. At the time of the Spanish invasion of the colony, Moore was with JEO's troops. He was sent as a courier to Charles Town, beseeching help, and hence was not present at what came to be known as the battle of Bloody Marsh. But he got first-hand accounts of it from participants and in September wrote a lengthy report to Trustees that described the action in great detail. See GOG 2:626-35. Firsthand accounts by Spanish participants are readily available, but must be regarded with caution because they do not agree upon important details. Probably the best modern interpretation is that of Ivers.

9. A full account is given in Cate. For the most detailed Spanish account that is generally accessible, see GHS *Collections* 7:20-118.

10. GOG 2:618, 624; Reese, 82; GHS *Collections* 3:125-6, 128.

11. GHS *Collections* 3:128, January 22, 1742.

12. JHC 17 Geo. II 615, line 24 of itemized military estimate.

13. DeBrahm, 153. Cf GHQ 1939, 23:103-21. According to a letter published in the South Carolina Gazette in March, 1733, JEO brought Raleigh's *Journal* with him on the *Ann*.

No doubt seeing himself as an 18th-century Raleigh, he checked maps in order to discover support for the Yamacraw tradition about which he heard very early. (See CRG 3:405-6). Wright long ago noted the improbability of the Raleigh/Georgia tradition.

14. Bolton, 90-1; cf. Egmont, *Diary*, 3:265; Stephens, *Journal*, (CRG 5), 640. Because no issue of national significance was involved, Cobbett makes no mention of the lengthy affair that ended in Stephens' humiliation and JEO's vindication.

15. Egmont, *Journal* #2, 679; King, 59; Wright, 325. Scarcity of references to this all-important upward step in JEO's career may be attributed to the already-prevalent custom of addressing him as "General." Trustee records, letters, and public documents initially label Georgia's founder as Mr. Oglethorpe. Gradually he becomes James Oglethorpe, Esqr. Formation of his regiment caused him to be entitled Colonel Oglethorpe. At the same time, the limited and honorary title of "General" attached to him because of his success in seizing the only significant salaried post in Carolina or Georgia. See CRG; Egmont, *Diary*; Wright, 325ff.

16. Egmont, *Diary*, 3:244-45; Bolton, 97.

Chapter 13. BITTERSWEET YEARS

SOURCES — APC; CSP; Church; Cobbett; Egmont, *Diary*; Egmont, *Journal* #2; Ettinger; Force; CRG 1; CRG 2; CRG 3; *Gentleman's*; JHC; King; JEO, "Accompt;" CRG 24; CRG 25; CRG 6; Saye; Taylor, *Walpole*; Taylor; plus

"The Particulars of the Manor of West-Brooke, With the Valuable and very Improveable Freehold Estates . . . in Godalming, . . . Surrey, of the late General Oglethorpe, deceased," offered at auction by Mr. Spurrier on Friday, the 2nd of May 1788." Four printed pages with marginal annotations by the attorney representing Oglethorpe's heirs. ["Particulars"]. Guildford Muniment Room, Castle Arch, Guildford, Surrey.

A copy of this document was provided through the courtesy of Frances Harrold, Georgia State University, Atlanta.

/Potter, Davie M., Jr., "The rise of the plantation system in Georgia," GHQ 1932, 16:114-35./ [Potter].

NOTES — 1. JHC 17 Geo II, 21 March 1744, 615.

2. JHC 17 Geo II, 615; war office estimate is dated March 13, and was spread upon the record on March 21, 1744.

This document is unusual in several respects. According to it, JEO's total out-of-pocket outlay for Georgia's defenses amounted to £91,705. Value of provisions delivered to his regiment was listed at £3,565. During the five-year period involved, treasury remittances to him amounted to £22,030. That left a net claim of £66,109.

Note that the war office specified that no provision was made for interest, fees, or commissions during the five-year period. Neither was there any account of "Damages sustained by Re-exchange, and other Charges arising by Non-payment of the unsatisfied Bills drawn for Part of these extraordinary Services."

Was it a hasty entry by a war office clerk — or a studied response inserted through the agency of powerful friends — that caused this expense account to be labelled as having been incurred in "the Preservation and Defence of his Majesty's Dominions on the Continent of *North America* [italics in original]," and not simply for poor, weak Georgia?

Note also that time spent on the journey home was included in the analysis.

Annual pay of the Highland Independent Company was listed at £1,910 — 3 — 4 for three consecutive years. This total was derived from an assumption that the company led by Captain John McIntosh was made up of: 2 lieutenants, an ensign, 4 sergeants, 4 corporals, 2 drummers, a surgeon, and 100 effective men. Including McIntosh, pay of this company ran to £5 — 4 — 8 per day, making a 365-day total of £1,910 — 3 — 4; see JEO's "Accompt."

Yet Ivers found that effective strength of the Highland Independent Company fluctuated widely and was sometimes as low as 16; Ivers, 139, 149.

This method of accounting was not, however, unusual in the 18th-century. During the entire post-Oglethorpe period of Trustee era Georgia, for example, Parliament assumed that the king's forces in the colony never varied by so much as one man, hence authorized annual payments based on this premise. See JHC 1745-51; King, pp. 61-3.

No separate entry was made for an all-important draft by Capt. Mark Carr, JEO's Virginia agent, July, 1741. Though the value of this instrument was only £100, its appearance in London and its rejection by authorities precipitated the crisis in which JEO drew dozens of bills that were disallowed, Longon's revised intructions not yet having been received.

No other single matter in the entire Georgia experiment more vividly underscores the communications problem. Treasury officials issued regulations, but before they could reach Georgia an additional £12,000 in bills of exchange had been drawn; see Jones 1:367, Wright, 284-5.

Peregrine Fury, secretary to Chelsea Hospital and JEO's military agent in Britain, handled bills of exchange for a time. As Chancellor of the Exchequer, Walpole initially permitted these instruments to go directly to the treasury for payment. After the incident of the £100 Carr bill, Walpole directed that future instruments be laid before the lords justices because "they related to a new credit." See Wright, 284-5, and DNB.

3. Unaccountably, Egmont, *Diary*, 3:293, reports that Parliament "acted with great honor" to Oglethorpe on March 20 — rather than on March 22 (JHC). Many biographers treat this Egmont notation as definitive. According to it, JEO received immediate reimbursement in full. Yet in reality, matters did not proceed nearly so smoothly as that.

4. Two warrants were issued to the paymaster-general by the treasury. The first, in amount £40,000 was paid to JEO on May 8, 1744. The balance of £26,109 — 13 — 10 was paid on July 5.

JEO, a self-confessed poor keeper of records, employed an accountant to whom he paid £300 for three years of work on itemized records — often reported to the fractional part of one penny — that were sometimes detailed and dated, sometimes general and undated. See JEO, "Accompt."

In August, 1751, auditors were still struggling with details of some items. At issue were "some thousands of pounds" claimed by JEO but not yet approved; here, the items involved may have been included in his "Accompt," which was submitted in support of reimbursements already made to him. See CRG 1:565-6.

5. JHC 17 Geo II, 22 March, 1744, p. 634.

6. Egmont, *Diary*, 3:293.

7. A major facet of the unresolved mystery centers in the huge personal expenditures JEO claimed to have made.

His salary as colonial general was £1,000 per year. Net rental income from his British real property ranged above or below £300 per year, with estimated yearly value of all income from such property not more than £500 ("Particulars").At the time his British real properties were offered at auction in 1788, a careful estimate of value ranged from a low of £13,956 ["Particulars]. Even the smaller of these sums was not realized; the anticipated sale was not then consummated. With little economic fluctuation in Britain during a period of more than half a century, mortagages yielding 100% of property value would not, in the 1730's and 1740's, have put more than £15,000 at JEO's disposal.

He held some securities — no great number — of undetermined value. He owned nearly 30,000 acres in Carolina. He may have gained a valuable monopoly in the skin trade.

Haslemere borough, with its two seats in Parliament, was worth perhaps £15,000 to £25,000 (see King). JEO's fraction of that borough, at the time he financed Georgia's military defense, could not have exceeded £12,500 in value.

After mortgaging everything he owned and pledging his future salary, there was a very substantial difference between JEO's available cash and his out-of-pocket expenditures. He bought a great deal of merchandise for future payment. JEO and his agent, Verelst, carefully spread his purchases among many merchants. Having no central credit bureau, merchants and lenders of London had no way to determine JEO's total outstanding obligations at any given time.

His detailed record of interest and charges accrued on bills of exchange is complete only for the period May 21-23, 1744. 19 creditors are listed; among them, total debts of £7,094 are spread. No individual debt exceeds £2,522 — and the smallest is a mere £6. Interest on unpaid principal sums, plus accrued interest on other outstanding loans and bills then (May 31, 1744) amounted to £2,454 — 17 — 10 (JEO, "Accompt").

Even with carefully-distributed accounts among many merchants and lenders taken into consideration, JEO reports expenditures of approximately twice his total assets. Where did he get money over and above that yielded by mortgages plus borrowing plus purchasing for future payment?

From Egmont, an Oglethorpe scholar ventures to suggest.

Certainly not! Though Egmont was quite wealthy, he was neither generous nor adventuresome. Had he lent JEO money, details of every transaction would have been recorded — along with minute information respecting financial transactions large and small: purchase of lottery tickets, return from investments, sale and purchase of land.

Two of JEO's sisters were wealthy — one by marriage, another as a result of having sold extensive holdings in the Mississippi Company at the height of that bubble. But neither woman shared JEO's political loyalties and neither ever showed the slightest interest in the Georgia enterprise. That one or both would have made huge loans on so wildly speculative a basis as the distant hope of a Parliamentary grant of reimbursement is highly questionable.

Could Egmont have been right in his intuitive guess that JEO held secret instructions from the crown? Was King George II the source of some of the funds used in baiting and then defeating the Spanish?

Until additional evidence is uncovered, this aspect of JEO's great Georgia gamble must be treated as an unsolved mystery.

8. Typical entries were selected from hundreds that appear in the "Accompt," itemized to ¼ penny. Dates are omitted here; some are not included in the record, and others cannot be deciphered because of the narrow margins of sheets.

As submitted for audit on August 2, 1745, the total account — extending over a period of five eventful years in Georgia — substantially exceeded Parliament's reimbursement to him. For reasons unknown, JEO did not swear to the accounting and sign it until October 27, 1747. Even this action meant only that the tedious process of a final audit could now begin.

9. Cobbett devotes more than 100 columns to Parliament's responses to various aspects of The Pretender's threats during the spring of 1744, when JEO's case got hasty and favorable action.

10. Documented financial dealings between JEO and Lady Sambrooke center in the 1750's. Their relationship has led to speculation that she may have provided some small part of the funds he used in Georgia's struggle against Spain.

11. It is impossible to overlook JEO's dominant role in the long and bitter contest over control of the skin trade. Speedy resolution of that contest, once he left Georgia for good, adds some weight to undocumented charges made by merchants of Britain concerning his "monopoly." Formally and informally, JEO did indeed take personal charge of the vast

business — just as he assumed command of nearly every enterprise in which he was involved. Whether or not he personally profited from the flow of skins down the Savannah river, and if so to what degree, it is impossible to determine. Yet this huge commercial enterprise is a possible source of some of the money Georgia's founder spent in her defense. It was no accident that he arranged for his Savannah river ferry, licensed by Carolina, to be situated at a strategic spot. Had he wished to do it, JEO really was in a position to exact a toll upon every skin shipped from Fort Augusta — biggest trading center of its sort in North America.

12. Taylor, Tables I-XI, pp. 305-17.

13. Some of the Indians with whom JEO was upon friendly terms were practicing slavery when the *Ann* reached Savannah. He made no attempt to alter the structure of their society. Indeed, when Mary Musgrove's Indian slave, Justice, was killed in an accident, JEO sent her a replacement for him — a servant indentured to the Georgia Trust (see Temple, 83).

14. Incredibly detailed and complex, the revised statute that sought to give a religious veneer to the acceptance of slavery is detailed in full in CRG 1:56-62. See also CRG 2:504 and Potter.

15. Jones 1:460.

16. CRG 1:567.

Chapter 14. LION OF LONDON

SOURCES — ABHS; APC; Carroll; Church; Cobbett; DNB; Egmont, *Diary*; Ettinger; CRG 1; CRG 2; CRG 3; *Gentleman's;* JHC; King; JEO, "Accompt;" CRG 6; Saye; Sirman; Spalding; Taylor, *Walpole; Westbrook*; Wright; plus

/Corry, John P., "Some new light on the Bosomworth claims," GHQ 1941, 25:195-224./ [Corry].

[Coulter, E.M., "Mary Musgrove, 'Queen of the Creeks,' " GHQ 1927, 11:1-30./ [Coulter, "Musgrove"].

Dedman, The Rev. Stanley, typescript. (Dedman was the long-time librarian of Godalming, Surrey.) [Dedman].

*Dugmore, Ruth, "Puttenham under the Hog's Back." Undated local history, held in Godalming Library along with mss. relating to transaction in which title to lands changed hands. [Dugmore].

*Manuscripts and papers, the Losely Collection, Muniment Room, Guildford, Surrey. [Losely].

NOTES — 1. Cobbett, 27 Geo. II, devotes columns 194-248 to the 1753 Commons' "Enquiry into the management of the last Lottery."

2. Egmont, Diary, 3:293, reports that "This day the House of Commons granted the sums expended by General Oglethorpe in defence of Georgia, amounting to above 60,000 l, without any division, and with great honour to himself." This notation is usually taken at face value, and treated as writing an end to Oglethorpe's claims for reimbursement in an enterprise many close to him considered a sure road to ruin.

Earlier, it has been noted that Egmont errs by two days in reporting that House action took place on Tuesday, March 20, instead of two days later. Even then it did not constitute direct and immediate repayment to JEO. Following the customary pattern, the total sum was voted to order of the king. Subsequently the treasury issued two warrants to Thomas Winnington, Paymaster General. The first, dated May 8, 1744, was for £40,000. The second, dated July 5, 1744, was for the remaining £26,109 — 13 — 10. (PRO; T52/42, pp. 424, 452).

A search conducted by keepers of the Public Record Office ended at this point, since both remittances were immediately forwarded to JEO. But it has already been observed that the matter was not nearly so simple as it appears on the surface. A lengthy obituary in *Gentleman's*, closest contemporaneous public reference to the issue, noted that at his death JEO had not received full compensation for his expenditures in Georgia.

Searching the record in preparation for writing the JEO biography in DNB, prior to 1917, John Andrew Doyle concluded that many JEO bills had been disallowed. "Nor," said he, "is there any proof that Oglethorpe was ever reimbursed." Spalding cites Egmont as authority for the fact that "the greater part of the debt was . . . apparently repaid in 1744," but holds that JEO's accounts were not "finally authorized to be 'quit' by Chancellor of the Exchequer, William Pitt," until 1792 — eight years after his death. (See Spalding, 189f, n. 11.) Ettinger followed the trail only until 1791, at which point he found reports of a formal accounting "that showed Oglethorpe owed the govenment £841 as overdrawn." (See Ettinger, 252, n. 4.)

Final resolution of this tangled question to the satisfaction of everyone is doubtful.

Regardless of how close JEO came to collecting in full before his death, the substantial losses he incurred from interest charges and from surcharges attached to disallowed bills were large enough to account for the fact that he never was affluent. Though he spent many years in his wife's manor, she managed her own property and retained control of her cash-flow.

A disastrous fire at Westbrook manor destroyed many of JEO's personal records. Possibly, but not positively, the man who stressed his intense dislike for the keeping of accounts may have made memoranda that would have clarified this matter, had they survived the fire.

3. Under terms of JEO's will, his entire estate passed to his widow. Their long-standing agreement concerning real property stipulated that if they had no son or daughter and if she survived him, Westbrook and other properties in Surrey would be transferred to the nearest bloodrelative of JEO.

Very soon after his death two of his nephews laid claim to all properties once held by their uncle. The Marquis de Bellegarde, son of JEO's sister Fanny, pursued the matter to the point of seeking to determine the disposition of holdings he believed JEO to have had in Georgia. Chevalier de Mézières, son of JEO's sister Eleanor, filed a rival claim to the New World properties, forwarding his inquiries concerning them through Thomas Jefferson — then U.S. Minister to France. Inquiries concerning Georgia were misdirected, since JEO never held title to any land in the colony. Apparently the nephews overlooked the possibility of claiming JEO's extensive Carolina holdings, doubtless being unaware of their existence.

Both nephews were thwarted in their designs. JEO's widow, who survived him by two years, bequeathed the Surrey holdings to Eugene, Marquis of Bellegarde — a great-nephew of her husband. Barred by law from taking title to the English estates because of his French citizenship, the Marquis received the total cash return from liquidation of JEO's estate. It was first placed on the market in 1788, to be sold in its entirety at auction. This sale failed, however, and holdings were sold piecemeal under authority granted to Granville Sharpe and William Gill, executors representing the estate of Mrs. Oglethorpe. (See *Gentleman's*, 1787, 1025f; "Particulars;" *Westwood*.)

4. Ellis was named executive head of the colony to serve "during the absence of Mr. Reynolds." So appointed on August 3, 1756, he was not elevated in rank until May 17, 1758 —meaning that during 21 months as a royal colony, Georgia had no governor. At the departure of Ellis on November 2, 1760, he turned leadership over to James Wright. Settlement of the Musgrove-Bosomworth claims was perhaps the most notable event of Ellis' administration.

5. Though usually treated as having been of full European blood, Musgrove was himself the son of Col. John Musgrove by an Indian woman.

6. At the time of his appointment, Bosomworth was no stranger to Savannah and its

environs. He first went to Georgia in 1741 in order to serve as clerk to William Stephens, but upon arrival in the colony refused to serve in the post. For nearly a year he was Secretary of Indian Affairs for Georgia. Subsequent to the battle of Bloody Marsh he went to New York and then back to England, where he gained ordination from the Bishop of London. In the post of resident clergyman, or minister to the colony, his salary — paid by the Society for the Propagation of the Gospel — was £50, plus use of a parsonage, two servants, and 300 acres of land.

7. An alternate form, Coosaponakessa, appears in CRG 22, pt. 1: 256ff. Educated at Pon Pon, Carolina, she was one of the few Christians in the Indian region. She is believed to have been approximately ten years older than JEO.

8. Official records indicate that John Musgrove received £100 for his services as interpreter during the British visit of Tomochichi and party; see CRG 2:75. His wife claimed £100 per year for the entire period of Georgia's existence under the Trust, and eventually got it.

9. Bosomworth's claims, entered in his wife's name, indicated that during the period of JEO's leadership Mary received only £200 in salary. The valuable diamond ring said to have been conferred upon her by JEO was a personal gift. Relatively small payments reported in JEO's "Accompt" for brief special services were apparently overlooked by persons charged with investigating and settling the Bosomworth claims.

10. Note that Wright's Georgia holdings were almost as extensive as those of JEO in Carolina. As governor of a crown colony, Wright was not prohibited from making personal profit.

By the time of the American Revolution, property values had so increased that worth of the Wright plantations was estimated at £160,000. Briefly under house arrest by patriots under leadership of Joseph Habersham, Wright escaped and soon returned with strong military forces. He resumed his role as governor, confiscated the property of many rebels, and maintained control of Savannah for three years. Upon the defeat of British forces in America by George Washington, Wright once more went to England. There he made a determined but futile attempt to prevent confiscation of his Georgia holdings. (Presumably but not positively, any Carolina tracts still held by JEO at the time of the Revolution were also confiscated.)

On December 5, 1772, Wright was created a baronet as a reward for his services in Georgia. (See DNB.) His 1762 success in defeating attempts of South Carolina leaders to gain control of part or all of Georgia, plus his legal extension of Georgia's southern boundary from the Altamaha river to the Saint Mary's, rested entirely upon achievements of JEO in earlier decades.

11. England's first official census was conducted in 1801. During the era in which Georgia was founded, Wales was grouped with England for purposes of population estimates. In 1730 the probable population of England and Wales, combined, was 5,796,000. (See ABHS.) Georgia's 1980 population was 5,464,265; with the 1970-80 growth rate being 19%, the projected 1982 population of the state founded by JEO is 5,671,907.